Landscape
Urbanism

The Landscape Urbanism Reader

Charles Waldheim, editor

Princeton Architectural Press, New York

Published by
Princeton Architectural Press
37 East Seventh Street
New York, New York 10003

For a free catalog of books, call 1.800.722.6657.
Visit our web site at www.papress.com.

The publication of this book was supported by a grant from the Graham
Foundation for Advanced Studies in the Fine Arts.

Editing: Scott Tennent
Design: Brett Yasko

Cover photo: Brett Yasko, 2005.
Frontispiece: Joan Roig and Enric Batlle, Trinitat Cloverleaf Park, Barcelona, 1992.
Photo by Luis On; courtesy Joan Roig and Enric Batlle.
Pages 286–87: Photo by Alan Berger.

Special thanks to: Nettie Aljian, Dorothy Ball, Nicola Bednarek, Janet Behning,
Penny (Yuen Pik) Chu, Russell Fernandez, Jan Haux, Clare Jacobson, John King,
Mark Lamster, Nancy Eklund Later, Linda Lee, Katharine Myers, Lauren Nelson,
Jennifer Thompson, Paul Wagner, Joseph Weston, and Deb Wood of Princeton
Architectural Press —Kevin C. Lippert, publisher

Library of Congress Cataloging-in-Publication Data
The landscape urbanism reader / Charles Waldheim, editor.—1st ed.
p. cm.
ISBN-13: 978-1-56898-439-1 (alk. paper)
ISBN-10: 1-56898-439-1 (alk. paper)
1. Urban landscape architecture. I. Waldheim, Charles.
SB472.7.L36 2006
712.09173'2—dc22   2005036346

This book collects the work of many colleagues and collaborators from a range of institutions internationally. The authors, and the network of institutions and assistants supporting their work, are each deserving of acknowledgment; without their generous contributions this book would not be possible. Equally essential has been the patient commitment to the project by Princeton Architectural Press, particularly the editorial vision of Kevin Lippert and Clare Jacobson, the extraordinary care, editorial insight, and patient hard work of Scott Tennent, as well as the advice of Nancy Levinson. The book is also the product of the hard work, patience, and shared commitment of many other individuals whose names do not appear apart from these acknowledgments. The notes that follow are an attempt to acknowledge those who contributed to it in less obvious, yet equally significant, ways.

The landscape urbanism project and this publication owe a debt of gratitude to Rick Solomon, the late director of the Graham Foundation, for his early and consistent support for the topic, its relevance, and value. The Graham Foundation, in addition to providing funding for this publication, supported the initiative by co-sponsoring an eponymous conference and exhibition. This book, the conference, and the exhibition were conceived in parallel to the implementation of an academic program in landscape urbanism in the School of Architecture at the University of Illinois at Chicago. The Graham Foundation, and Solomon in particular, offered both financial viability and operational legitimacy to this nascent initiative, providing time and space for it to find its voice and audiences. Without Solomon's support for the topic, the emerging discourse surrounding landscape urbanism could scarcely expect to have the relevance and audience that it presently enjoys in North America and Western Europe.

The landscape urbanism initiative, and this publication, would not have been possible without the vigorous support and advocacy of the School of Architecture and College of Architecture and the Arts at the University of Illinois at Chicago. Two directors of the School, Ken Schroeder and Katerina Rüedi Ray, were particularly responsible for initiating and nurturing these activities. Ken Schroeder first proposed an application to the Graham Foundation for such an initiative, and invested in me an authority over its stewardship incommensurate with my experience. Katerina Rüedi Ray was a vocal and visible advocate of the initiative, and made a space for discussions of landscape and urbanism in a context otherwise predisposed to questions of architectural essentialism. In addition to the institutional support of the School, the Landscape Urbanism Program benefited enormously from the contributions of a number of committed and supportive colleagues at the University of Illinois at Chicago. Among them, Stuart Cohen,

Bob Bruegmann, Peter Lindsay Schaudt, Richard Blender, Bruno Ast, and Roberta Feldman each helped to articulate the precise role that discussions of contemporary landscape might play in the School. Likewise, I am equally indebted to my colleagues at the University of Illinois at Urbana-Champaign, especially Terry Harkness for his advice and consent.

For the intellectual impetus of the program, I also relied on the counsel and advice of numerous colleagues in North America and Europe. Among them, James Corner was characteristically generous with his time and insights. Corner's research into contemporary landscape and its increasing relevance for questions of the city has been central to the formulation of landscape urbanism over the past many years. Equally present was the body of literature concerning the role of landscape at the regional scale, particularly the work of Ian McHarg. Also significant, although admired at a distance, were the published texts of various authors and critics cited herein on the topic of contemporary urbanism, most particularly the work of Kenneth Frampton, Peter Rowe, and Rem Koolhaas.

The academic program in Landscape Urbanism inaugurated a visiting critic position, named in honor of the Danish émigré and Chicago landscape designer Jens Jensen. I remain uniquely indebted to the Jensen critics who contributed to the program, including James Corner, Terence Harkness, George Hargreaves, and Kathryn Gustafson, for sharing their teaching methods, critical insights, and time. I am equally indebted to a number of colleagues and friends who joined me in teaching design studios and theory seminars on topics of landscape and urbanism at the University of Illinois at Chicago including Clare Lyster, Sarah Dunn, and Igor Marjanović, among others.

The original Landscape Urbanism conference, April 25–27, 1997 at the Graham Foundation in Chicago, provided the first occasion to publicly frame the topic before a live audience. That event, and the discussion that followed, benefited from presentations by Ian McHarg, James Corner, Mohsen Mostafavi, Linda Pollak, Brigitte Shim, Adriaan Geuze, Joan Roig, Grant Jones, and Kathy Poole, among others. The eponymous exhibition traveled from the Graham Foundation to the Storefront for Art and Architecture in New York before embarking on a U.S tour during 1997 and 1998. That show, and the audiences it formed, were dependent upon the work of James Corner / Field Operations, Julia Czerniak and Timothy Swischuk, Alex Wall, Adriaan Geuze / West 8, Anuradha Mathur and Dilip da Cunha, Alfons Soldavilla / Llorens-Soldevilla, Joan Roig and Enric Batlle / Batlle-Roig, Marcia Codinachs and Mercé Nadal / Codinachs-Nadal, Patrik Schumacher and Kevin Rhowbottom, Eric Owen Moss, Michael Van Valkenburgh, Linda Pollak and Sandro Marpillero / Marpillero-Pollak, William Conway and Marcy Schulte / Conway-Schulte, Brigitte Shim and Howard Sutcliffe / Shim-Sutcliffe, Georgia Daskalakis and Omar Perez / Das:20, Jason Young, Brian Rex, Paul Kariouk, and Shawn Rickenbacker, among others.

The discussions surrounding the conference, exhibition, and academic program were in and of themselves significant in providing an outlet for the emerging discourse, and I am particularly mindful of my indebtedness to many individuals who have offered time and attention to the topic at various moments over the past several years. Among them, Kenneth Frampton, Dan Hoffman, Grahame Shane, Alan Berger, Jane Wolff, Richard Sommer, Hashim Sarkis, Jacqueline Tatom, Alex Krieger, Richard Marshall, Elizabeth Mossop, Rodolphe el-Khoury, Detlef Mertins, Robert Levit, Peter Beard, Kelly Shannon, Marcel Smets, Sébastien Marot, Christophe Girot, Kristine Synnes, Paola Viganò, and Stefan Tischer have each offered insights on the topic.

My understanding of the topic has benefited greatly from opportunities to offer studios and seminars on the topic of landscape urbanism as a visitor at a variety of institutions internationally. For those opportunities, and for discussions attendant to the work in those contexts, I remain indebted to Alex Krieger, Niall Kirkwood, and Peter Rowe at the Harvard Design School; Rodolphe el-Khoury and Larry Wayne Richards at the University of Toronto; Christophe Girot and Jacqueline Parish at the ETH, Zurich; as well as Kari Jormakka and Bernhard Langer at the TU, Vienna. Equally, my work has depended upon the support and advice of my current colleagues and friends at the University of Toronto including George Baird, Larry Richards, An Te Liu, Rob Wright, Pierre Bélanger, Rodolphe el-Khoury, Robert Levit, Brigitte Shim, Mary Lou Lobsinger, and Andy Payne. I would also like to acknowledge the contributions of countless students that have shared the development of this topic with me in lectures, design studios and seminars in a variety of institutional contexts over the past several years. For their tireless hard work and unflagging interest in the topic, I am truly thankful. Finally, this work and the environment in which it has been possible would have been inconceivable absent the ongoing support of my family. Thanks to Siena and Cale for reminding me that everything really is possible.

—Charles Waldheim

Landscape Urbanism describes a disciplinary realignment currently underway in which landscape replaces architecture as the basic building block of contemporary urbanism. For many, across a range of disciplines, landscape has become both the lens through which the contemporary city is represented and the medium through which it is constructed.

A Reference Manifesto

Charles Waldheim

FIG. 1 "Territory for the New Economy." Andrea Branzi, Strijp Philips, Eindhoven, The Netherlands, 1999–2000

"Interdisciplinarity is not the calm of an easy security; it begins *effectively*...when the solidarity of the old disciplines breaks down—perhaps even violently, via the jolts of fashion—in the interests of a new object and a new language..."

—Roland Barthes

Across a range of disciplines, landscape has become a lens through

which the contemporary city is represented and a medium through which it is constructed [FIG. 1]. These sentiments are evident in the emergent notion of "landscape urbanism."

Today, in the context of global capital, post-Fordist models of flexible production, and informal labor relations, urbanization continues to decrease the density of North American settlement. The architectural objects left in the wake of this process are often absorbed by tourism and culture, offering many buildings an alternative post-industrial narrative as part of leisurely destination environments. Many cities in North America formerly known for their autochthonous architectural culture are presently engaged in rebranding themselves for larger economies of tourism, recreation, and destination entertainment, packaging architectural objects and fragments of the traditional urban fabric as optional excursions into themed environments. The architecture of the city becomes commodified as a cultural product, ironically rendering many cities less and less distinguishable from one another. In place of regional and historical distinctions, many industrial cities have long since lost most of their inhabitants to their decentralized suburban surroundings. In place of traditional, dense urban form, most North Americans spend their time in built environments characterized by decreased density, easy accommodation of the automobile, and public realms characterized by extensive vegetation. In this horizontal field of urbanization, landscape has a newfound relevance, offering a multivalent and manifold medium for the making of urban form, and in particular in the context of complex natural environments, post-industrial sites, and public infrastructure.

The Landscape Urbanism Reader gathers essays from fourteen authors across a range of disciplines internationally, to articulate the origins and aspirations of this burgeoning field of cultural production. It, and the "new language" it puts forth, attempt to describe the rapidly changing context for landscape in discussions of the contemporary city. The emerging discourse it documents speaks to the relative inadequacy of the traditional disciplinary, professional, and critical categories to account for the renewed interest in landscape found in the work of many architects, landscape architects, and urbanists over the past several years. This collection assembles a variety of essays looking back to the very recent past and, through the shock of fashion, to the advantage of a new object, a new language.

The formulation of a "reference manifesto" at once proclaims an emergent moment of cultural production and traces its etymology, genealogy, and critical commitments. The phrase produces an interesting double-bind, demanding that this volume describe emergent conditions before they fully clarify themselves while simultaneously documenting their various sources and referents. These dual aspirations place the book in a curious critical position, necessitating new modes of description, new forms of scholarship, new models of discourse. The anthology form this publication adopts, an often undervalued format, affords space for a range of divergent voices while at the same time focusing those critical energies on a collective object of study. It presupposes a varied and in some cases incongruous set of contributors, from a spectrum of disciplinary and scholarly backgrounds. Some are established scholars, others emerging voices. All have found the discourse surrounding landscape urbanism to be significant to their own work, and have devoted considerable time and energy to the articulation of its potentials in this collection. The essays collected here, and the projects and propositions they point to, provide clear evidence of landscape's invocation as a medium through which the contemporary city might be apprehended and intervened upon.

In his essay "Terra Fluxus," James Corner describes the intellectual and practical underpinnings of the landscape urbanist agenda, framing the recent renewal of interest in landscape within the historical disciplinary formations of architecture, urban design, and planning. Corner's proposal puts forth four interpractical themes from which to organize the emerging landscape urbanist practice: ecological and urban processes over time, the staging of horizontal surfaces, the operational or working method, and the imaginary. He argues that only through the imaginative reordering of the design disciplines and their objects of study might we have some potential traction on the formation of the contemporary city. Following Corner, my essay "Landscape as Urbanism" focuses on the discourses surrounding landscape and urbanism over the past quarter-century, constructing a lineage for the emergent practice beginning with the restructuring of the industrial economy in the West, the rise of postmodernism, and the ongoing transformation of the industrial city through flexible production and consumption, global capital, and decentralization. Here, landscape urbanist tendencies emerge within the discourse of architects in response to the economic, social, and cultural shifts surrounding de-industrialization. Practices of landscape urbanism emerge as a useful framework in these contexts, most appropriately adopted for sites experiencing the abandonment, toxicity, and social pathologies left in the wake of industry as it decamped for more favorable locations.

Grahame Shane extends this line of inquiry relating the decentralization of industry to contemporary interests in landscape urbanism. In his essay, Shane surveys the growing body of literature attendant to landscape urbanism, while tracing the institutions and individuals implicated in its discourse, especially as they relate to the disciplinary formations and discourses of urban design. Richard Weller's essay, "An Art of Instrumentality," surveys contemporary landscape practice in relation to de-industrialization, infrastructure, and the rapidly expanding commodification of the traditional urban realm. From this vantage point he cites Corner and the work of others in conceptualizing landscape urbanism as a practice providing newfound relationships between landscape architecture and other professional and disciplinary modes of urbanization, including civil engineering, real estate development, and the design professions.

With "Vision in Motion: Representing Landscape in Time," Christophe Girot seizes upon the temporality, subjectivity, and centrality of visual images in the landscape medium to argue for new modes of representation, particularly time-based media in apprehending the subjects of landscape urbanism. Girot's theoretical reflections derive from his own teaching and research on the role of video in capturing the subjects of urban landscape, particularly over time. Julia Czerniak uses the framework of landscape urbanism to inform her reading of the topic of "site" across disciplinary, professional, and generational boundaries. Her essay "Looking Back at Landscape Urbanism: Speculations on Site," while implying that the landscape urbanist moment has passed, prompts readers to consider the complex conceptual apparatus that is the site for a design project, referencing the available literature of recent notions of site and proposing a renewed relevance for questions of site in relation to urbanization and landscape practice. Linda Pollak continues this interest in the essential or fundamental precepts of urban landscape work with her essay "Constructed Ground: Questions of Scale," which examines Henri Lefebvre's analysis of nested scales of space to inform her reading of several contemporary urban landscapes relative to their social and scalar dimensions.

With her essay "Place as Resistance: Landscape Urbanism in Europe," Kelly Shannon chronicles the rise of landscape urbanism in European landscape practice, particularly as a mechanism for resisting the commodification of urban form. Based on Kenneth Frampton's interest in landscape as a medium of resistance to placeless urbanization, Shannon's essay traces the evolution of Kenneth Frampton's interests in a regionalism of resistance, first through architectonic form, and more recently through the landscape medium. The essay cites numerous contemporary European examples of landscape design offering a specific regional identity in the face of ongoing urbanization. Elizabeth Mossop extends the conversation of landscape in relation to urban infrastructure with an analysis of the various relationships available between the two. Noting examples from Europe, North America, Australia, and Asia, Mossop assembles a convincing array of precedents in support of the notion that practices of landscape urbanism are most evident in relations between the horizontal ecological field and the networks of infrastructure that urbanize them. Extending the theme of urban infrastructure, Jacqueline Tatom chronicles the history and future of the urban highway as a locus of landscape practice. Citing a range of historical cases from the nineteenth and twentieth centuries, Tatom folds more contemporary interests in the integration of highways into the fabric of cities, especially as social, ecological, and ultimately cultural artifacts.

Alan Berger, in his essay "Drosscape," advances a conceptual and analytical framework for coming to terms with the enormous territories left abandoned in the wake of de-industrialization. Theorizing these sites as part of a broader economy of waste, Berger advocates landscape urbanism as an inter-practical framework for approaching the appropriation of territories left in the wake of industrial abandonment. With "Landscapes of Exchange: Re-articulating Site," Clare Lyster describes the changing scale of economic activity as one basis for a model of urban form and an explanation for contemporary interest in landscape urbanism. Following from several historical examples of urban form, Lyster locates the operational and logistical imperatives of just-in-time production and other contemporary paradigms for post-industrial commerce as analogs for horizontal landscapes of exchange. Pierre Bélanger continues this interest in the surfaces of contemporary commerce and offers an historical inquiry into the development of North America's landscape of paved surfaces. Bélanger chronicles the technical and social milestones in the unrelenting onslaught of asphalt across the continent, from highways and ports to inter-modal transit hubs and foreign trade zones, in the making of a horizontal network of urbanized surfaces. The collection concludes with Chris Reed's meditations on the changing conditions for public works practice in North America. Citing a range of public projects from the nineteenth and twentieth centuries, Reed describes the role of landscape urbanist practices as an analog to the organizational, political, and procedural conditions through which public projects are conceived and commissioned.

Taken together, these essays describe the positions, practices, and projective potentials of landscape urbanism. Equally, they articulate the expanding international relevance of what can now be understood as the single most significant shift in the design disciplines' descriptions of the city in the past quarter century.

The Landscape Urbanism Reader assembles the fullest account to date of the origins, affinities, aspirations, and applications of this emerging body of knowledge. In so doing, it chronicles the shifting attentions of those disciplines aspiring to describe, delineate, and design the contemporary city. The book records the subtle shifts and sharp shocks of a deep, ongoing, disciplinary breakdown, in favor of a new object, a new language.

Notes

Epigraph. Roland Barthes, "From Work to Text," *Image Music Text*, trans. Stephen Heath (New York: Hill and Wang, 1977), 155.

Terra Fluxus

James Corner

FIG. 1 The High Line, New York, 2004; view of hard and organic surfaces bleeding into one

In the opening years of the twenty-first century, that seemingly old-fashioned term landscape has curiously come back into vogue [FIG. 1]. The reappearance of landscape in the larger cultural imagination is due, in part, to the remarkable rise of environmentalism and a global ecological awareness, to the growth of tourism and the associated needs of regions to retain a sense of unique identity, and to the impacts upon rural areas by massive urban growth. But landscape also affords a range of imaginative and metaphorical associations, especially for many contemporary architects and urbanists. Certainly, architecture schools have embraced landscape in recent years, even though not long ago architects could not (or would not) even draw a tree, let alone demonstrate interest in site and landscape. Today, however, it is not merely an interest in vegetation, earthworks, and site-planning that we see espoused in various schools of design and planning, but also a deep concern with landscape's conceptual scope; with its capacity to theorize sites, territories, ecosystems, networks, and infrastructures, and to organize large urban fields. In particular, thematics of organization, dynamic interaction, ecology, and technique point to a looser, emergent urbanism, more akin to the real complexity of cities and offering an alternative to the rigid mechanisms of centralist planning.

Leading schools of landscape architecture have traditionally understood the scope of landscape as a model for urbanism, embracing large-scale organizational techniques alongside those of design, cultural expression, and ecological formation. Recently, a few landscape architects have shed their professionally defined limits to expand their skills across complex urbanistic, programmatic, and infrastructural areas. So it seems that certain elements within each of the design professions—architecture, landscape architecture, urban design, and planning—are moving toward a shared form of practice, for which the term *landscape* holds central significance, as described through the formulation *landscape urbanism*. What is the precise nature of this hybrid practice, and how are each of the terms *landscape* and *urbanism* altered?

This new disciplinary collusion was anticipated in the Landscape Urbanism symposium and exhibition in 1997, originally conceived and organized by Charles Waldheim, and has been further articulated through a range of publications.[1] It is a proposition of disciplinary conflation and unity, albeit a unity that contains, or holds together, difference—difference in terms of the ideological, programmatic, and cultural content of each of those loaded and contested words, "landscape," "urbanism" [FIG. 2].

Clearly, much of the intellectual intent of this manifestolike proposition, and the essays collected under that formulation here, is the total dissolution of the two terms into one word, one phenomenon, one practice. And yet at the same time each term remains distinct, suggesting their necessary, perhaps inevitable, separateness. Same, yet different; mutually exchangeable, yet never quite fully dissolved, like a new hybrid ever dependent upon both the x *and* y chromosome, never quite able to shake off the different expressions of its parents.

Such a dialectical synthesis is significant, for it differs from earlier attempts to speak of urban sites as landscapes, or from attempts to situate landscape in the city. The more traditional ways in which we speak about landscape and cities have been conditioned through the nineteenth-century lens of difference and opposition. In this view, cities are seen to be busy with the technology of high-density building, transportation infrastructure, and revenue-producing development, the undesirable effects of which include congestion, pollution, and various forms of social stress; whereas landscape, in the form of parks, greenways, street trees, esplanades, and gardens, is generally seen to provide both salve and respite from the deleterious effects of urbanization. A most canonical instance of this, of course, is Olmsted's Central Park, intended as relief from the relentless urban fabric of Manhattan—even though the catalytic effect that Central Park exerted on surrounding real estate development links it more closely with a landscape urbanist model. In this instance, landscape *drives* the process of city formation.

Danish émigré and Chicago landscape architect Jens Jensen articulated this sentiment when he said, "Cities built for a wholesome life…not for profit or speculation, with the living green as an important part of their complex will be the first interest of the future town-planner."[2] "Complex" is an important term here, and I shall return to it; suffice it to say that for Jensen, as for Olmsted—and even for Le Corbusier in his Plan Voisin—this "green complex" comes in the form of parks and green open spaces, accompanied by the belief that such environments will bring civility, health, social equity, and economic development to the city.

More than aesthetic and representational spaces, however, the more significant of these traditional urban landscapes possess the capacity to function as important ecological vessels and pathways: the hydrological and stormwater system underlying the necklacelike structure of Boston's Back Bay Fens, for example, or the greenway corridors that infiltrate Stuttgart and bring mountain air through the city as both coolant and cleanser. These kinds of infrastructural landscapes will surely continue to be important to the overall health and well-being of urban populations. These precedents also embody some of the more significant potentials of landscape urbanism: the ability to shift scales, to locate urban fabrics in their regional and biotic contexts, and to design relationships between dynamic environmental processes and urban form.

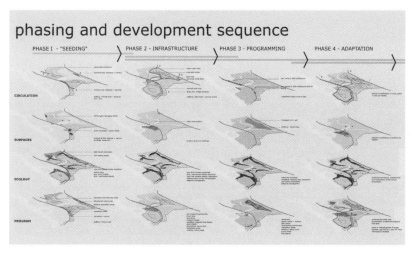

phasing and development sequence

FIG. 2 Fresh Kills Lifescape, Staten Island, 2004; phasing diagrams

The challenge in looking to these precedents for insight into our contemporary conditions is their invocation of a cultural image of "Nature," an image to which landscape is so firmly attached. Nature, in the above-mentioned examples, is mostly represented by a softly undulating pastoral scene, generally considered virtuous, benevolent, and soothing, a moral as well as practical antidote to the corrosive environmental and social qualities of the modern city. This landscape is the city's "other," its essential complement drawn from a nature outside of and excluding building, technology, and infrastructure.

A more complex and contradictory example is the Los Angeles River, which runs from the Santa Susana Mountains through downtown L.A. The "river" is actually a concrete channel built by the U.S. Corps of Engineers in response to the serious flood threat posed by the springtime snow-melts combined with surface runoff from surrounding developments. The channel is designed to optimize the efficiency and speed at which the water is discharged. Its advocates view "nature" here as a violent and threatening force—and rightly so. On the other hand, landscape architects, environmentalists, and various community groups want to convert the channel into a green corridor, replete with riparian habitat, woodlands, birdsong, and fishermen. For these groups, "nature" has been defaced by the engineer's zeal for control. It is, I believe, a well-intentioned but misguided mission, and it underscores the persistent opposition in people's minds.

This contest goes both ways. The debate is not only concerned with bringing landscape into cities but also with the expansion of cities into surrounding landscape—the source of the pastoral ideal, characterized by vast agrarian fields, wooded hillsides, and natural preserves. In 1955, the mega-mall urbanist Victor Gruen coined the term "cityscape," which he posited in contradistinction

FIG. 3 East Darling Harbor, Sydney, Australia, 2005; aerial view of new waterfront urban development as an exotic topographical landscape

to "landscape." Gruen's "cityscape" refers to the built environment of buildings, paved surfaces, and infrastructures. These are further subdivided into "techno-scapes," "transportation-scapes," "suburb-scapes," and even "subcityscapes"—the peripheral strips and debris that Gruen calls the "scourge of the metropolis." On the other hand, "landscape," for Gruen, refers to the "environment in which nature is predominant." He does say that landscape is not the "natural envi-ronment" per se, as in untouched wilderness, but to those regions where human occupation has shaped the land and its natural processes in an intimate and reciprocal way. He cites agrarian and rural situations as examples, invoking an image of topographic and ecological harmony, bathed in green vegetation and clear blue sky. For Gruen, cityscape and landscape were once clearly separated, but today the city has broken its walls to subsume and homogenize its sur-rounding landscape in an economic and "technological blitzkrieg"—the various "scapes" now in conflict and with boundless definition.[3]

This image of one thing overtaking another (with competing values attached to each, as in either landscape permeating the city or the city sprawling across its hinterland) is reminiscent of debates surrounding the design of Parc de la Villette, in which many landscape architects initially decried the lack of "landscape" in the park's design, seeing only the buildings or "follies." More recently, landscape architects have revised this sentiment, suggesting that upon further inspection, the still maturing landscape has come to prevail over the buildings. This senti-ment is very telling, for—as with Jensen, Olmsted, Le Corbusier, Gruen, and their contemporaries, or indeed for the various groups contesting the Los Angeles River today—it keeps the categories of building/city versus green landscape as separate entities: the follies at la Villette are somehow not recognized as being part of the landscape, just as the concrete river channel is not recognized as a landscape element, even though its landscape *function* is solely hydrological.

Moreover, we know full well that each of these categories—landscape and urbanism—belongs to a certain profession, or institutionalized discipline. Architects construct buildings and, with engineers and planners, they design cities; landscape architects build landscapes, in the form of earthwork, planting, and open-space design. Implicit in the sentiments of many landscape architects is indignation that the Parc de la Villette was designed not by a landscape architect but by an architect. Similarly, when a landscape architect wins a competition today that architects think belongs in their domain, there can be heard some rather cynical grumbling in that court too. So this antinomic, categorical separation between landscape and urbanism persists today not only because of a perceived difference in material, technical, and imaginative/moralistic dimensions of these two media, but also because of a hyper-professionalized classification, a construction further complicated through competing power relations.

For example, it has been argued by others that landscape tends to be repressed by architects and planners, or appropriated only to the extent that it frames and enhances the primacy of urban form. Landscape is employed here as a bourgeois aesthetic, or naturalized veil. Moreover, it is increasingly the case that vast developer-engineering corporations are constructing today's world with such pace, efficiency, and profit that all of the traditional design disciplines (and not only landscape) are marginalized as mere decorative practices, literally disenfranchised from the work of spatial formation.

Conversely, of course, many ecologically aligned landscape architects see cities as grossly negligent with regard to nature. While the accomplishments of environmental restoration and regulation are both urgent and impressive, the exclusion of urban form and process from any ecological analysis remains extremely problematic. Moreover, so-called "sustainable" proposals, wherein urbanism becomes dependent upon certain bioregional metabolisms, while assuming the place-form of some semi-ruralized environment, are surely naive and counterproductive. Do the advocates of such plans really believe that natural systems alone can cope more effectively with the quite formidable problems of waste and pollution than do modern technological plants? And do they really believe that putting people in touch with this fictional image called "nature" will predispose everybody to a more reverent relationship with the earth and with one another (as if relocating millions from cities to the countryside will actually somehow improve biodiversity and water and air quality) [FIG. 3]?

At the beginning of the twentieth century, only sixteen cities in the world had populations larger than a million people, yet at the close of the century more than five hundred cities had more than a million inhabitants, many boasting more than ten million residents and still expanding. Metropolitan Los Angeles has a current population of approximately thirteen million and is projected to double in the next twenty-five years. Given the complexity of the rapidly urbanizing metropolis, to continue to oppose nature against culture, landscape against city—and not only as negational absolutes but also in the guise of benign, complementary overlaps—is to risk complete failure of the architectural and planning arts to make any real or significant contribution to future urban formations.

With this preface, we can begin to imagine how the concept of landscape urbanism suggests a more promising, more radical, and more creative form of practice than that defined by rigid disciplinary categorizations. Perhaps the very complexity of the metabolism that drives the contemporary metropolis demands a conflation of professional and institutionalized distinctions into a new synthetic art, a spatio-material practice able to bridge scale and scope with critical insight and imaginative depth [FIG. 4].

By way of providing a schematic outline for such a practice, I can sketch four provisional themes: processes over time, the staging of surfaces, the operational or working method, and the imaginary. The first of these themes addresses processes over time. The principle is that the processes of urbanization—capital accumulation, deregulation, globalization, environmental protection, and so on—are much more significant for the shaping of urban relationships than are the spatial forms of urbanism in and of themselves. The modernist notion that new physical structures would yield new patterns of socialization has exhausted its run, failing by virtue of trying to contain the dynamic multiplicity of urban processes within a fixed, rigid, spatial frame that neither derived from nor redirected any of the processes moving through it. This emphasis on urban processes is not meant to exclude spatial form but rather seeks to construct a dialectical understanding of how it relates to the processes that flow through, manifest, and sustain it.

This suggests shifting attention away from the object qualities of space (whether formal or scenic) to the systems that condition the distribution and density of urban form. Field diagrams or maps describing the play of those forces are particularly useful instruments in furthering an understanding of urban events and processes. For example, the geographer Walter Christaller's diagrams of population distribution and city planner Ludwig Hilberseimer's diagrams of regional settlement patterns each articulate flows and forces in relation to urban form.[4]

In comparing the formal determinism of modernist urban planning and the more recent rise of neo-traditional "New Urbanism," the cultural geographer David Harvey has written that both projects fail because of their presumption that spatial order can control history and process. Harvey argues that "the struggle" for designers and planners lies not with spatial form and aesthetic appearances alone but with the advancement of "more socially just, politically emancipatory, and ecologically sane mix(es) of spatio-temporal production processes," rather than the capitulation to those processes "imposed by uncontrolled capital accumulation, backed by class privilege and gross inequalities of

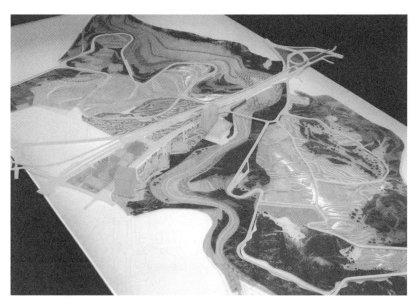

FIG. 4 Botanical Garden of Puerto Rico, San Juan, 2004; site plan depicting the garden as a new hybridized form, conjoining urban programs, research, technology, and information with nature, open space, and rain forest

political-economic power."[5] His point is that the projection of new possibilities for future urbanisms must derive less from an understanding of form and more from an understanding of process—how things work in space *and* time.

In conceptualizing a more organic, fluid urbanism, ecology itself becomes an extremely useful lens through which to analyze and project alternative urban futures. The lessons of ecology have aimed to show how all life on the planet is deeply bound into dynamic relationships. Moreover, the complexity of interaction between elements within ecological systems is such that linear, mechanistic models prove to be markedly inadequate to describe them. Rather, the discipline of ecology suggests that individual agents acting across a broad field of operation produce incremental and cumulative effects that continually evolve the shape of an environment over time. Thus, dynamic relationships and agencies of process become highlighted in ecological thinking, accounting for a particular spatial form as merely a provisional state of matter, on its way to becoming something else. Consequently, apparently incoherent or complex conditions that one might initially mistake as random or chaotic can, in fact, be shown to be highly structured entities that comprise a particular set of geometrical and spatial orders. In this sense, cities and infrastructures are just as "ecological" as forests and rivers.

Since the publication in 1969 of Ian McHarg's *Design With Nature*, landscape architects have been particularly busy developing a range of ecological techniques for the planning and design of sites. But, for a variety of reasons, some outlined earlier, ecology has been used only in the context of some thing called the "environment," which is generally thought to be of "nature" and exclusive of the city. Even those who have included the city in the ecological equation have done so only from the perspective of natural systems (hydrology, air-flow, vegetational communities, and so on). We have yet to understand cultural, social, political, and economic environments as embedded in and symmetrical with the "natural" world. The promise of landscape urbanism is the development of a space-time ecology that treats all forces and agents working in the urban field and considers them as continuous networks of inter-relationships.

One model for such a conflation that comes to mind in this context is Louis Kahn's 1953 diagram for vehicular circulation in Philadelphia. With regards to this project, Kahn wrote:

> Expressways are like rivers. These rivers frame the area to be served. Rivers have Harbors. Harbors are the municipal parking towers; from the Harbors branch a system of Canals that serve the interior; . . . from the Canals branch cul-de-sac Docks; the Docks serve as entrance halls to the buildings.[6]

Later, in Kahn's proposal for Market Street East came a whole repertoire of "gateways," "viaducts," and "reservoirs," each finding new expression in the urban field as iconographic figures illuminated in colored light at nighttime allowing for both navigation and the regulation of speed.

Kahn's diagrams suggest the need for contemporary techniques of representing the fluid, process-driven characteristics of the city, wherein the full range of agents, actors, and forces that work across a given territory might be brought into consideration, mobilized, and redirected. This work must necessarily view the entire metropolis as a living arena of processes and exchanges over time, allowing new forces and relationships to prepare the ground for new activities and patterns of occupancy. The designation *terra firma* (firm, not changing; fixed and definite) gives way in favor of the shifting processes coursing through and across the urban field: *terra fluxus*.

The second theme of the landscape urbanism project concerns itself with the phenomenon of the horizontal surface, the ground plane, the "field" of action. These surfaces constitute the urban field when considered across a wide range of scales, from the sidewalk to the street to the entire infrastructural matrix of urban surfaces. This suggests contemporary interest in surface continuities, where roofs and grounds become one and the same; and this is certainly of great value with regard to conflating separations between landscape and building—one thinks of the collaborations between Peter Eisenman and Laurie Olin in this regard. However, I would emphasize a second understanding of surface: surface understood as urban infrastructure. This understanding of the urban surface is evident in Rem Koolhaas's notion that urbanism is strategic and directed toward the "irrigation of territories with potential."[7] Unlike architecture, which consumes the potential of a site in order to project, urban infrastructure sows the seeds of future possibility, staging the ground for both uncertainty and promise. This preparation of surfaces for future appropriation differs from merely formal interest in single surface construction. It is much more strategic, emphasizing means over ends and operational logic over compositional design.

For example, the grid has historically proven to be a particularly effective field operation, extending a framework across a vast surface for flexible and changing development over time, such as the real estate and street grid of Manhattan, or the land survey grid of the Midwestern United States. In these instances, an abstract formal operation characterizes the surface, imbuing it with specificity and operational potential. This organization lends legibility and order to the surface while allowing for the autonomy and individuality of each part, and remaining open to alternative permutations over time. This stages the surface with orders and infrastructures permitting a vast range of accommodations and is indicative of an urbanism that eschews formal object-making for the tactical work of choreography, a choreography of elements and materials in time that extends new networks, new linkages, and new opportunities.

This understanding of surface highlights the trajectories of shifting populations, demographics, and interest groups upon the urban surface; traces of people provisionally stage a site in different ways at different times for various programmatic events, while connecting a variety of such events temporally around the larger territory. This attempts to create an environment that is not so much an object that has been "designed" as it is an ecology of various systems and elements that set in motion a diverse network of interaction. Landscape urbanism is here both instigator and accelerator, working across vast surfaces of potential. This approach, at once simple and conventional, affords residents a range of programmatic configurations as seasons, needs, and desires change. The thrust of this work is less toward formal resolution and more toward public processes of design and future appropriation. Concerned with a working surface over time, this is a kind of urbanism that anticipates change, open-endedness, and negotiation.

This leads in turn to the third theme of landscape urbanism, which is the operation or working method. How does one conceptualize urban geographies that function across a range of scales and implicate a host of players? Moreover, beyond issues of representation, how does one actually operate or put into effect the work of the urbanist, given the exigencies of contemporary development? There is no shortage of critical utopias, but so few of them have made it past the drawing board. It is both tragic and ironic that as designers we are all ultimately interested in the density of building but that most who actually accomplish this can only do so through the typically unimaginative and uncritical techniques of design as a service profession. On the other hand, the visionaries, it would seem, are as always provocative and interesting, but their utopias continually evade the problem of an operative strategy.

There is much more that the practice of landscape urbanism holds for questions of representation. I believe that landscape urbanism suggests a reconsideration of traditional conceptual, representational, and operative techniques. The possibilities of vast scale shifts across both time and space, working synoptic maps alongside the intimate recordings of local circumstance, comparing cinematic and choreographic techniques to spatial notation, entering the algebraic, digital space of the computer while messing around with paint, clay, and ink, and engaging real estate developers and engineers alongside the highly specialized imagineers and poets of contemporary culture—all these activities and more seem integral to any real and significant practice of synthetic urban projection. But the techniques to address the sheer scope of issues here are desperately lacking—and this area alone, it would seem to me, is deserving of our utmost attention and research.

This of course arrives at the fourth theme of landscape urbanism, which is the imaginary. There is simply no point whatsoever in addressing any of the above themes for their own sake. The collective imagination, informed and stimulated by the experiences of the material world, must continue to be the primary motivation of any creative endeavor. In many ways, the failing of twentieth-century planning can be attributed to the absolute impoverishment of the imagination with regard to the optimized rationalization of development practices and capital accumulation. Public space in the city must surely be more than mere token compensation or vessels for this generic activity called "recreation." Public spaces are firstly the containers of collective memory and desire, and secondly they are the places for geographic and social imagination to extend new relationships and sets of possibility. Materiality, representation, and imagination are not separate worlds; political change through practices of place construction owes as much to the representational and symbolic realms as to material activities. And so it seems landscape urbanism is first and last an imaginative project, a speculative thickening of the world of possibilities.

In conclusion, I would return to the paradoxical separateness of *landscape* from *urbanism* in the formulation that occasions this essay. Neither term is fully conflated into the other. I do believe that this paradox is not only inescapable but necessary to maintain. No matter how ambitious and far-reaching the above outlined practices may be, at the end of the day there will still always be doors, windows, gardens, stream corridors, apples, and lattes. There is an inevitable intimacy with things that characterizes rich urban experience. The failure of earlier urban design and regionally scaled enterprises was the oversimplification, the reduction, of the phenomenal richness of physical life. A good designer must be able to weave the diagram and the strategy in relationship to the tactile and the poetic. In other words, the union of landscape with urbanism promises new relational and systemic workings across territories of vast scale and scope, situating the parts in relation to the whole, but at the same time the separateness of landscape from urbanism acknowledges a level of material physicality, of intimacy and difference, that is always nested deep within the larger matrix or field.

In mobilizing the new ecologies of our future metropolitan regions, the critically minded landscape urbanist cannot afford to neglect the dialectical nature of being and becoming, of differences both permanent and transient. The lyrical play between nectar and NutraSweet, between birdsong and Beastie Boys, between the springtime flood surge and the drip of tap water, between mossy heaths and hot asphaltic surfaces, between controlled spaces and vast wild reserves, and between all matters and events that occur in local and highly situated moments, is precisely the ever-diversifying source of human enrichment and creativity. I can think of no greater *raison d'etre* for persisting with the advancement of landscape urbanism than this.

Notes

1. Landscape Urbanism Symposium and Exhibition, April 1997, Graham Foundation, Chicago. See also, for example, my essays in *Stalking Detroit*, ed. Georgia Daskalakis, Charles Waldheim, and Jason Young (Barcelona: Actar, 2001); *Landscape Urbanism: A Manual for the Machinic Landscape*, ed. Mohsen Mostafavi and Ciro Najle (London: Architectural Association, 2003); and David Grahame Shane, *Recombinant Urbanism* (London: John Wiley, 2005).
2. Jens Jensen, *Siftings* (Baltimore: Johns Hopkins University Press, 1990). On Jensen's work and life, see Robert E. Grese, *Jens Jensen: Maker of Natural Parks and Gardens* (Baltimore: Johns Hopkins University Press, 1992).
3. Victor Gruen, *The Heart of our Cities: The Urban Crisis, Diagnosis and Cure* (New York: Simon and Schuster, 1964). See also Gruen, *Centers for the Urban Environment: Survival of the Cities* (New York: Van Nostrand Reinhold, 1973).
4. See Walter Christaller's *Central Place Theory* (Englewood Cliffs, NJ: Prentice-Hall, 1966); and Ludwig Hilberseimer's *New Regional Pattern* (Chicago: P. Theobald, 1949).
5. David Harvey, *The Condition of Post-Modernity* (Cambridge, England: Blackwell, 1990.)
6. Louis Kahn "Philadelphia City Planning: Traffic Studies," Philadelphia, PA, 1951–53. These drawings and project papers are in the Louis I. Kahn Collection, Architectural Archives of the University of Pennsylvania.
7. Rem Koolhaas, "Whatever Happened to Urbanism," Koolhaas and Bruce Mau, *S, M, L, XL* (New York: Monacelli, 1995), 969.

Landscape
as
Urbanism

Charles Waldheim

FIG. 1 Rem Koolhaas/OMA, Parc de la Villette Competition, 1982; cartoon of programs

Over the past decade landscape has emerged as a model for contemporary urbanism, one uniquely capable of describing the conditions for radically decentralized urbanization, especially in the context of complex natural environments. Over that same decade the landscape discipline has enjoyed a period of intellectual and cultural renewal. While much of the landscape discipline's renewed relevance to discussions of the city may be attributed to this renewal or to increased environmental awareness more generally, landscape has improbably emerged as the most relevant disciplinary locus for discussions historically housed in architecture, urban design, or planning [FIG. 1].

Many of the conceptual categories and projective practices embodied in landscape urbanism and documented in this publication arise from outside those disciplines traditionally responsible for describing the city. As such, landscape urbanism offers an implicit critique of architecture and urban design's inability to offer coherent, competent, and convincing explanations of contemporary urban conditions. In this context, the discourse surrounding landscape urbanism can be read as a disciplinary realignment in which landscape supplants architecture's historical role as the basic building block of urban design. Across a range of disciplines, many authors have articulated this newfound relevance of landscape in describing the temporal mutability and horizontal extensivity of the contemporary city. Among the authors making claims for the potential of landscape in this regard is architect and educator Stan Allen, Dean of the School of Architecture at Princeton University:

> Increasingly, landscape is emerging as a model for urbanism. Landscape
> has traditionally been defined as the art of organizing horizontal sur-
> faces.... By paying close attention to these surface conditions—not only
> configuration, but also materiality and performance—designers can
> activate space and produce urban effects without the weighty apparatus
> of traditional space making.[1]

This efficiency—the ability to produce urban effects traditionally achieved through the construction of buildings simply through the organization of horizontal surfaces—recommends the landscape medium for use in contemporary urban conditions increasingly characterized by horizontal sprawl and rapid change. In the context of decentralization and decreasing density, the "weighty apparatus" of traditional urban design proves costly, slow, and inflexible in relation to the rapidly transforming conditions of contemporary urban culture.

The idea of landscape as a model for urbanism has also been articulated by landscape architect James Corner, who argues that only through a synthetic and imaginative reordering of categories in the built environment might we escape our present predicament in the cul-de-sac of post-industrial modernity, and "the bureaucratic and uninspired failings" of the planning profession.[2] His work critiques much of what landscape architecture has become as a professional concern in recent years—especially its tendency to provide scenographic screening for environments engineered and instrumentalized by other disciplines.[3] For Corner, the narrow agenda of ecological advocacy that many landscape architects profess to is nothing more than a rear-guard defense of a supposedly autonomous "nature" conceived to exist *a priori*, outside of human agency or cultural construction. In this context, current-day environmentalism and pastoral ideas of landscape appear to Corner, and many others, as naïve or irrelevant in the face of global urbanization.[4]

Landscape urbanism benefits from the canonical texts of regional environmental planning, from the work of Patrick Geddes and Benton MacKaye to Lewis Mumford to Ian McHarg, yet it also remains distinct from that tradition.[5] Corner acknowledges the historical importance of McHarg's influential *Design with Nature* yet, himself a student and faculty colleague of McHarg's at the University of Pennsylvania, rejects the opposition of nature and city implied in McHarg's regionally scaled environmental planning practice.[6]

THE ORIGINS OF LANDSCAPE URBANISM can be traced to postmodern critiques of modernist architecture and planning.[7] These critiques, put forth by Charles Jencks and other proponents of postmodern architectural culture, indicted modernism for its inability to produce a "meaningful" or "livable" public realm,[8] for its failure to come to terms with the city as an historical construction of collective consciousness,[9] and for its inability to communicate with multiple audiences.[10] In fact, the "death of modern architecture," as proclaimed by Jencks in 1977, coincided with a crisis of industrial economy in the United States, marking a shift toward the diversification of consumer markets.[11] What postmodern architecture's scenographic approach did not, in fact could not, address were the structural conditions of industrialized modernity that tended toward the decentralization of urban form. This decentralization continues apace today in North America, remarkably indifferent to the superficial stylistic oscillations of architectural culture.

In the wake of the social and environmental disasters of industrialization, postmodern architecture retreated to the comforting forms of nostalgia and seemingly stable, secure, and more permanent forms of urban arrangement. Citing European precedents for traditional city form, postmodern architects practiced a kind of preemptive cultural regression, designing individual buildings to invoke an absent context, as if neighborly architectural character could contravene a century of industrial economy. The rise of the urban design discipline in the 1970s and '80s extended interest in the aggregation of architectural elements into ensembles of nostalgic urban consumption. During this same time, the discipline of city planning abdicated altogether, seeking refuge in the relatively ineffectual enclaves of policy, procedure, and public therapy.[12]

The postmodern *rappelle á l'ordre* indicted modernism for devaluing the traditional urban values of pedestrian scale, street grid continuity, and contextual architectural character. As has been well documented, the postmodern impulse can be equally understood as a desire to communicate with multiple audiences or to commodify architectural images for diversifying consumer markets. But this dependence upon sympathetically styled and spatially sequenced architectural objects could not be sustained, given the rise of mobile capital, automobile culture, and decentralization. And yet the very indeterminacy and flux of the contemporary city, the bane of traditional European citymaking, are precisely those qualities explored in emergent works of landscape urbanism. This point is perhaps best exemplified in Barcelona's program of public space and building projects in the 1980s and early '90s, which focused primarily on the traditional center of the Catalan capital. Today the push in Barcelona to redevelop the airport, logistical zone, industrial waterfront, metropolitan riverways, and water-treatment facilities has less to do with buildings and plazas than with large-scale infrastructural landscapes. These examples, along with recent work in the Netherlands, reveal the role of large-scale landscape as an element of urban infrastructure. Of course many traditional examples of nineteenth century urban landscape architecture integrate landscape with infrastructure—Olmsted's Central Park in New York and Back Bay Fens in Boston serve as canonical examples. Contrasting this tradition, contemporary practices of landscape urbanism reject the camouflaging of ecological systems within pastoral images of "nature." Rather, contemporary landscape urbanism practices recommend the use of infrastructural systems and the public landscapes they engender as the very ordering mechanisms of the urban field itself, shaping and shifting the organization of urban settlement and its inevitably indeterminate economic, political, and social futures.

LANDSCAPE IS A MEDIUM, it has been recalled by Corner, Allen, and others, uniquely capable of responding to temporal change, transformation, adaptation, and succession. These qualities recommend landscape as an analog to contemporary processes of urbanization and as a medium uniquely suited to the open-endedness, indeterminacy, and change demanded by contemporary urban conditions. As Allen puts it, "landscape is not only a formal model for urbanism today, but perhaps more importantly, a model for process."[13]

Tellingly, the first projects to reveal this potential for landscape to operate as a model for urban process were produced not in North America but rather in

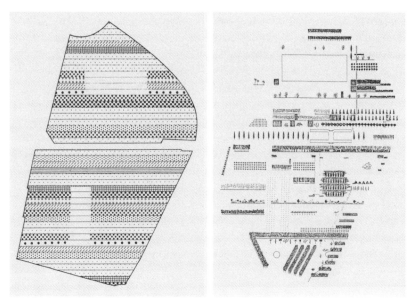

FIGS. 2, 3 Parc de la Villette Competition: diagram of strips (LEFT); planting diagram (RIGHT)

Europe. Among the first projects to orchestrate urban program as a landscape process was the 1982 Competition for Parc de la Villette. In 1982, la Villette invited submissions for an "Urban Park for the 21st Century" over a 125-acre site, once the site of Paris's largest slaughterhouse. The demolition of the Parisian *abattoir* and its replacement with intensively programmed public activities is precisely the kind of project increasingly undertaken in post-industrial cities across the globe. Just as more recent design competitions in North America such as Downsview and Fresh Kills, la Villette proposed landscape as the basic frame-work for an urban transformation of what had been a part of the working city, left derelict by shifts in economies of production and consumption. The competition for la Villette began a trajectory of postmodern urban park, in which landscape was itself conceived as a complex medium capable of articulating rela-tions between urban infrastructure, public events, and indeterminate urban futures for large post-industrial sites, rather than simply as healthful exceptions to the unhealthy city that surrounded them.[14]

470 entries from over 70 countries were submitted for la Villette, the vast majority of which retraced familiar profiles for public parks and typologies for the recovery of the traditional city, while two submissions clearly signaled a par-adigm shift still underway in the reconception of contemporary urbanism. The winning scheme, by the office of Bernard Tschumi, represented a conceptual leap in the development of landscape urbanism; it formulated landscape as the most suitable medium through which to order programmatic and social change

over time, especially complex evolving arrangements of urban activities. This continued Tschumi's longstanding interest in reconstituting event and program as a legitimate architectural concern in lieu of the stylistic issues dominating architectural discourse in the postmodern era, as he stated in his competition entry:

> The '70s witnessed a period of renewed interest in the formal constitution of the city, its typologies and its morphologies. While developing analyses focused on the history of the city, this attention was largely devoid of programmatic justification. No analysis addressed the issue of the activities that were to occur in the city. Nor did any properly address the fact that the organization of functions and events was as much an architectural concern as the elaboration of forms or styles.[15]

Equally significant was the influence of the second-prize entry submitted by the Office of Metropolitan Architecture and Rem Koolhaas [FIGS. 2, 3]. The unbuilt scheme explored the juxtaposition of unplanned relationships between various park programs. Koolhaas's organizational conceit of parallel strips of landscape, itself having become something of a canonical cliché, radically juxtaposed irreconcilable contents, invoking the vertical juxtaposition of various programs on adjacent floors of Manhattan skyscrapers as described in Koolhaas's *Delirious New York*.[16] As conceived by Koolhaas/OMA, the infrastructure of the park would be strategically organized to support an indeterminate and unknowable range of future uses over time:

> [I]t is safe to predict that during the life of the park, the program will undergo constant change and adjustment. The more the park works, the more it will be in a perpetual state of revision.... The underlying principle of programmatic indeterminacy as a basis of the formal concept allows any shift, modification, replacement, or substitutions to occur without damaging the initial hypothesis.[17]

Through their deployment of postmodern ideas of open-endedness and indeterminacy, Tschumi's and Koolhaas's projects for Parc de la Villette signaled the role that landscape would come to play as a medium through which to articulate a postmodern urbanism: layered, non-hierarchical, flexible, and strategic. Both schemes offered a nascent form of landscape urbanism, constructing a horizontal field of infrastructure that might accommodate all sorts of urban activities, planned and unplanned, imagined and unimagined, over time.

IN THE WAKE OF LA VILLETTE'S INFLUENCE, architectural culture has become increasingly aware of landscape's role as a viable framework for the contemporary city. Across a diverse spectrum of cultural positions landscape has emerged as the most relevant medium through which to construct a meaningful and viable public realm in North American cities. Consider how the thinking of architectural historian and theorist Kenneth Frampton has shifted in recent years. In the 1980s, Frampton lamented the impediments to making meaningful urban form given the power of speculative capital and the rise of automobile culture:

> Modern building is now so universally conditioned by optimized technology that the possibility of creating significant urban form has become extremely limited. The restrictions jointly imposed by automotive distribution and the volatile play of land speculation serve to limit the scope of urban design to such a degree that any intervention tends to be reduced either to the manipulation of elements predetermined by the imperatives of production, or to a kind of superficial masking which modern development requires for the facilitation of marketing and the maintenance of social control.[18]

Against the forces of "optimized technology," Frampton argued for an architecture of "resistance." During the following decade, however, Frampton's call for architecture as an instrument of local resistance to global culture gave way to a more subtly shaded position that concedes the unique role of landscape in providing a modicum of market-based urban order. In this later formulation, landscape rather than object formalism affords the greater (albeit still slim) prospect of constructing meaningful relations within the detritus of market production:

> The dystopia of the megalopolis is already an irreversible historical fact: it has long since installed a new way of life, not to say a new nature . . . I would submit that instead we need to conceive of a remedial landscape that is capable of playing a critical and compensatory role in relation to the ongoing, destructive commodification of the man-made world.[19]

To invoke Frampton and Koolhaas together is perhaps curious, for Frampton's interest in local cultural resistance to globalization could not be further afield from Koolhaas's project of engagement with the very mechanisms of global capital. Indeed Koolhaas's practice of spinning a neo-avant gardist position from the working of global brands is by now familiar. Despite their divergent cultural politics, by the mid '90s, Koolhaas and Frampton had come to occupy curiously convergent positions, concurring on the fact that landscape had supplanted architecture's role as the medium most capable of ordering contemporary urbanism. As Koolhaas put it in 1998: "Architecture is no longer the primary element of urban order, increasingly urban order is given by a thin horizontal vegetal plane, increasingly landscape is the primary element of urban order."[20]

Arguably a third significant cultural position, a *realpolitik* of laissez faire economic development and public-private partnerships in planning processes, is articulated by Peter Rowe in *Making a Middle Landscape*.[21] Interestingly, Rowe's conclusions are not dissimilar; he advocates a critical role for the design disciplines in the making of a meaningful public realm in the exurban "middle" between traditional city center and greenfield suburb beyond. Rowe's position is summarized by Frampton, who identifies two salient points: "first, that priority should now be accorded to landscape, rather than to freestanding built form and second, that there is a pressing need to transform certain megalopolitan types such as shopping malls, parking lots, and office parks into landscaped built forms."[22]

If landscape urbanism offers strategies for design, is also provides a cultural category—a lens through which to see and describe the contemporary city, many of which, absent intervention by designers and without the benefit of planning, have been found to emulate natural systems. Again, the work of Koolhaas is notable, but not exceptional.[23] The clearest example of this tendency can be found in Koolhaas's essay on Atlanta:

> Atlanta does not have the classical symptoms of the city; it is not dense;
> it is a sparse, thin carpet of habitation, a kind of supramatist composition
> of little fields. Its strongest contextual givens are vegetal and infrastruc-
> tural: forests and roads. Atlanta is not a city; it is a *landscape*.[25]

The tendency to view the contemporary city through the lens of landscape is most evident in projects and texts which appropriate the terms, conceptual categories, and operating methodologies of field ecology: that is, the study of species as they relate to their natural environments.[25] This reveals one of the implicit advantages of landscape urbanism: the conflation, integration, and fluid exchange between (natural) environmental and (engineered) infrastructural systems.

While this newfound relevance for landscape in conceptions of urbanism first manifested itself in the work of architects, it has been quickly corroborated from within the profession of landscape architecture itself. Though still largely marginalized by the dominant culture of mainstream landscape architecture, it is increasingly seen as a viable aspect of the profession's future in much of the academy and for a variety of progressive professional practices. This is possible in part given the critical reassessment that landscape architecture is presently enjoying, in many ways analogous to the transformations within architectural culture with the rise of postmodernism. In fact, it is perfectly reasonable to understand the recent renaissance of landscape discourse as the impact of postmodern thought on the field.

As the discipline of landscape architecture is examining its own historical and theoretical underpinnings, the general public is increasingly conscious of environmental issues, and thus more aware of landscape as a cultural category. Simultaneously many landscape architecture practices in North America have become proficient in professional activities that were once the domain of urban planners. This has allowed landscape architects to fill a professional void, as planning has largely opted out of responsibility for proposing physical designs. Landscape architects have also been increasingly involved in work for both

FIG. 4 Joan Roig and Enric Batlle, Trinitat Cloverleaf Park, Barcelona, 1992; aerial view

post-industrial sites and the easements of various infrastructural systems such as electrical, water, and highway systems. As Australian landscape architect Richard Weller describes the landscape profession's newfound relevance:

> Postmodern landscape architecture has done a boom trade in cleaning up after modern infrastructure as societies—in the first world at least— shift from primary industry to post industrial, information societies. In common landscape practice, work is more often than not conducted in the shadow of the infrastructural object, which is given priority over the field into which it is to be inserted. However, as any landscape architect knows, the landscape itself is a medium through which all ecological transactions must pass: it is *the* infrastructure of the future.[26]

The efficacy of landscape as a remediating practice—a salve for the wounds of the industrial age—is evident in the work of many contemporary landscape architects. Projects by Peter Latz at Duisburg Nord Steelworks Park in Germany and Richard Haag at Gas Works Park in Seattle, are useful illustrations of this

FIGS. 5, 6 Adriaan Geuze/West 8 Landscape Architects: East Scheldt, 1992 [LEFT];
Schelpenproject, 1992; detail [RIGHT]

tendency. Many landscape architects have taken up this work for brownfield sites in North America as the body of technical knowledge, modes of practice, and availability of funding have increased in recent years. Projects by Hargreaves Associates, Corner/Field Operations, and Julie Bargmann's DIRT Studio are representative here, among others. Another key strategy of landscape urbanism is the integration of transportation infrastructure into public space. This is exemplified by Barcelona's program of public space and peripheral road improvements, including projects such as Trinitat Cloverleaf Park by Enric Batlle and Joan Roig, among others [FIG. 4]. While this genre of work—the use of landscape in the stitching of infrastructure into urban fabrics—has well-established precedents, the Barcelona peripheral roadwork is distinct. It offers public parks conceived and constructed simultaneously with the public conveyance of the highway, subtly inflecting its design away from an optimized artifact of civil engineering toward a more complex synthesis of requirements, in which neither civil engineering nor landscape dominate.

One of the more outspoken proponents of landscape as urbanism is Adriaan Geuze, principal of West 8 Landscape Architects, based in Rotterdam. West 8 has worked on projects at various scales, articulating multiple roles for landscape in the shaping of contemporary urbanism.[27] Several of these have imaginatively reordered relationships between ecology and infrastructure, deemphasizing the middle scale of decorative or architectural work and favoring instead the large-scale infrastructural diagram and the small-scale material condition.

West 8's Shell Project, for instance, organizes dark and light mussel shells and the corresponding flocks of similarly shaded dark and light birds naturally adapted to feed from them [FIGS. 5, 6]. These surfaces form parallel strips of shoulders along the highway connecting the constructed islands of the East Scheldt storm-tide barrier. This project organizes an ecology of natural selection and renders it for public perception via the automobile. By contrast, historical precedents for

FIGS. 7, 8   Adriaan Geuze/West 8 Landscape Architects, Schiphol Amsterdam Airport
Landscape, 1992–96: green gaze collage [LEFT]; birches [TOP RIGHT]; clover [BOTTOM RIGHT]

urban parkways typically reproduce a pastoral image of "nature" without intervening in their ecological surroundings in any substantial way. Likewise, West
8's ambitious scheme for the Schiphol Amsterdam Airport Landscape abandons
the professional tradition of specifically detailed planting plans, deploying
instead a general botanical strategy of sunflowers, clover, and beehives [FIGS. 7, 8].
This work, by avoiding intricate compositional designs and precise planting
arrangements, allows the project to respond to future programmatic and political changes in Schiphol's planning, positioning landscape as a strategic partner
in the complex process of airport planning rather than (as is usually the case)
simply an unfortunate victim of it. Another example of landscape urbanism as
a professional framework is West 8's redevelopment plan for Borneo and
Sporenburg in Amsterdam Harbor. The planning and design of this large-scale
redevelopment is conceived as an enormous landscape urbanism project, orchestrated by West 8, into which the work of numerous other architects and designers is inserted. The project suggests the potential diversity of landscape urbanist
strategies through the insertion of numerous small landscaped courts and yards,
and the commissioning of numerous designers for individual housing units.
Taken together, the range of West 8's recent production illustrates the potential
for landscape architecture to supplant architecture, urban design, and urban
planning as design disciplines responsible for reordering post-industrial urban
sites [FIGS. 9–12].

SEVERAL RECENT INTERNATIONAL DESIGN competitions for the reuse of
enormously scaled industrial sites in North American cities have used landscape as
their primary medium. Downsview Park, located on the site of an underutilized
military airbase in Toronto, and Fresh Kills, on the site of the world's largest
landfill on Staten Island, New York, are representative of these trends and offer
the most fully formed examples of landscape urbanism practices to date applied

FIGS. 9–11
Adriaan Geuze/West 8 Landscape Architects
Schouwburgplein Rotterdam, 1995; layers (LEFT),
Borneo en Sporenburg, Amsterdam Harbor
Redevelopment, 1995–96; housing program (BELOW)
Nieuw Oost Amsterdam, 1994; plan (BOTTOM)

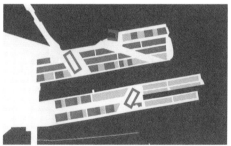

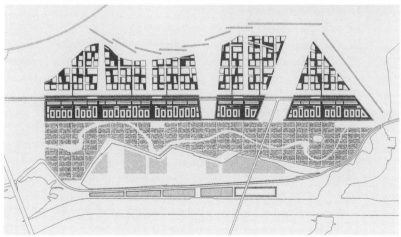

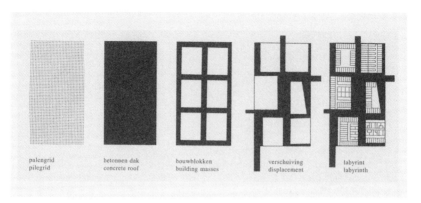

FIG. 12 Nieuw Oost Amsterdam; plan diagrams

to the detritus of the industrial city.[28] While significant distinctions exist between these two commissions, as do questions regarding their eventual realization, the body of work produced for Downsview and Fresh Kills represents an emerging consensus that designers of the built environment, across disciplines, would do well to examine landscape as the medium through which to conceive the renovation of the post-industrial city. James Corner's projects for Downsview (with Stan Allen) [FIGS. 13, 14] and Fresh Kills [FIGS. 15, 16] are exemplary in this regard, illustrating mature works of landscape urbanism through their accumulation and orchestration of absolutely diverse and potentially incongruous contents. Typical of this work, and by now standard fare for projects of this type, are detailed diagrams of phasing, animal habitats, succession planting, and hydrological systems, as well as programmatic and planning regimes. While these diagrams initially overwhelm with information, they present an understanding of the enormous complexities confronting any work at this scale. Particularly compelling is the complex interweaving of natural ecologies with the social, cultural, and infrastructural layers of the contemporary city.

While both Koolhaas/OMA (in partnership with designer Bruce Mau) and Tschumi submitted entries as finalists at Downsview, they found their historical fortunes reversed, more or less precisely. The imageable and media friendly Mau and Koolhaas/OMA scheme "Tree City" was awarded first prize and the commission; while the more sublime, layered, and intellectually challenging scheme of the office of Bernard Tschumi will doubtless enjoy greater influence within architectural culture, particularly as the information age transforms our understandings and limits of the "natural." Tschumi's "The Digital and the Coyote" project for Downsview presented an electronic analog to his longstanding interest in urban event, with richly detailed diagrams of succession planting and the seeding of ambient urbanity in the midst of seemingly desolate prairies. Tschumi's position at Downsview is symmetrical with his original thesis for la Villette. Both

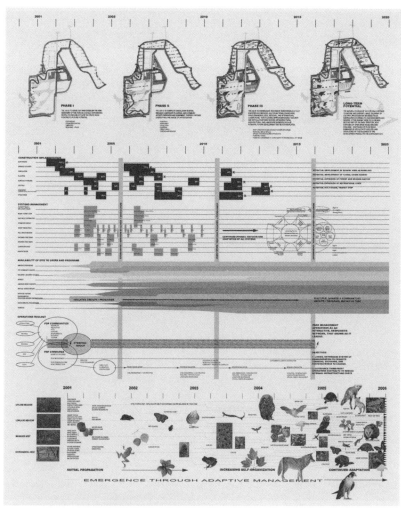

FIGS. 13, 14
James Corner and Stan Allen/Field
Operations, Downsview Park
Competition, Toronto, 2000
plan diagrams (ABOVE); model (LEFT)

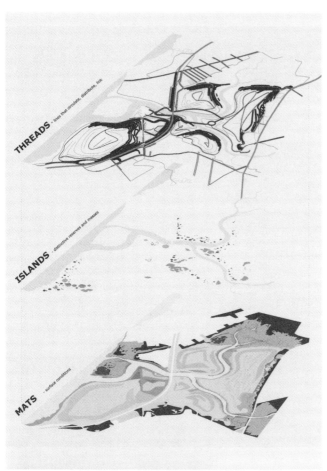

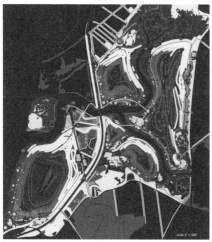

FIGS. 15, 16
James Corner/Field Operations,
Fresh Kills Landfill Competition,
New York, 2001
site diagrams (LEFT); site plan (RIGHT)

projects were based on a fundamental indictment of the nineteenth-century Olmstedian model, offering in its place an understanding of landscape conflated with a pervasive and ubiquitous urbanism. As Tschumi put it in his project statement for Downsview:

> Neither theme park or wildlife preserve, Downsview does not seek to renew using the conventions of traditional park compositions such as those of Vaux or Olmsted. The combination of advanced military technologies with water courses and flows and downstreams suggests another fluid, liquid, digital sensibility. Airstrips, information centers, public performance spaces, internet and worldwide web access all point to a redefinition of received ideas about parks, nature, and recreation, in a 21st century setting where everything is "urban," even in the middle of the wilderness.[29]

The Downsview and Fresh Kills projects are notable for the presence of landscape architects on interdisciplinary teams of consultants, whereas the la Villette competition named a single lead architect to orchestrate the entire project. Striking and consistent in this regard are the central involvement of ecologists as well as information or communication designers on virtually all teams. This is clearly distinct from the overarching role of architects in previous regimes of urban design and planning, where these concerns were either absent altogether (ecology) or simply subsumed within the professional practice of the architect (information design).

While it remains unclear if either of the winning schemes by Mau and Koolhaas/OMA for Downsview and Corner/Field Operations for Fresh Kills will be fully realized, we must see this as a challenge of political imagination and cultural leadership rather than as a failure of the competition processes or the projects they premiated. These projects and the work of their competitors, taken collectively, point to transformations currently underway which are profoundly changing the disciplinary and professional assumptions behind the design of the built environment. Particularly evident is the fact that projects of this scale and significance demand professional expertise at the intersections of ecology and engineering, social policy and political process. The synthesis of this range of knowledge and its embodiment in public design processes recommend landscape urbanism as a disciplinary framework for reconceiving the contemporary urban field.

Notes

1. Stan Allen, "Mat Urbanism: The Thick 2-D," in Hashim Sarkis, ed., *CASE: Le Corbusier's Venice Hospital*, (Munich: Prestel, 2001), 124.
2. See James Corner, "Terra Fluxus," in this collection. See also James Corner, ed., *Recovering Landscape* (New York: Princeton Architectural Press, 1999).

3. See Corner's introduction to *Recovering Landscape*, 1–26.

4. One marker of a generational divide between advocacy and instrumentalization has been the recent emergence of complex and culturally derived understanding of natural systems. An example of this can be found in the shift from pictorial to operational in landscape discourse that has been the subject of much recent work. See for example James Corner, "Eidetic Operations and New Landscapes," in *Recovering Landscape*, 153–69. Also useful on this topic is Julia Czerniak, "Challenging the Pictorial: Recent Landscape Practice," in *Assemblage* 34 (December 1997): 110–20.

5. Ian McHarg, *Design with Nature* (Garden City, New York: Natural History Press, 1969). For an overview of Mumford's work, see Mark Luccarelli, *Lewis Mumford and the Ecological Region: The Politics of Planning* (New York: Guilford Press, 1997).

6. See Corner, "Terra Fluxus," in this collection.

7. Early critiques of modernist architecture and urban planning ranged from the populist Jane Jacobs, *Death and Life of Great American Cities* (New York: Vintage Books, 1961), to the professional Robert Venturi, *Complexity and Contradiction in Architecture* (New York: Museum of Modern Art, 1966).

8. Kevin Lynch, *A Theory of Good City Form* (Cambridge, Mass.: MIT Press, 1981). Also see Lynch's earlier empirical research in *Image of the City* (Cambridge, Mass.: MIT Press, 1960).

9. The most significant of these critiques was Aldo Rossi. See Rossi, *The Architecture of the City* (Cambridge, Mass.: MIT Press, 1982).

10. Robert Venturi and Denise Scott-Brown's work is indicative of these interests. See Venturi, Scott-Brown, and Steven Izenour, *Learning From Las Vegas: The Forgotten Symbolism of Architectural Form* (Cambridge, Mass.: MIT Press, 1977).

11. Charles Jencks, *The Language of Post-Modern Architecture* (New York: Rizzoli, 1977). On Fordism and its relation to postmodern architecture, see Patrik Schumacher and Christian Rogner, "After Ford," in Georgia Daskalakis, Charles Waldheim, and Jason Young, eds., *Stalking Detroit* (Barcelona: ACTAR, 2001), 48–56.

12. Harvard University's Urban Design Program began in 1960, and the discipline grew in popularity with increased enrollments, increased numbers of degrees conferred and the addition of new degree programs during the 1970s and '80s.

13. Allen, "Mat Urbanism: The Thick 2-D," 125.

14. For contemporaneous critical commentary on la Villette, see Anthony Vidler, "Trick-Track," *La Case Vide: La Villette* (London: Architectural Association, 1985), and Jacques Derrida, "Point de Folie-Maintenant l'architecture," *AA Files* 12 (Summer 1986): 65–75.

15. Bernard Tschumi, La Villette Competition Entry, "The La Villette Competition," *Princeton Journal* vol. 2, "On Landscape" (1985): 200–10.

16. Rem Koolhaas, *Delirious New York: A Retroactive Manifesto for Manhattan* (New York: Oxford University Press, 1978).

17. Rem Koolhaas, "Congestion without Matter," *S, M, L, XL* (New York: Monacelli, 1999), 921.

18. Kenneth Frampton, "Towards a Critical Regionalism: Six Points for an Architecture of Resistance," in Hal Foster, ed., *The Anti-Aesthetic* (Seattle: Bay Press, 1983), 17.

19. Kenneth Frampton, "Toward an Urban Landscape," *Columbia Documents* (New York: Columbia University, 1995), 89, 92.

20. Rem Koolhaas, "IIT Student Center Competition Address," Illinois Institute of Technology, College of Architecture, Chicago, March 5, 1998.

21. Peter Rowe, *Making a Middle Landscape* (Cambridge, Mass.: MIT Press, 1991).

22. Kenneth Frampton, "Toward an Urban Landscape," 83–93.

23. Among these see, for example, Lars Lerup, "Stim and Dross: Rethinking the Metropolis," *After the City* (Cambridge, Mass.: MIT Press, 2000), 47–61.

24. Rem Koolhaas, "Atlanta," *S, M, L, XL* (New York: Monacelli, 1999), 835.

25. Among the sources of this material of interest to architects and landscape architects is field ecologist Richard T. T. Forman. See Wenche E. Dramstad, James D. Olson, and Richard T. T. Forman, *Landscape Ecology Principles in Landscape Architecture and Land-Use Planning* (Cambridge, Mass. and Washington, D.C.: Harvard University and Island Press, 1996).

26. Richard Weller, "Landscape Architecture and the City Now," unpublished manuscript based on "Toward an Art of Infrastructure in the Theory and Practice of Contemporary Landscape Architecture," keynote address, *MESH* Conference, Royal Melbourne Institute of Technology, Melbourne, Australia, July 9, 2001.

27. On the work of Adriaan Geuze/West 8 see, "West 8 Landscape Architects," in *Het Landschap/The Landscape: Four International Landscape Designers* (Antwerpen: deSingel, 1995), 215–53, and Luca Molinari, ed., *West 8* (Milan: Skira, 2000).

28. Downsview and Fresh Kills have been the subject of extensive documentation, including essays in *Praxis*, no. 4, *Landscapes* (2002). For additional information see Julia Czerniak ed., *CASE: Downsview Park Toronto* (Cambridge/Munich: Harvard/Prestel, 2001), and Charles Waldheim, "Park=City? The Downsview Park Competition," in *Landscape Architecture Magazine* vol. 91, no.3 (March 2001): 80–85, 98–99.

29. Bernard Tschumi, "Downsview Park: The Digital and the Coyote," in Czerniak, ed., *CASE: Downsview Park Toronto*, 82–89.

The Emergence of Landscape Urbanism

Grahame Shane

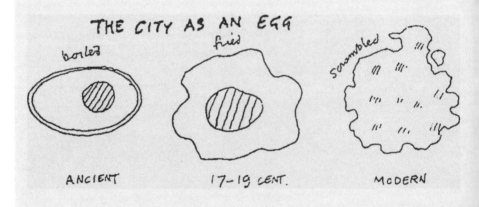

FIG. 1 Cedric Price, "Three Eggs Diagram"

Traditional urban histories make a distinction between the Neolithic agrarian revolution that produced compact cities around the world and the modern, industrial revolution that allowed cities to break beyond their former bounds [FIG. 1].[1] More recently historians like Spiro Kostof, in his books the *The City Shaped* and *The City Assembled* followed cues offered by Kevin Lynch in *Good City Form*, to develop an argument for a third city form, one that Lynch called "organic," moving beyond his teacher Frank Lloyd Wright and the car-based, agrarian-industrial model of Broadacre City from the mid-1930s.[2] Sébastien Marot, in his *Suburbanism and the Art of Memory*, gives this complex of ideas an ironic twist, reintroducing a sense of layering, history, and poetry into the suburban landscape.[3]

In this brief essay I trace the recent trajectory of the idea of landscape urbanism and the expanded field of urban design as the successor to this elusive third term in the emerging essay collections, such as this volume, *Landscape Urbanism: A Manual for the Machinic Landscape*, edited by Mohsen Mostafavi and Ciro Najle, or *Stalking Detroit*, edited by Georgia Daskalakis, Charles Waldheim, and Jason Young.[4] Collected in the latter, the essay "After Ford," by Patrik Schumacher and Christian Rogner, of the Design Research Laboratory at the Architectural Association (AA) in London, provides a most convincing explanation for the relation between modern urbanism and Fordist economic imperatives, as well as the surreal spectacle of decay and abandonment found today in many North American industrial cities. In Neo-Marxian terms, Schumacher and Rogner brilliantly describe the interior logic of Fordist mass production and the consequences for the traditional, closed form of the city. They map three phases in the evolution of Fordism as a technical and spatial system, matching each phase to a logical and organizational structure.[5]

The development of the industrial city begins with the invention of the mass-production line through the application of Frederick Winslow Taylor's principles of scientific management to industrial production. Le Corbusier published Albert Kahn's 1909 Ford Highland Park Plant as an icon of modernism and an exemplar of this industrial form in the landmark publication *Towards a New Architecture*, published in 1927.[6] According to Schumacher and Rogner, the traditional industrial city's destruction began in what they term Phase 2, when the "assembly line concept is applied to the overall urban complex," creating a miniature "city as machine."[7] Here Ford dispersed the production line flows and assembly points in single-story sheds designed by Kahn across enormous suburban property, creating the world's largest industrial complex. Both Hitler and Stalin admired this system of rapid industrialization, leading Kahn to build five hundred plants in Russia between 1929 and 1932. Finally the effects of Fordism and the "city machine" model of organization dissolved the industrial city itself into the landscape.[8] Schumacher and Rogner mark Phase 3 with Ford's dispersal of production patterns—first regionally, then nationally, then globally. This dispersal created a more open, decentralized, self-organizing, and postmodern "matrix" pattern, still operating today.

The problems of this postmodern organization in the landscape became obvious in the 1990s with the proliferation of sprawling cities, gated enclaves, residential communities, megamalls, and theme parks. As Schumacher and Rogner write, the extension of this dispersed system "fueled the rapid decompression of urban industrial cities and the decentralization of both mass production and mass consumption."[9]

The question facing American postindustrial cities in the wake of Fordism is what to do about the abandoned factories, acres of vacant workers' housing, and redundant commercial strips. How should once mighty cities shrink and recede back into the landscape? The British architect Cedric Price proposed a mobile university in train carriages on abandoned railway tracks to revive a similar "rust belt" area in his Potteries Think Belt project (1964–65). David Green of Archigram, in his Rockplug (1969) and L.A.W.U.N. (1970) projects, imagined the complete dissolution of the "machine city" into a series of mobile housing units with automated service robots and buried networks set in an idyllic landscape. The term *garden suburb* took on a new, ironic, and electronic meaning: a territory inhabited by sophisticated urban nomads in inflatable capsules, needing access to global systems.[10] Following this lead, the Urban Street Farmer Group in London in the early 1970s envisioned a huge recycling process conducted on a street-by-street basis, creating urban agriculture. In 1987 Richard Register, in his Ecocity Berkeley project, provided a considered ecological framework for such urban shrinkage, with many low-tech ecological lessons applicable to the dissolution of former industrial cities into the landscape.[11] In this context, "landscape urbanism" has recently emerged as a rubric to describe the design strategies resulting in the wake of traditional urban forms. Lynch, in his *Good City Form*, used the term "ecological" to describe his third, hybrid city morphology. He cited earlier classic ecological texts, such as E. P. Odum's 1963 book *Ecology*, to further describe his emerging sense of the urban landscape as a system of flows and feedback loops.[12]

Charles Waldheim further articulated this ecological understanding in the organization of a March 1997 conference and exhibition titled Landscape Urbanism. Waldheim coined the term "landscape urbanism" to describe the practices of many designers for whom landscape had replaced architectural form as the primary medium of citymaking. This understanding of decentralized post-industrial urban form highlighted the leftover void spaces of the city as potential commons. Waldheim saw landscape urbanism, like landscape architecture, as an interstitial design discipline, operating in the spaces between buildings, infrastructural systems, and natural ecologies. In these contexts, landscape urbanism became a useful lens through which to view those "unseen," residual *terrain vagues* once inhabited by conceptual and land artists like Robert Smithson or advocated as marginal spaces worthy of attention by the architect Ignasi de Solà-Morales Rubio.[13]

The Landscape Urbanism exhibition contained an international survey of public urban spaces, but one project that stood out in particular was James Corner's premiated but sadly unbuilt project for Greenport Harborfront, Long Island (1997). His office, Field Operations, proposed creating a sense of urban activity around the annual raising and lowering of the town's ancient sailing ship *Stella Maris* up and down a newly created slip, with a historic children's carousel housed in an adjacent band shell. Corner envisioned this staged, twice annual event as an attractor for people and the media, who would flock to the town in its off season, inhabiting the newly created commons on the harbor front to watch the ship's spectacular movements. In the winter, the ship would become a monumental, sculptural presence lit at night in the center of the small port's commons; in the summer it would return to its accustomed quayside, where its masts would tower above the rooftops.[14]

Corner's project illustrates his concept of a "performative" urbanism based on preparing the setting for programmed and unprogrammed activities on common land. Three other projects included in the exhibition, each using Detroit as their subject, paired with commentary by a landscape architect, provide further insights into this emerging strategy.[15] Waldheim proposed the most comprehensive of landscape urbanism practices in "Decamping Detroit," advocating a four-stage decommissioning of land from the city's legal control: Dislocation (disconnection of services), then Erasure (demolition and jumpstarting the native landscape ecology by dropping appropriate seeds from the air), followed by Absorption (ecological reconstitution of part of the Zone as woods, marshes, and streams), and finally Infiltration (the recolonization of the landscape with heteropic villagelike enclaves).[16] As Corner writes in his commentary, this project "prompts you to reflect on the reversal of the traditional approach to colonization, from building to unbuilding, removal, and erasure."[17] This reversal of normal processes opens the way for a new hybrid urbanism, with dense clusters of activity and the reconstitution of the natural ecology, starting a more ecologically balanced, inner-city urban form in the void.

In the context of post-Fordist decentralization and the abandonment of industrial city centers, Corner proposes "landscraping" as a solution to the disappearance of the city documented in *Stalking Detroit*. Corner sees the creation of the voids of inner-city Detroit as a result of Ford's (and Chrysler's and General Motors's) organizational and territorial evolution as industrial corporations. He conceives of the resultant voids as "constructions" produced by an industrial logic and as reserves of "indeterminacy"—places of potential action. This "logistical and performative" future action, as in the past, will emerge from social codes and conventions that regulate the relationships between urban stakeholders or actors in industrial societies.[18] These codes become embedded in "infrastructural regimes" that Corner argues, like Schumacher and Rogner, are best depicted as diagrams of organization. These diagrams show "the mechanisms necessary for something to be enacted (including erasure)."[19] The disappearance of the city into the landscape thus becomes a part of its larger evolution over time that can be designed, just as John Soane in the 1820s imagined his new Bank of England in London as a future ruin. Corner looks forward to "moving from both modernist and New Urbanist models of ordering the city (both of which believe that formal models alone will remedy the problems of the city, stylistic differences not withstanding), to more open-ended, strategic models."[20]

Corner traces this performative approach back to the work of Rem Koolhaas and Bernard Tschumi, who in turn drew on the time-centered work of Cedric Price and Archigram. Corner saw Tschumi's Parc de la Vilette project (1982) as a "prepared ground" for Paris, with pavilions and exceptional park regulations allowing walking on the grass, football, bicycling, kite-flying, picnicking, and even equestrian events. Koolhaas (with Xaveer de Geyter) protected the beautiful landscape territory of Melun-Sénart by "linear voids" of nondevelopment in his New Town Competition entry (1987). Another Dutch precedent for Corner is West 8, led by landscape architect Adriaan Geuze, whose West Market Square in Binnerotte, Rotterdam (1994–95), provides a working example of this strategy.[21] The municipality of Binnerotte owns, maintains, and programs the space, which is also free at times to be occupied by local people of all ages, under the surveillance of cameras and local police.

For Corner these spaces are "prepared grounds," flexible and open, like the British commons or Indian *maidan*, allowing the "ad hoc emergence" of "performative social patterns and group alliances that eventually colonize these surfaces in provisional yet deeply significant ways."[22] A historic British commons like Hampstead Heath in London, with its seasonal, traveling carnivals, sporting events and clubs, disorganized fireworks displays on Guy Fawkes Day, and tradition of healthy walks, bicycling races, nude sunbathing, and swimming—not to mention youth gang fights and gay cruising—operates in this way within the dense surrounding urban fabric of the inner city. The Boston Commons and New York's Central Park perform a similar, much more policed, heterotopic function.

Corner points to the Anglo-Saxon performative tradition described at length by W. G. Hoskins in the classic 1955 work *The Making of the English Landscape*.[23] Here the creation of the urban grew out of a constant battle with the landscape, with generations building layers of traces in the countryside over centuries. Both Ebenezer Howard in his *Garden Cities of Tomorrow* and Patrick Geddes in his

Cities in Evolution, each published nearly a half-century prior to Hoskins, sensed that the Industrial Revolution altered this delicate ecological and agrarian balance of village around a commons.[24] They dreamt of merging the Industrial City with the old landscape tradition of small-scale, complementary town and country developments (a merger best represented by Howard's "Three Magnets Diagram"). Howard proposed that the State would ensure an even distribution of facilities in small New Towns constructed beyond a no-build Green Belt. Corner's predecessor at the University of Pennsylvania, Ian McHarg continued this argument in *Design with Nature*. He added the layering capacity of computer graphics to help in isolating the "no build" voids based on aesthetic, ecological, and agricultural values.[25]

Corner also draws on a landscape ecology tradition that defines the landscape very broadly as a mosaic of "the total spatial and visual entity of human living space" that integrates the environment, living systems, and the man-made.[26] Carl Troll, who coined the phrase *landscape ecology* in 1939 in Germany, wrote, "Aerial photo research is to a great extent landscape ecology.... It is the consideration of the geographical landscape and the ecological cause-effect network in the landscape."[27] Landscape ecology grew up as an adjunct of land planning in Germany and Holland after the Second World War, reaching America only in the 1980s, when Corner was a student at Penn. In America during the 1990s, European land management principles merged with post-Darwinian research on island biogeography and diversity to create a systematic methodology for studying ecological flows, local biospheres, and plant and species migrations conditioned by shifting climatic and environmental factors (including human settlements). Computer modeling, geographic information systems, and satellite photography formed a part of this research into the patches of order and patterns of "disturbances" (hurricanes, droughts, floods, fires, ice ages) that help create the heterogeneity of the American landscape.[28]

In *Taking Measures Across the American Landscape*, Corner and pilot-photographer Alex S. MacLean, track from an aerial perspective the impact of the enormous productive industrial economy engendered by Fordism, as well as the landscape created by this pattern of production and consumption in suburban sprawl.[29] As landscape ecologists, Corner and MacLean try to show an entire national agricultural and industrial ecology at work. Corner's multilayered drawings document both the man-made industrial-agricultural "machine city" and natural ecological systems at a sublime scale, creating vast patches of control and order in the American landscape. Anuradha Mathur and Dilip da Cunha, Corner's colleagues at the University of Pennsylvania, perform a similar survey and systematic analysis of the Mississippi's flow pattern over the centuries and the recent efforts of the Army Corps of Engineers to control them in their 2001 book *Mississippi Floods: Designing a Shifting Landscape*.[30] Here the temporal and performative nature of the human battle with the enormous forces of the river earns pride of place. The engineers even had prisoners of war in the 1940s construct a gigantic concrete scale model of the vast river basin so that they could measure the flows of water and efficacy of their proposed levees, canals, and dams. Alan Berger, a graduate of Penn, uses similar graphic and analytic techniques to reveal the vast, overlooked landscape patterns created by mining, agricultural, industrial, and hydraulic operations in his book *Reclaiming the American West*.[31]

All of landscape urbanism's triumphs so far have been in such marginal and "unbuilt" locations. These include Victoria Marshall and Steven Tupu's premiated design for ecological mudflats, dunes, canals, and ramps into the water in the Van Alen East River Competition (1998), which would have simultaneously solved the garbage disposal problem of New York and reconstituted the Brooklyn side of the East River as an ecology to be enjoyed as productive parkland.[32] In the Downsview Park, Toronto Competition (2000), Corner, with Stan Allen, competed against Tschumi, Koolhaas and Bruce Mau (who won), and two other teams, providing a showcase for their "emergent ecologies" approach.[33] This was further elaborated upon in Field Operations' winning design for the Freshkills Landfill Competition at Staten Island (2001). Corner analyzed the human, natural, and technological systems' interaction with characteristic aerial precision. They presented the project as a series of overlaid, CAD-based activity maps and diagrams that stacked up as in an architect's layered axonometric section. These layered drawings clearly showed the simultaneous, differentiated activities and support systems planned to occupy the site over time, creating a diagram of the complex settings for activities within the reconstituted ecology of the manmade landfill.[34] Mathur and da Cunha's entry in the same competition used a similar approach but emphasized the shifting and changing ecological systems of the site over time, seeking suitable places for human settlements including residences.

In a recent conference on landscape urbanism held at the University of Pennsylvania in April 2002, Dean Gary Hack questioned the interstitial and small-scale strategies of the participants. Hack identified a key problem for landscape urbanists as they face the challenge of adapting to complex urban morphologies beyond that of an Anglo-Saxon village and its commons. Suburbanites are willing to pay a premium to visit staged urban spectacles, which can take the form of the Palio annual horse race in Siena, a parade on Disneyworld's Main Street, or a weekend in a city-themed Las Vegas casino like the Venetian, with its simulation of the Grand Canal as a mall on the third floor above the gaming hall. The desire for the city as compressed hustle and bustle in small spaces remains strong. Mohsen Mostafavi, the chairman of the Architectural Association in London, delivered the keynote speech, showing the Barcelona-style, large-scale infrastructural work of the first three years of the AA Landscape Urbanism program.[35]

The recent discourse surrounding landscape urbanism does not yet begin to address the issue of urban morphologies or the emergence of settlement patterns over time. It concentrates on their disappearance and erasure. The problem of this approach is its amnesia and blindness to preexisting structures, urban ecologies, and morphological patterns. A common ground is useless without people to activate it and to surround it, to make it their commons. Housing, however transient or distant, is an essential part of this pattern of relationship, whether connecting to a village green or a suburban mall. With this logic the 1987 International Building Exhibition (IBA) in Berlin sponsored the recolonization of vacant inner-city lots with high-density, low-rise infill blocks, in anticipation of the construction of Potsdamer Platz and the demolition of the Berlin Wall. Adaptive reuse, as in the conversion of dockland warehouses or multistory factories to lofts and apartments, is another successful strategy that has provided housing and workplaces to activate inner-city areas. Even in Detroit, Henry Ford's grandson is rebuilding the Ford River Rouge Plant as a model hybrid "green" facility.[36]

Landscape urbanists are just beginning to battle with the thorny issue of how dense urban forms emerge from landscape and how urban ecologies support performance spaces. The linear organization of the village main street leading to a common space, with its row-house typology and long thin land subdivisions, is one of the oldest global urban patterns, studied by the pioneer urban morphologist Michael R. G. Conzen in the 1930s.[37] Urban morphologists look for the emergence of such characteristic linkages between activity and spatial patterns in human settlements. Such linkages, when repeated over time, form islands of local order structuring the larger patterns of global, ecological, and economic flows.[38] The pattern of the town square and approach street is another, more formal example of an urban morphology, focusing on a single center, setting up the central agora or forum as in a Greek or Roman city grid (and echoed in the typology of the courtyard house). The Islamic city, with its irregular cul-de-sac structure, accommodating the topography, emerged as a variation on this classical model, with the mosque, bazaar, school, and baths replacing the forum and temples at the center.[39] Medieval European cities, also with cul-de-sacs but based on a row-house typology, formed another morphological variation of the classical city, with market halls and cathedrals on the city square.

In *The Making of the American Landscape*, edited by Michael P. Conzen of the University of Chicago, contributors illustrate how the morphology of the city shifted from a dense single center to a "machine city."[40] This bipolar structure was based on railways creating a regional division between the dense center and the suburban villa edge, involving the separation of consumption from production, industry from farmland, rich from poor, and so on. In the second phase, the "machine city" of the modernists (best exemplified by the morphology of Le Corbusier's 1933 Ville Radieuse, with its slab blocks and towers set in parkland) replaced the old, dense Industrial City. With the advent of the automobile, a third morphology emerged in a multicentered pattern and isolated pavilion building typologies, a pattern that was further extended by airports on the regional periphery. Joel Garreau identified this in 1991 as the postmodern "Edge City" morphology of malls, office parks, industrial parks, and residential enclaves.[41]

In Europe, Cedric Price jokingly described these three city morphologies in terms of breakfast dishes. There was the traditional, dense, "hard-boiled egg" city fixed in concentric rings of development within its shell or walls. Then there was the "fried egg" city, where railways stretched the city's perimeter in accelerated linear space-time corridors out into the landscape, resulting in a star shape. Finally there was the postmodern "scrambled egg city," where everything is distributed evenly in small granules or pavilions across the landscape in a continuous network. Koolhaas and younger Dutch firms like MVRDV continue this tradition of urban, morphological analysis with a light, analogical touch. The organizing group of the 2001 International Conference of Young Planners meeting in Utrecht, for instance, used Price's metaphors to study the impact of media and communications on the city.[42] Franz Oswald, from the ETH Zurich Urban Design program, also examines the "scrambled egg" network analogy in the Synoikos and Netcity projects, both of which study the distribution of urban morphologies in central Switzerland as layers in a cultural, commercial, industrial, and informational matrix within the extreme Alpine topography and its watersheds.[43] Schumacher, at the AA's Design Research Laboratory, has also extended his work from *Stalking Detroit* into an investigation of the role of personal choice in a dynamic, typological, and morphological matrix forming temporary housing structures in the city.[44] His colleagues in the landscape urbanism program have also shifted to a more urban orientation, studying Venice and its lagoon.[45]

This rationalist, morphological, and landscape tradition seems to be centered in Venice. Here Bernardo Secchi and Paola Viganò continue the typological analysis begun in the 1930s, but now applied to the voids of the postmodern city-region, the "Reverse City." Viganò's *La Città Elementare* (*The Elementary City*, 1999) is exemplary of this larger European landscape urbanism movement. For Viganò, large landscape infrastructures form the basis for later urbanization.[46] Le Corbusier's work at the Agora in Chandigarh is exemplary in its monumental manipulation of the terrain, orientation to the regional landscape, and attempt to form an urban space. Xaveer de Geyter Architects' After Sprawl, with its fifty-by-fifty-kilometer "Atlases" of European cities made by various university groups, gives an easily accessible cross section of a wider landscape urbanism and morphological network linked to Venice.[47]

The recent publication of *Landscape Urbanism: A Manual for the Machinic Landscape* shows the further evolution of landscape urbanism practices since Waldheim's founding of the landscape urbanism program in the School of Architecture at the University of Illinois, Chicago, in 1997. The instrumentality of the Industrial Revolution is here linked to a pre-modern, deep ecological sensitivity to light, to watershed, to ground cover, to topography, even topology, merging the cosmic with the industrial in a vast, sublime, machinic order. Foreign Office Architects (FOA), for instance, turn the concept of the green roof into a dynamic, flowing, baroque parkland setting in their Osaka Ocean Liner Terminal Project. Pier and park, two previously separate urban morphologies, are hybridized so as to become inseparable. Juan Abalos and Inaki Herreros, with their big "garden windows" (several stories high and cut into suburban, modernist blocks), or Jesse Reiser and Nanako Umemoto, with their flowing pedestrian paths and ramps, create radical new hybrid morphologies—part landscape, part city, with few precedents.[48]

The emerging practices surrounding landscape urbanism offer many lessons for urban designers wanting to link structures to specific flows of populations, activities, construction materials, and time. The greatest strength of these practitioners lies in a determination not to accept the readymade formulas of urban design, whether "New Urbanist" or "generic" urbanist megaforms à la Koolhaas. Landscape urbanists want to continue the search for a new basis of a performative urbanism that emerges from the bottom up, geared to the technological and ecological realities of the postindustrial world. This implies an opportunity to open urban design out beyond the current rigid and polarized situation to a world where the past building systems and landscape can be included as systems within urban design. Designers recognize and play with these morphologies that are traces of human habitation, creating layers of meaning for current production. Landscape urbanists, equipped with a sense of shifting and changing urban morphologies, create new and unforeseen recombinations and hybridizations, liberating the urban design discipline from the current, hopeless, binary opposition of past and present, town and country, in and out.

Notes

1. I am grateful to my colleagues at Columbia University, Professors Brian McGrath and Victoria Marshall, to Chairman Mohsen Mostafavi at the Architectural Association, and to Ciro Najle of the Landscape Urbanism Program there, as well as to Charles Waldheim for introducing me to this concept. I also thank Bill Saunders and Antonio Scarponi for their comments on an earlier, longer version of this article published electronically in the Harvard Design Magazine, Fall 2003.

2. See Spiro Kostof, in the The City Shaped (London and New York: Thames and Hudson, 1991), and The City Assembled (London and New York: Thames and Hudson, 1992). Also Kevin Lynch, Good City Form (Cambridge and London: MIT Press, 1981), 73–98.

3. See Sebastien Marot, Suburbanism and the Art of Memory (London: The Architectural Association, 2003). Marot bases his complex synthesis and hybrid discipline on Frances Yates, The Art of Memory (London: Routledge and K. Paul, 1966), Colin Rowe, Collage City (Cambridge, Mass. and London, England: MIT Press, 1978) and the land artist Robert Smithson.

4. Mohsen Mostafavi and Ciro Najle, eds., *Landscape Urbanism: A Manual for the Machinic Landscape* (London: Architectural Association, 2003), and Georgia Daskalakis, Charles Waldheim, Jason Young, eds., *Stalking Detroit* (Barcelona: Actar Editorial, 2001).

5. Patrik Schumacher and Christian Rogner, "After Ford," in Daskalakis, Waldheim, and Young, eds., *Stalking Detroit*, 48–56.

6. Le Corbusier, *Towards a New Architecture* (Harmondsworth, England: Penguin Books, 1970).

7. Schumacher and Rogner, "After Ford," 50.

8. Ibid., 49

9. Ibid., 50. See also David Harvey, *The Condition of Post-Modernity* (Oxford: Blackwell, 1987) and Edward Soja, *Post-modern Geographies* (London, New York: Verso, 1989).

10. For Cedric Price's Think Belt, see Royston Landau, *New Directions in British Architecture* (New York: Braziller, 1968), 80–87; for Archigram see *A Guide to Archigram 1961–74* (London: Academy Editions, 1994).

11. Richard Register, *Ecocity Berkeley* (Berkeley, CA: North Atlantic Books, 1987).

12. Lynch, *Good City Form*, 115.

13. Ignasi de Solà-Morales Rubió, "Terrain Vague," in *Anyplace* (Cambridge, Mass.: MIT Press, 1995), 118–23.

14. See http://www.vanalen.org/exhibits/greenort.htm, and Guy Debord, *The Society of the Spectacle*, trans. D. Nicholson-Smith (New York: Zone Books, 1995).

15. Daskalakis, Waldheim, and Young, eds., *Stalking Detroit*. In "Projecting Detroit," Daskalakis and Omar Perez of the Das 20 Architecture Studio propose building two long, low, ramped, enormous glass fingers across Woodward Avenue, the main axis of Detroit—fingers that would reflect the ruins of the baroque Grand Circus, marking the edge of the old core (79–99). Jason Young leads a group of associates in a series of site-specific interventions, all expressing "Line Frustration" with the lines of demarcation in the city, including the Eight Mile line. They stress the importance of the media image of the inner city and propose a Media Production Center for one site (130–143).

16. Corner, "Landscraping," in Daskalakis, Waldheim, and Young, eds., *Stalking Detroit*, 122–25.

17. Ibid., 122

18. Ibid.

19. Ibid.

20. Ibid., 123.

21. See Bart Lootsma and Inge Breugeum , eds., *Adriaan Geuze: West 8: Landschapsarchitectuur* (Rotterdam: Uitgeverij 010, 1995), 44–45.

22. Corner, "Landscraping," 124.

23. W. G. Hoskins, *The Making of the English Landscape* (New York: Payson & Clarke, Ltd., 1955).

24. Ebenezer Howard, *Garden Cities of Tomorrow* (London: S. Sonnenschein & Co., Ltd., 1902), and Patrick Geddes, *Cities in Evolution* (London: Williams & Norgate, 1915).

25. Ian McHarg, *Design with Nature* (Garden City, NY: Published for the American Museum of Natural History, the Natural History Press, 1969).

26. See James Corner, "Eidetic Operations and New Landscapes," in Corner, ed., *Recovering Landscape: Essays in Contemporary Landscape Architecture* (New York: Princeton Architectural Press, 1999), 153–69, and Corner's courses at http://www.upenn.edu/gsfa/landscape/index.htm.

27. Quotation from Monica G. Turner, Robert H. Gardner, and Robert V. O'Neill, *Landscape Ecology in Theory and Practice: Pattern and Process* (New York: Springer, 2001), 10.

28. See ibid., 10, and Richard T. T. Forman and Michel Godron, *Landscape Ecology* (New York: Wiley, 1986), 619; see also Richard T. T. Forman, *Landscape Mosaics:*

The Ecology of Landscapes and Regions (Cambridge, England: Cambridge University Press, 1996).

29. James Corner and Alex S. MacLean, *Taking Measures Across the American Landscape* (New Haven, CT: Yale University Press, 1996).

30. Anuradha Mathur and Dilip da Cunha, *Mississippi Floods; Designing a Shifting Landscape* (New Haven, CT: Yale University Press, 2000).

31. Alan Berger, *Reclaiming the American West* (New York: Princeton Architectural Press, 2002).

32. See http://www.vanalen.org/competitions/east_river/projects.htm.

33. For Downsview see http://www.vanalen.org/exhibits/ downsview.htm and http://www.juncus.com/release1/index.htm. Also see Julia Czerniak, "Appearance, Performance: Landscape at Downsview," and Kristina Hill, "Urban Ecologies: Biodiversity and Urban Design," in Czerniak, ed., *CASE: Downsview Park, Toronto* (Cambridge and Munich: Harvard Design School and Prestel, 2001), and Stan Allen, "Infrastructural Urbanism," in *Points + Lines: Diagrams and Projects for the City* (New York: Princeton Architectural Press, 1999), 48–57.

34. http://www.nyc.gov/html/dcp/html/fkl/index.html and http://www.juncus.com/release2/ index.htm.

35. Mohsen Mostafavi and Ciro Najle, "Urbanism as Landscape?," in *AA Files* 42 (London: Architectural Association, 2000), 44–47.

36. See http://www.mcdonoughpartners.com/projects/p_ford_rouge.html.

37. See Terry R. Slater "Starting Again: Recollections of an Urban Morphologist," in Slater, ed., *The Built Form of Western Cities* (Leicester and New York: Leicester University Press, 1990), 22–36, and http://www.bham.ac.uk/geography/umrg.

38. See Anne Vernez Moudon, "Getting to Know the Built Landscape: Typomorphology," in Karen A. Franck and Lynda H. Schneekloth, eds., *Ordering Space: Types in Architectural Design* (New York: Van Nostrand Reinhold, 1994), 289–311.

39. Stephano Bianco, *Urban Form in the Islamic World* (New York: Thames and Hudson, 2000), 153.

40. Michael P. Conzen, ed., *The Making of the American Landscape* (Boston: Unwin Hyman, 1990).

41. Joel Garreau, *Edge City* (New York: Doubleday, 1991).

42. International Society of City and Regional Planners, 2001, "Honey, I Shrank the Space," Congress note at http://www.isocarp.org/2001/keynotes/index.htm.

43. See http://www.orl.arch.ethz.ch/FB_Staedtebau/home.html.

44. Patrik Schumacher, "Autopoesis of a Residential Community," in [+RAMTV] and Brett Steel, eds., *Negotiate My Boundary!: Mass-Customization and Responsive Environments* (London: Architectural Association, 2002), 12–15. See also http://www.arch-assoc.org.uk/aadrl.

45. See http://www.aaschool.ac.uk/lu

46. For Bernardo Secchi, see *Prima lezione di urbanistica* (Rome, Bari: Editori Laterza, 2000). For Paola Viganò, see *La Città Elementare* (Milan: Skira, 1999) and Viganò, ed., *Territories of a New Modernity* (Naples: Electa, 2001). See also Stephano Munarin and Maria Chiara Tosi, *Tracce di Città; Esplorazioni di un territoria abitato: l'area venet* (Milan: Franco Angeli, 2001).

47. Xaveer de Geyter Architects, *After Sprawl* (Rotterdam: Nai Publishers/DeSingel, 2002).

48. See Alejandro Zaera-Polo, "On Landscape" (132–34); Iñaki Abalos and Juan Herreros, "Journey Through the Picturesque (a Notebook)" (52–57); and Jesse Reiser and Nanako Umemoto, "In Conversation with RUR: On Material Logics in Architecture, Landscape and Urbanism" (102–10); in Mostafavi and Najle, eds., *Landscape Urbanism: A Manual for the Machinic Landscape.*

An Art of Instrumentality: Thinking Through Landscape Urbanism

Richard Weller

FIG. 1 "Semantic Reserves"

In a classical sense it is virtually impossible to romance the city as a collective work of art. Rather, the contemporary, globally interconnected metropolis is a rapacious, denatured tangle of infrastructure problems and planning issues increasingly subject to base motivations. And yet, even if we are to instrumentally evolve the city in accord with its environmental limitations and social crises, it would remain merely mechanistic, without art.

To conflate art and instrumentality, two terms generally thought so distant as to not relate, I am purposefully returning to landscape architecture's idealism and definition as a holistic enterprise, something that is at best both art and science.[1] Aware that there is much in art and science that landscape architecture will never be, and that landscape architecture seems relatively ineffectual in reshaping the world, this positioning of the discipline seems nonetheless theoretically correct and worthy in its aspiration.[2]

Landscape architecture's relative impotence in leading any reshaping of the world to date cannot just be blamed on the evil genius of capitalism and the traditional hegemony of engineering and architecture. Landscape architecture's scope and influence, whilst in all likelihood increasing, is still weakened by its own inability to conceptually and practically synthesize landscape planning and landscape design, terms which stereotypically signify science and art, respectively. In common parlance, planning concerns infrastructure (both mechanical systems and land-use designation) which, while essential to everything else the city comprises, bears a low semantic load in and of itself. On the other hand, design is perceived and practiced as the rarefied production of highly wrought objects or specific sites that bear a high semantic load. For its focus on intentional meaning, design sacrifices the scale and instrumentality of its agency, whereas that which planning gains in scale and efficacy it inversely loses in artful intent. Although this is not always the case, and perhaps too diagrammatic, this axiom of landscape architecture's bilateral crisis is the crux of the problem.[3] This is hardly a new observation, and therefore this essay (with its tangential subtext of associated montages) doesn't claim to identify new problems exactly—rather, it explores some new ways of getting at the old.[4]

These new ways can be gathered under the rubric of landscape urbanism. Although still a fuzzy cluster of rhetorical positioning and largely unsubstantiated by work on the ground, landscape urbanism warrants serious discussion because it alone seems theoretically prepared and practically capable of collapsing the divide between planning and design. This also entails a compression of

FIG. 2 "Art, instrumentality, and landscape architecture"

divisions between architecture and landscape, between fields and objects, between instrumentality and art. Significantly, landscape urbanism is emerging as a cross disciplinary sensibility, not to say a movement which positions landscape as the datum from which to critically negotiate the denatured field conditions of the contemporary metropolis.

Born of architecture's recent interest in landscape and landscape architecture's own critical self-appraisal in recent years, the ground of the contemporary metropolis is no longer modernity's repressed other (as Elizabeth Meyer once rightly identified),[5] but potentially the twenty-first century's *mother of the arts*. And yet what makes the emergence of landscape at this time unusual is that it occurs precisely as that which has been traditionally referred to as landscape is almost completely denatured, if not erased, by urbanity. Therefore, to arrive at an understanding of landscape urbanism and be able to review its design ramifications, this essay also attempts to chart what is meant by landscape in the city now [FIG. 2].

Postmodern landscape architecture has done a boom trade in cleaning up after modern infrastructure as societies, in the first world at least, shift from primary industry to post-industrial information societies. In common landscape practice—and here I am referring to a perception of landscape architecture by what is published and awarded in Europe, America, and Australia—landscape architects seem mostly employed to deal with spaces where infrastructure is not. They are employed to say where infrastructure should not be, and are generally expected to create the illusion that mechanical infrastructure is not where it is.

FIG. 3 "Ecology"

A pastoral modernity holds sway in the public imagination, and thus landscape remains popularly defined as the absence of infrastructure, a condition which says much about the prevailing power of eighteenth-century English aesthetics and very little of the truth about contemporary reality. Further, it seems reasonable to say that by virtue of economic rationalism and the hegemony of architecture and engineering, the infrastructural object or system in question in any development is given a kind of autonomous priority over the landscape (socio-ecological field) into which it is to be inserted. However, as any landscape architect knows, the landscape itself is a medium through which all ecological transactions must pass, it is the infrastructure of the future and therefore of structural rather than (or as well as) scenic significance [SEE FIG. 1].

To know where things should not exist and how to make voids in an increasingly cluttered world—as landscape architects do—is important, but, as is oft bemoaned, landscape architecture often ends up just arranging the wreaths for its own funeral, crying crocodile tears for the nature and neighborhoods of yesteryear. Alternatively, landscape design as a fine art, with pretensions to the critical disposition of art, is often seen as the decadent creation of what James Corner refers to as "semantic reserves"—sites where, as he puts it, only "the connoisseurs and the intelligentsia enjoy the associative play of narrative references."[6]

Landscape design's indulgences in the semantics of the garden are paralleled by planning's tendency toward reductionism, and grandiloquent narratives of reconciliation between culture and nature.[7] The gap between landscape planning and landscape design that weakens landscape architecture is in some ways demanded by professional specialization, but it is also a consequence of landscape architecture being stretched so far across the intellectual and actual geography of what is meant by *landscape*.

What is meant by landscape cannot be considered unless one works through what can be meant by ecology, and it is perhaps there that we find a new conceptual imaging of landscape, one which landscape urbanist sensibilities apprehend as a hybridization of natural and cultural systems on a globally interconnected scale. Such an apprehension, it will be argued, necessarily interweaves the untenable polarizations of design and planning stereotypes.

FIG. 4 "Power Pictures"

The science of ecology and its popular manifestation as environmentalism has practical and philosophical implications for landscape architecture and society at large [FIG. 3]. The conceptual shift brought about by ecology (and, more generally, the physics and biology of the twentieth century) is that the world is one of interconnection and codependency between organisms and environments, between objects and fields. Although translating into a victimized "nature," in the popular imagination, ecology is increasingly synonymous with new and more sophisticated models of universal (dis)order such as chaos and complexity theory, kaleidoscopes through which both romantics and scientists find previously unrecognizable order unfolding over time in spite of entropy.[8] Ecology is profoundly important not only because by progressing science from the measurement of mechanical objects to the mapping of non-linear systems it moves science closer to life, but also because it places cultural systems within the epic narrative of evolution. In this sense ecology is not only a meta-science measuring that which was previously beyond measurement, but also a discourse which implicitly leads to questions of meaning and value, questions of art.

Much recent thinking on ecology and urbanism is inspired by the creative potential of contemporary scientific metaphors. Terms such as diversification, flows, complexity, instability, indeterminacy, and self-organization become influential design generators, shaping the way we consider and construct places.[9] Writing on ecology in 1996, James Corner says "similarities between ecology and creative transmutation are indicative of an alternative kind of landscape architecture, one in which calcified conventions of how people live and relate to land, nature, and place are challenged and the multivariate wonders of life are once again released through invention."[10] He urges landscape architecture to develop a creative relationship with ecology in order to exploit a "potential that might inform more meaningful and imaginative cultural practices than the merely ameliorative, compensatory, aesthetic, or commodity oriented."[11] Pertinently, he identifies the problem that creativity in landscape architecture has "all too frequently been reduced to dimensions of environmental problem solving and aesthetic appearance."[12] The association of ecology with creativity, and in turn creativity with degrees of instrumentality, is long overdue.

Among other things, the conditions of ecological crisis make that which was invisible radically apparent, and with this vision we see our true nature and transcend preoccupations with urban morphology and the simplistic traditional aesthetics of objecthood. But this vision is not easy; for example, take a simple object like a house, unpack its constituent parts, and then trace them both back and forward in time—that is, from their source to their entropic end(lessness). The result, insofar as it is even thinkable, is a complex four-dimensional mapping, and even then it is one which barely represents the true complexity of the materializations and tangential processes involved.

If not to "save the world" and simplistically fit culture into nature, landscape architecture is right to ally itself with ecology. Landscape architecture—insofar as it is implicitly concerned with materials and processes subject to obvious change—seems well placed to give form to an ecological aesthetic. Landscape architecture is *not* frozen music. The axiom of ecology, and something now confirmed by the butterfly effect of chaos theory, is that all things are interconnected. Therefore every act, every design, is significant. Add to this the fact that every surface of the earth is not a given, but rather a landscape manipulated by human agency, then clearly landscape architecture can only blame itself if it does not become more powerful.

Landscape architecture's potential power is vested in the grand narrative of reconciling modernity to place [FIG. 4]; but the contemporary city is no longer bounded, and therefore landscape architecture must track it to the ends of the earth. Landscape urbanism is therefore not just about high-density urban areas and civic spaces, it is about the entire landscape off which the contemporary global metropolis feeds and into which it has ravenously sent its rhizomatic roots, a growth framed in the aerial photo or the satellite image. In the frame of the aerial image, landscape architecture finds its grand narrative of reconciling modernity to place.

But aerial images are contradictory (Faustian) representations because, while they hold out the prospect of directing that which is below, they are also images that invite hubris. Aerial images lay everything bare, and yet by their reduction of things to a marvellous pattern they smooth out the complexity and contradiction of being in a body; they conceal the real socio-political and ecological relations of the working landscape.

A book that critically engages aerial imagery and frames the magnitude of what a relevant practice of landscape architecture might be is Corner's *Taking Measures Across the American Landscape*.[13] Unlike Ian McHarg's plans and panoramas which, as Charles Waldheim identifies, were predicated on a nature-culture polarity, Corner's montages anticipate and marvel over a synthetic future of

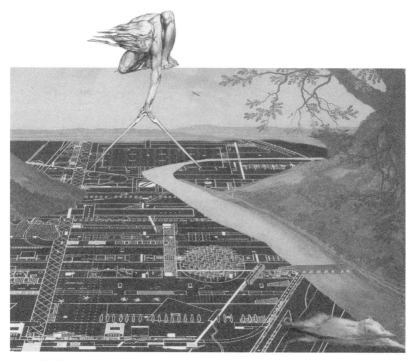

FIG. 5 "SCAPE"

constructed ecology.[14] And yet, even if poststructuralists are right to observe the problem of McHarg's basis in dichotomous semiotics, surely they can also award his planning the potential outcome of synthesis. Unlike McHarg's *Design With Nature, Taking Measures* is not a book with a plan. Corner does not design the ground he sees, neither does he propose a method for others to do so. Whereas McHarg's didactic overviews of how to redesign the world below had an answer for everything (except why the plan can never be achieved), Corner's collages of maps, photos, and site data seem to remain merely representational—just graphic recordings of particular intersections of topos and technology, a brand of hermeneutic site analysis.

If we can in retrospect see the impossibility of McHarg's ecological and methodological fundamentalism, can we not also foresee an overly aesthetic, self-conscious postmodernism in Corner's all too beautiful images? Just as McHarg's method could be learned by rote and practiced with a heavy hand by everyone, Corner's representational elegance and theoretical sophistication seems destined to remain voyeuristic, a detached perspective his own recent favoring of *landschaft* (working milieu) over *landskip* (constructed scene) contradicts.[15] Be that as it may, *Taking Measures* frames working landscapes and takes poetics to the planner's perspective, and when held alongside McHarg's work, we are aptly reminded that landscape architecture is at best an art of instrumentality, or better still, an *ecological* art of instrumentality. If they are to be taken seriously, landscape urbanists need to conjoin McHarg and Corner and ground both.[16]

The historian and theorist of landscape architecture John Dixon Hunt leads us in a step toward such a union by noting that the rarefied practice of design of gardens and parks (semantic reserves) provide models for the making of whole places.[17] This point has been borne out by the ways in which the unbuilt scheme for Parc de la Villette in Paris by Rem Koolhaas and the Office for Metropolitan Architecture (OMA) continues to be used in landscape urbanist literature as a benchmark for new ways of conceptualizing the whole landscape. Described by Alex Wall as "a field of social instruments," OMA's design for Parc de la Villette moved landscape design—as the installation of various infrastructures for an array of programmatic potential rather than a completed aesthetic composition replete with symbolic narratives and mimetic elements—to the center of debate over the last twenty years.[18] Unconcerned by Koolhaas's poor ecological credentials in 1999, James Corner stretched OMA's Parc de la Villette to the breaking point, suggesting that it might represent "a truly ecological landscape architecture," that such a landscape "might be less about the construction of finished and complete works, and more about the design of 'processes,' 'strategies,' 'agencies,' and 'scaffoldings'—catalytic frameworks that might enable a diversity of relationships to create, emerge, network, interconnect, and differentiate."[19]

As Marc Angelil and Anna Klingmann explain it, Koolhaas reads the city as simply "SCAPE©"—a condition in which architecture, infrastructure, and landscape are undifferentiated and subject to the same forces [FIG. 5].[20] It is this conception of the urban environment and its associated landscapes that has gripped a new generation of (particularly and understandably European) designers. The conflation of culture and nature into a hybrid weave across Europe underpins Alex Wall's description of the contemporary landscape as "a catalytic emulsion, a surface literally unfolding events in time," and as a "functioning matrix of connective tissue that organizes not only objects and spaces but also the dynamic processes and events that move through them."[21]

Acknowledging OMA's Parc de la Villette as seminal, Wall speaks of landscape as if it were a powerboard—a surface through which to run internet cables, sewage systems, and whatever else is needed to, as he puts it, "increase its capacity to support and diversify activities in time [FIG. 6].[22] For Wall, as for many aligning themselves with landscape urbanism, the conditions of late capitalism—that is, placelessness, and the mobility of capital, goods, and people—have forced a shift from *seeing* cities in formal spatial terms to *reading* them as four-dimensional dynamic systems of flux. As opposed to neoconservative new urbanism, which would have us reconstruct images along classical or vernacular lines, Wall says that the contemporary landscape is one made up of "network flows, nonhierarchical ambiguous spaces, spreading rhizomelike dispersals and diffusions, strategically staged surfaces, connective tissue, ground as matrix and accelerant, unforseen programs, and other polymorphous conditions."[23] This speeding and slippery account of the late capitalist landscape enthusiastically advances a conception of landscape as service matrix. According to Wall, the emphasis in design shifts "from forms of urban space to processes of urbanization, processes that network across vast regional—if not global—surfaces."[24] In line with the central theme of this essay, Wall is speaking of the ambitions of landscape planning and representing them as a design discourse.

The meaning of "city" in this context changes. The city in mind here is not a place or just "a" system, but a part of all processes and systems, a field which covers and makes up the world at any given time. Similarly, for the philosopher and historian Manuel de Landa the city is a coagulation of fluctuating systems, a slowing or acceleration of larger temporal processes.[25] The city and its global landscapes are an admixture of cultural, technological, and natural systems, an admixture that encrusts in urban form and its institutions, accretions of mind and matter that can be viewed as crystallizations (as Robert Smithson saw it) within larger evolutionary phenomena.[26] Accepting that de Landa's location of cultural history within natural history is a historiography befitting an ecological sensibility, then it is now more appropriate to describe urban centers as relative intensifications of processes that stretch across the Earth's surface, a surface with depth that can be understood as a complex field charged with articulations, relationships, and potentials. All at once the contemporary city is landscape, building, and infrastructure spread across urban, rural, and wilderness territories, a theoretical positioning of the city as no longer in dialectic with "nature," but by the same token a positioning which can once again naturalize and therefore justify everything humans make of the world.

Wall's visions owe more to modernism, futurism, and contemporary systems thinking than to the more orthodox landscape architectural pedigree of English gardens, democratic parks, garden cities, and Jane Jacobs, and it is this difference that makes it interesting. Indeed, the conditions upon which this new landscape urbanism is being constructed have previously inspired landscape architecture's Arcadian antipathy toward the city and motivated its traditional desire for groundedness, orientation, and emplacement. Any new discourse of landscape architecture—such as Wall's—must then be appreciated in terms of what is arguably the failing of orthodox landscape architecture to either resist and critique the postmodern city or, on the other hand, to creatively reimagine it.

In theory, Wall's stated intention is to engage and then structure the forces of the city in a critical rather than compliant manner. In fact, Wall sounds like a good old critical regionalist when he explains that his conception of the landscape as a dominant matrix "may be the only hope of withstanding the excesses of popular culture—restless mobility, consumption, density, waste, spectacle,

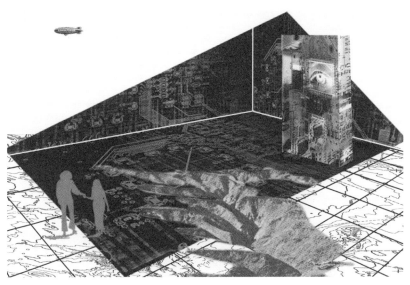

FIG. 6 "Continuous Matrix"

and information while absorbing and redirecting the alternating episodes of concentration and dispersal caused by the volatile movement of investment capital and power."[27] He does not, however, sound like a critical regionalist when he divulges an aesthetic predilection for "the extensive reworking of the surface of the earth as a smooth, continuous matrix that effectively binds the increasingly disparate elements of our environment together."[28] To a degree, he then finds himself at cross purposes.

Wall says landscape urbanist design strategies are "targeted not only toward physical but also social and cultural transformations, functioning as social and ecological agents."[29] Apart from the reference to ecology, he could indeed be speaking of modernism—and perhaps landscape architecture is yet to really have its own modernism, an ecological modernity, an ecology free of romanticism and aesthetics. Even if Koolhaas's ecological credentials are dubious, he and the landscape urbanists are ecological insofar as they read relationships between things as much as objects in and of themselves, as has been architecture's want. In privileging the field over the object, architects, in theory and in scope, are now becoming landscape architects. But one wonders whether they mean to assert that landscape is the infrastructure to which all other infrastructure elements or networks are answerable, or whether they are just more effectively getting on with the job of covering the entire Earth with the brutalist mechanics of the city.

As the next in many recent steps of reinvention, architecture now looks to the so-called landscape, but it does so not for a primal setting in contradistinction

FIG. 7 "Datascapes"

to its modern reason, nor for critical regionalism's *genius loci*; rather, architecture looks to landscape as the broader informational field of contemporary socio-ecological and cultural conditions for greater control. Part fact and part self-fulfilling prophecy, the denatured, post-dialectical "scape" of the global city and its infra- and supra-structural system is also one increasingly accepted and apprehended by landscape architects.

With renewed confidence, the discipline of landscape architecture realizes that through its ability to deal with large-scale dynamic systems it may be best equipped to deal with many of the problems planners and architects have unsuccessfully struggled with in designing cities.[30] A new generation of landscape architects are prepared to negotiate the mechanics of the city, philosophically and practically treating both its culture and its nature as a singular dynamic ecology without edge. In this field condition the two disciplines of architecture and landscape architecture find each other entangled together in *the weave of the world*.

In terms of working this weave, one thing seems certain: everything is uncertain—a condition which fits with the definition of chaos as the predictability of unpredictability. Experience teaches that attempts at mastery of the whole are vainglorious. Rather, Koolhaas speaks only of staging uncertainty, of diversification and redistributions, of "irrigating territories with potential."[31] Arguably justified by the fact that indeterminacy is the (quantum) quintessence of our times, such vague invocations are (perhaps necessarily) common to conversations about landscape urbanism. They also stem from a tide of Koolhaasian rhetoric which, in suggesting that architecture is a washed away sandcastle, effectively expands architecture's territory into landscape. Sink or swim? Landscape or architecture? Both, Koolhaas seems to answer.[32]

Emerging from a Koolhaasian sensibility, a new generation of designers are moving away from the dialectics and the romantics of design as a tension between form and function, idea and reality. Whilst to an extent ever-present, such romantic dialectics now seem cumbersome and inappropriate to getting on in a culture of *too much data*. There, the design process becomes a question of computation, not semiotics, a question of negotiating statistical limits, not hermeneutic intrigues. Such work is being gathered under the rubric of "datascapes," which Bart Lootsma explains as simply "visual representations of all the measurable forces that may influence the work of the architect or even steer or regulate it."[33] Such work is part of the oeuvre of landscape urbanists [FIG. 7].

Not unlike landscape architecture's recourse to site analysis to justify its outcomes, datascapes are thought to have great persuasive, commercial, and bureaucratic force because the subjectivities of the designer can be embedded in seemingly objective data. Whereas more romantic conceptions of the design process see the autonomous designer pained by the collision between ideal form and world, the datascapist does the inverse and begins with the outer limits of a project. They accept that a project is always already a site of negotiation. Deferring a preconceived design outcome, datascaping actively embraces restrictions and regulations. For example, Lootsma tells us that some of the most important threads running through West 8's landscape design work are "such apparently uninteresting things as traffic laws and the civil code—things often seen as annoying obstacles by designers who put their own creativity first."[34] Lootsma goes on to claim that for a designer, setting aside subjectivity and following the bureaucratic rules of a given place needn't mean neofunctionalism nor constitute mindless robotics (although there is always that risk), but rather, that the designer "commits a genuinely public act in which everyone can participate and perhaps even subvert."[35] Exactly how this is so, or where it has been tested and proven, remains unclear.

Winy Maas of MVRDV, a practice now synonymous with datascaping, also willingly embraces all the economic and regulatory constraints affecting any design project. Maas argues that in focusing on and working almost exclusively with this factual material, a project's form can be pushed beyond artistic intuition or formal predilections, and further, that the result is somewhere "between critique and ridicule of a world unable to grasp the dimensions and consequences of its own data."[36] Similarly, Corner believes "the datascape planner reveals new possibilities latent in a given field simply by framing the issues differently... in such a way as to produce novel and inventive solutions."[37] Although some of the design results and claims made for datascaping seem as faddish as they are inflated, we can productively ask that if the datascaper can now, according to Corner and Maas, take bland data and make novel and inventive solutions, why has the data-rich landscape design process as we know it not been able to?

Firstly, the purpose and medium of landscape design should not (and does not) always lend itself to the pursuit of anthropocentric novelty. But having made that qualification, consider that where landscape architects have paid close attention to their data they have perhaps expected it to do *all* the work. Positivist rather than hermeneutic sensibilities have reduced the catalytic role of the author in any design process. Alternatively, also consider that much landscape architecture, while paying lip service to site analysis data, does *not* in fact work with the data carefully enough and allow it to come forcefully to the surface. For example, designers are often more intent on the mimesis of a preconceived, expected, or desired image; and regardless of what site data might indicate, they will arrive at something picturesque.

Datascaping implies that the creative and critical operation of design is redirected from visual and ideological determinations, toward more attentive mapping of interrelated social, political, and economic dynamics that manifest themselves in any given place. In this sense, datascaping as a methodology is, to use a less fashionable word, planning. It is also potentially ecological. But whilst it is easy to understand how datascapes are descriptive of design/planning problems and programs, it is not so easy to see how they are generative of inventive (as opposed to crudely neofunctionalist) design responses.

MVRDV's Datatown is a case in point. Based strictly on statistical extrapolation, MVRDV quadruple the current population of Holland inside its existing boundary and visualize the resultant spatial complications. *Datatown*, the book, is full of bombastic images of multilevel carbon sink forests and livestock herded into skyscrapers, as would be necessary to maintain the current quality of life for circa 260 million Europeans within a 400-by-400-kilometer landscape.[38] Brilliantly dystopian, this is nonetheless datascaping in its crudest form. At no point do the authors do anything but extrapolate existing statistical conditions and follow function with form; the result being the opposite extreme of McHarg's ideal of a static culture finally finding its niche within the landscape's limits. While both models deny creativity and foreclose the openness necessary to a coevolving nature-culture synthesis, one is left wondering what sort of world lies in between these extremes, and if this is the world that landscape urbanism has in mind.

To conclude, Lootsma tells us that the datascape "is less about philosophy, theory, and aesthetics, and more about how the visionary and the pragmatic may be combined in creative and paradoxical ways."[39] He distinguishes a new generation from the old, declaring that datascaping is concerned with "critical pragmatism," not critical regionalism.[40] We know that the grand narrative of reconciling modernity with place rules the passion of critical regionalism—so the question to ask of Lootsma's critical pragmatism is "critical of what?" and "pragmatic toward what end?" Lootsma, Wall, and Corner all answer that the purpose of design is to "realign the conditions of late capitalism toward more socio-ecologically enriching ends."[41] This would seem a return to Kenneth Frampton's critical regionalist ethics, and it is worth noting that, almost as a postscript to his powerful thesis of resistance in the 1980s, Frampton has himself recognized that any hope of directing the uncontrollable global megalopolis lies in landscape as a structural force, not only an aesthetic source of local authenticity.[42]

If ecology and society are as simple as datascapes suggest, then every site can now be mapped in ways that gain closer access to the four-dimensional, socio-ecological reality of the situation. The computer can work in time, simulating and visualizing dynamic processes of change under specific conditions—modeling complex ecological and cultural flows in relation to design interventions. An intersection of the deleteriously divided art and instrumentality of landscape architecture, the polarity with which this essay began, is foreseeable in the computation of datascapes as the cyborgian designer works within a more fluid field of data, ideas, and form. Instead of master plans, which guide the arrow of time to a fixed point, landscape urbanists, while cognizant of the whole, make partial interventions, strategic moves which might incite loops of non-linear change throughout a system. Perhaps then here is a clue for how planning's pretences to the whole and design's preoccupation with parts can come together in a more finely tuned and instrumental landscape architecture.[43] It might not save the world, but one is tempted to think of this as an evolutionary leap in landscape architecture's favor, a move toward an ecological art of instrumentality.

Notes

1. Reference to landscape architecture as both an art and a science and a discipline periodically tensioned by bias toward one or the other is common to landscape architectural literature, indeed it is one of the recurrent themes in the American Society of Landscape Architecture's centennial publication, Melanie Simo, *100 Years of Landscape Architecture: Some Patterns of a Century* (Washington, D.C.: ASLA Press, 1999). Similarly, in concluding his comprehensive reader in landscape architectural theory, Simon Swaffield notes that calls for landscape architecture to be both practiced and theorized as an art and science were first heard in the 1950s, and that this ambition remains central to the discipline in the new millennium. Simon Swaffield, ed., *Theory in Landscape Architecture: A Reader* (Philadelphia: University of Pennsylvania Press, 2002), 229.

2. I think it was the American Landscape architect Peter Walker who once pointed out that despite laying claims to the earth, landscape architects affect only a tiny percentage of its surface—a seemingly self-evident point. One could add that this influence is likely to increase as every piece of land is increasingly in need of professional management.

3. The division of landscape architecture's body of knowledge and the divide amongst its practitioners has been, since the 1970s in particular, commonly discussed as a rift between planning and design. This again is a theme which weaves throughout Melanie Simo's *100 Years of Landscape Architecture*, cited above. It is also a theme which has structured debates in most national landscape journals. The issue is also revisited by Elizabeth Meyer, "The Post Earth Day Conundrum: Translating Environmental Values into Landscape Design," and Anne Whinston Spirn, "Ian McHarg, Landscape Architecture and Environmentalism," both in Michel Conan, ed., *Environmentalism in Landscape Architecture* (Washington D.C.: Dumbarton Oaks, 2000), 112–14, 187–90.

4. This essay is a refined and shortened version of a keynote address originally delivered at the 2001 MESH Conference, a biennial Australian landscape architecture conference on this occasion held at the Royal Melbourne Institute of Technology. Some of the illustrations associated with this paper were originally published in 2001 in *Landscape Review* vol. 7, no 1 (2001): 3–44, alongside an essay tracing the work of James Corner.

5. Elizabeth K. Meyer, "Landscape Architecture as Modern Other and Postmodern Ground," in Harriet Edquist and Vanessa Bird, eds., *The Culture of Landscape Architecture* (Melbourne: Edge Publishing, 1994).

6. James Corner, "Eidetic Operations and New Landscapes," in Corner, ed., *Recovering Landscape: Essays in Contemporary Landscape Architecture* (New York: Princeton Architectural Press, 1999), 158.

7. The implied mastery of modernist planning underpinned by belief in predictability and utopia is of course now replaced by its obverse, strategies of partial intervention in anticipation of unpredictability and dystopia.

8. Robert E. Cook gives a neat account of how contemporary models of ecology are influenced by advances in chaos theory and complexity science. Robert E. Cook, "Do Landscapes Learn? Ecology's 'New Paradigm' and Design in Landscape Architecture," in Conan, ed., *Environmentalism in Landscape Architecture*, 118–20.

9. See James Corner, "Ecology and Landscape as Agents of Creativity," in G. Thompson and F. Steiner, eds., *Ecological Design and Planning* (New York: John Wiley & Sons, 1997), 100.

10. Ibid., 82.

11. Ibid.

12. Ibid.

13. James Corner and Alex MacLean, *Taking Measures Across the American Landscape* (New Haven: Yale University Press, 1996).

14. Charles Waldheim, "Landscape Urbanism: A Genealogy," *PRAXIS Journal* no. 4 (2002): 4–17.

15. Corner's essay "Eidetic Operations and New Landscapes" is structured around a dialectic between *landschaft* and *landskip*.

16. I have argued elsewhere that Corner's practice is in fact concerned with exactly this issue. See Richard Weller, "Between Hermeneutics and Datascapes: A Critical Appreciation of Emergent Landscape Design Theory and Praxis through the Writings of James Corner, 1990–2000," *Landscape Review* vol. 7, no. 1 (2001): 3–44.

17. John Dixon Hunt, *Greater Perfections: The Practice of Garden Theory* (Philadelphia: University of Pennsylvania Press, 2000), 220.

18. Alex Wall, "Programming the Urban Surface," in Corner, ed., *Recovering Landscape*, 237.

19. Corner, "Ecology and Landscape as Agents of Creativity," 102.

20. Marc Angelil and Anna Klingmann, "Hybrid Morphologies: Infrastructure, Architecture, Landscape," *Daidalos: Architecture, Art, Culture* no. 73 (1999): 16–25.

21. Alex Wall, "Programming the Urban Surface," 233.

22. Ibid.

23. Ibid., 234.

24. Ibid.

25. Manuel De Landa, *A Thousand Years of Non-linear History* (New York: Zone Books, 2000). De Landa traces inherently unpredictable flows of genes, words, and materials across the last millennium so as to reveal, among other things, their consequential manifestations in urban form. Relevant to this essay is the way in which De Landa's history conflates natural and cultural systems and reads them as of a coevolving ecosystem, whereas we are accustomed to history as a progression narrative of events, ideas and identities acting against the backdrop of the natural world.

26. Robert Smithson, "The Crystal Land" in Nancy Holt, ed., *The Writings of Robert Smithson* (New York: New York University Press, 1979), 19–20.

27. Wall, "Programming the Urban Surface," above n 19, p 247.

28. Ibid., above n 19, p 246.

29. Ibid., above n 19, p 243.

30. Adriaan Geuze has made this point. "Architects and industrial designers often see their designs as a final product of genius whose aesthetic entirely originated in their minds. A design like that is thrown off by the slightest damage. Landscape architects have learned to put that into perspective, because they know their designs are continually adapted and transformed. We have learned to see landscape not as a fait accompli, but as the result of countless forces and initiatives." Geuze, as quoted in Bart Lootsma, "Biomorphic Intelligence and Landscape Urbanism," *Topos* no. 40 (2002): 12.

31. Rem Koolhaas, "Whatever Happened to Urbanism?" in Koolhaas and Bruce Mau, *S, M, L, XL* (New York: Monacelli Press, 1995), 971.

32. Ibid.

33. Bart Lootsma, "Synthetic Regionalization: The Dutch Landscape Toward a Second Modernity," in Corner, ed., *Recovering Landscape*, 270.

34. Ibid., 266.

35. Ibid.

36. Winy Maas, "Datascape: The Final Extravaganza," *Daidalos: Architecture, Art, Culture* no. 69/70 (1999): 48–49.

37. Corner, "Eidetic Operations and New Landscapes," 165.

38. Winy Maas, Jacob van Rijs, and Nathalie de Vries, *Metacity/Datatown* (Rotterdam: 010 Publishers, 1999).

39. Lootsma, "Synthetic Regionalization," 257.

40. Ibid., 264.

41. Ibid., 273.

42. See Kenneth Frampton, "Towards an Urban Landscape" *Columbia Documents* no. 4 (1994: 83–94; as well as Frampton, "Seven points for the Millennium: an untimely manifesto," *Architectural Review*, online: http//www.arplus.com/Frampton.htm.

43. Stan Allen has looked in to this, see Allen, "From Object to Field," *Architecture After Geometry; Architectural Design Profile* vol. 67, no. 127, ed. Peter Davidson and Donald L. Bates (1997): 24–32.

Vision in Motion: Representing Landscape in Time

Christophe Girot

FIG. 1 Tuileries Gardens, Paris

"Form is qualified above all else by the specific realms in which it develops, and not simply by an act of reason on our part, a wish to see form develop regardless of circumstance."

—Henri Focillon

Landscape urbanism is a term that has been coined to depict the study of urbanized landscapes of the second half of the twentieth century. It is, so to speak, the reactive child of all the teachings of our rationalist, functionalist, and positivist forefathers. It is light years away from the inductive thinking of earlier urban designers who drew and built their ideal cities on almost virgin lands. Landscape urbanism is meant first and foremost to decipher what happened in city landscapes of the last decades and to consequently act upon them. It addresses a complex and almost inextricable condition that is strangely recurrent at all four corners of the globe, although at closer look there remain undeniable topographic, climatic, and cultural differences in the patterns that are observed and developed [FIG. 1].

The advent of new media such as digital video has propelled visual research and communication to yet unforeseen levels in the various design disciplines, particularly those dealing with outdoor space. As a result, landscape urbanism, landscape architecture, and urban design are all benefiting tremendously from such progress. In the present context of landscape urbanism in Europe today, the potential impact of the moving image on both urban design and decision-making processes is considerable. It is of particular interest to urban landscape architecture to consider the extent to which such a mode of visual thinking can affect the shaping of future sites [FIG. 2].

THE CITY AS ENIGMA

We have moved from a conscious form-giving model of the city at the beginning of the twentieth century to a self-generated urbanity based essentially on quantitative programs and regulatory norms at the beginning of the twenty-first. The aesthetic of the city at present, if one can still speak in such terms, results at best from an *ad hoc* process, where older landscape identities collide relentlessly with the harsh imperatives of land value, development, productivity, and mobility. The resulting environment is hard to decipher, quite disorienting,

FIG. 2 Affoltern, Zurich

often insensitive, and unpleasant to the eye. Decades of successive upheavals have disfigured the secular qualities of almost every European landscape we know. These environments, when preserved, have been transformed or commodified at best into medieval-style shopping zones with their lot of branded boutiques, arts, craft markets, and flower baskets [FIG. 3].

In their milestone article on the dynamic evolution of the Italian landscape, entitled *Mutamenti del Territorio* ("Mutations of the Territory"), Stefano Boeri and Giovanni Lavarra postulate for an aggregated analysis of the landscape that demarks itself completely from the canons of the established institutional paradigms of representation in the European urban realm.[1] According to them, these canons are principally maintained via the plan (*la vizione zenitale agregata*), and the perspective image (*visione soggettiva e sequenziale*). They postulate, not without a tinge of iconoclastic sarcasm, that there exists a material phenomenology of the European territory based on specific conformities, asperities, and idiosyncrasies. This landscape heritage has until now always been able to digest and transform successive waves of importations into what they call the "European urban phrase." What is most interesting in this thought provoking text is the realization that the European urban landscape is a longstanding moving continuum, a complex flux of interwoven systems and epochs, a syncresis of countless moments compressed into a single space. Boeri and Lavarra claim that the

FIG. 3 Katzen See, Zurich   FIG. 4 Affoltern, Zurich

European landscape has self-regulated over centuries the specific acceptance and rebuttal of diverse transformations. If we accept the premise that landscape has undergone such diverse and complex alterations, we need then to decipher the implicit "genetics" of its evolution in order to explicate a vision for the future. And it is precisely this ability to read, integrate, and synthesize such complexities into design thinking that is lacking today.

The urban landscape is the multifaceted mirror of our epoch. For better or for worse, this is the raw material that we work with, and it is particularly important to reflect and act upon it with the proper tools. Scientific and planning models, in all their mathematical beauty, represent but a small part of the picture. There is a need to reinstate a balance between scientific and empirical, heuristic research on the landscapes of cities. Three main forces—degeneration, permanence, and transformation—both physically and ideologically act on the city, repeatedly contradicting each other. Each force, acting on a given site, can be observed synchronously but needs to be understood and engaged in different ways. It is rather ironic that present landscape thinking has chosen to cling exclusively to the notion of permanence, which is the third and much weaker force at stake. This idiosyncrasy can be explained in great part by the still prevalent fascination for the picturesque heritage, but it is also due to a patent absence of alternative modes of thinking and designing [FIG. 4].

Furthermore, urban development is the result of abstract and political processes that are seldom generative of what was expected or told.[2] The point is not so much to contest or contradict our tools of work but rather to understand how they have been misused, abused, and manipulated in both the design and decision-making processes. We know that the contemporary city is no longer the product of a single thought or plan, the vision of some prince, but rather the diffuse result of successive layers of decisions rarely having anything to do with each other. The established tools of representation influence not only the entire decision-making process and the media, but also subsequently the entire design and building process. The discrepancy between drawings and plans used as tools

FIG. 5 Evry Cathedral, Evry

of commercial and political seduction and the same documents used as a basis
for the production and construction of environments has demonstrated con-
cretely the limitations about the way we think of a city and its landscape today.
The highly publicized new town of Evry in France is a good case in point; despite
the great architectural and landscape architectural talents involved in various
aspects of the city project, this new piece of urbanity feels foreign to the place
and lacks a definite identity and cohesion. It is as if the sum of the individual
parts were not equal to the whole. Generally speaking, the absence of an overview
in design and the acute tendency toward a juxtaposition of totally antagonistic
programs produces hermetic urban environments that have led to the present
paradox: modern cities have literally dispersed and camouflaged the natural sub-
strate of their sites. Many of these substrates have been altered beyond recognition: waters have been covered or diverted, topographies erased or manipulated,
forests shredded or fragmented—the list is without end. The fact of the matter
is that the acute pragmatism and the short-term goals of current planning
trends has remained in great part oblivious to the sensitive physical and visual
realms of landscape [FIG. 5].

    To this portrait one can add an ever more reduced and questionable produc-
tion of designs for landscapes. One can say that over half of the urban environments produced escape the hands of architects, landscape architects, and urban
designers. Allow the thousand industrial, commercial, and residential zones, having sprouted across France along with their customary road engineering acces-
sories—roundabouts, deviations and so on—to serve as poignant examples. The

FIG. 6 Tableau No. 55, Bustamante

documentary film *Divina Obsesion*, by Volko Kamensky, shows to what extent a single technical street feature such as roundabouts on city peripheries has deeply affected our reading of the common French landscape.[3] We have entered a period of blind entropic projection, with its array of unforeseen results. Some theorists have taken on this fatality as a doctrine. The *laissez faire* aesthetic of the contemporaneous city requires, according to them, no vision; it just happens and evolves in an *ad hoc* manner. The denigration of vision and its relegation to the domain of *post facto* appreciation confirms the half-blind aberration we work and live in. Our understanding of remaining natural structures and their inherent potential in rapidly developing urban environments comes more often than not as hindsight. Here, landscape is no longer considered a main structural element but rather as the cherry on the cake, the last green frill on some built tract of land. This extremely reductive attitude in turn affects not only the imageability of a place but also its inherent quality and value [FIG. 6].

TOWARD A NEW UNDERSTANDING

The conclusions to draw from this analysis do not mean, however, that the deconstructed fragmentation of the city should be taken as model. The situationist discourse of the last few years has had no significant impact in the realm of landscape except for its further degradation. Nor does it necessarily mean that we always have to refer to the traces of a given site to legitimate some form of action. Such a retroactive stance, solely based on memory, is in no way a guarantee of quality—all the while denying the possibility for other, more diversified

FIG. 7 Champs Elysées, Paris

means of interpretation. The high-ly intellectualized analysis of a site and its past is necessarily exclusive and partial, and carries the risk of stifling a given condition. Whether it be the *laissez faire* discourse of chaos theory, the iconoclastic stand of a *tabula rasa* approach to urban design, or the melancholic com-plaint of better things past, the fact is that these dogmas have still not delivered any satisfactory remedial solutions to the current state of urbanism. It would be preferable, as suggested by Boeri and Lavarra, to accept differentiated readings of the urban landscape, readings which may reveal some inherited qualities from the past but may also be capable of repairing and clarify-ing opacities of the present. We need now to reinvent a language of the present, with strong new landscape identifiers, capable of integrating the complexity and contradiction of each place. These actions must respond amongst others to these very landscapes that have been either irremediably altered or effaced by the forces at work. There is a need for a completely re-founded vision of con-temporary urban landscapes, a creative gaze capable of providing a clearer understanding and line of action for each place [FIG. 7].

A new way of looking at our urban landscapes could deliver a better, more complete understanding of the multiplicity of phenomena at hand. It could also greatly improve the potential for an appropriate and concerted response to a site. It is therefore important to plead for an open, differentiated, and non-dog-matic reading of landscape, where both past traces and potential futures can be grasped synchronously. A site should be thought of within an evolving self-ref-erential frame, a visual frame meant to qualify and strengthen the natural poten-tial of a city over time. The quest for such a comprehensive vision of landscape is, however, almost impossible to attain with the current means at our disposal. We know that our conventional tools for recording and projecting landscape deliver all but an extremely partial and reductive glimpse of the world.

As in quantum mechanics, where the appreciation of a phenomenon under observation depends entirely on the position of the observer, the subjective point of view should become an integral part of the design process. There must be a new assessment of urban phenomena with respect to how they are planned, perceived, and experienced. We must question how and why we differentiate and substantiate the modern city the way we do. Having reached the limits of a strictly utilitarian viewpoint, a so to speak "objective" assessment, we are left with a sizeable enigma: how do we explain and appreciate the various urban environments that we have been left with? Can we really live and identify with them? It is necessary, at present, to recreate a topological understanding of the city, capable of revealing what is left of our humanity in the diverse environments that have emerged. We must therefore find a more substantiated way of looking at urban landscapes that is able to articulate such complexity into an understandable whole, easily communicable to the broadest range of people [FIG. 8].

CHANGING VISION
Both vision (that is to say the individual projection on a site) and action (the individual or collective use of an environment) contribute to our understanding of a place. Add to these the forces of nature and topography, and we have landscape. Landscape in general, and urban landscape in particular, is simply the sum total of successive dwelling periods on the land. But the complex blending of our cognitive and conceptual realms has led to a veritable dead end in landscape design. How far from reality can the landscape design tools that we work with be? The gradual withdrawal from landscape as a place to landscape as a piece of paper or a computer screen must be questioned, not only in terms of its conceptual shortcomings but also in terms of the very landscapes that result. The finest discourse in plans, whether layered or simple, cannot hide this inherent absence of site. Beautiful landscapes existed many centuries before cartography was even invented or perfected. These much older landscapes were built and thought out directly on the terrain over years. In the absence of a plan, vision became the guiding force of the project. Techniques such as onsite geometry and measurement, hydrology, construction, and horticulture supplied the necessary support for the site-specific vision at hand. The central question today is whether we are even capable of returning to a site-induced vision. Working on a history of plans is not the same as working on a vision of the land. We need to reconsider the primacy of vision over plan, a vision in motion, far removed from the established canons, capable of reflecting and inflecting upon the complex urban realm.

A better integration and understanding of contemporary visual thinking in the early design process, with its direct and indirect correlation in project development and communication, could contribute significantly to this field. Such a vision could concern not only the creative process in urban and landscape design but also the entire chain of decisions leading to the understanding and approval of a specific project. This new way of looking probably lies at the very margins of our habitual conceptual frameworks, where the actual blending of different times in space produces a new dimension. The tool of digital video, combined

FIGS. 8, 9 Porte d'Ivry, Paris

to some extent with the more classical means of topographic and architectonic representation, would enable one to formulate such a synthetic vision of a site, where the relativity of time, space, and motion are all present. The compression of these aspects into a single gaze would, in fact, provide the basis for a four-dimensional understanding of landscape. This new tool could deliver an almost immediate assessment of very complex settings, redefining completely our art of observation [FIG. 9].

LANDSCAPE IN MOTION

It is important to reconsider the perceptual limitations that pertain to landscape thinking in general. Why, for instance, has movement remained so marginal in our visual and sensitive assessment of urban environments? Aren't the fleeting sounds of the city just as significant as the tweet of a bird in our appreciation of a given place? It is now possible to imagine a new form of thinking that can integrate the travelling continuum of space and time, rather than present a series of immutable frames in our understanding of landscape. This means that the very tools of observation we are accustomed to are to be replaced by new ones that are more in tune with the way that we apprehend today's reality. The subject of digital landscape video has emerged in recent times as the ideal tool for such complex observations. It is slowly emerging as a genre of its own, distinct from the video art piece and the musical clip. Landscape video is neither filmic nor artistic, holding an argumentative discourse about site-specific qualities and events that are neither staged nor planned. The video material that is gathered shows samples of a place without cosmetics; its content is, for that matter, extremely raw and potent. In landscape video everything can be blended together indiscriminately—beauty spots can be seen next to no-man's lands. The traditional depiction of a place dissolves inevitably into a broader vision of urban and natural interrelationships and continuities [FIG. 10].

An aerial video over a neighborhood shows demonstratively, in the most intricate visual detail, the main structural framework of a landscape. It has the

FIG. 10 Pont National, Paris   FIG. 11 Nuclear Treatment Plant, La Hague, France

great advantage of revealing the specific identity of a site where houses and streets are immediately recognizable, and rivers and woods can be reconsidered. The image is almost immediate and true to the place, all the while integrating different times and movements in order to show its continually changing facets. Different seasons can be juxtaposed on a given site; transformations and alterations over decades can be compiled and visualized. A landscape seen in a variety of speeds and motions introduces a strong sense of relativity to our understanding of established identities. Recording behavior at different times of day reveals the multifaceted complexity of our cultural environment. What has systematically been called the impoverishment of landscape could now be understood as a form of diversification and enrichment [FIG. 11].

Landscape video also operates a transformation on the audience; the immediate recognizability of the images changes the perception of the viewer, as the video mirrors what one may witness day to day. It is this very act of reflecting that transforms the common gaze of inhabitants into an active, critical viewpoint. Offering a new visual understanding of even the most banal urban environments, this tool can be used critically to change both habits and mentalities. Different than the artistic photographs of similar places, video depicts a continuum rather than a series of frames, and can thus liberate itself entirely from the burden of the still. Here the "sightly" and "unsightly" blend into an overall landscape image, taking away from even the most beautiful vistas some of their splendid isolation. A five-minute presentation about a given site incorporates critical amounts of information and argumentation available, via the pervasive medium of the screen, to a much broader range of people.

Video is becoming a new genre in landscape. A new post-doctoral research program based in Hanover, entitled "Micro Landscapes," under the direction of Brigitte Franzen and Stefanie Krebs, received substantial funding from the VW Foundation in its aim to pinpoint the importance of new dynamics and movement in contemporary landscape design, including the tool of video.[4] Stefano Boeri pursues his work on landscape video with his proposal for the 2003

FIG. 12   Le Landemer, Normandy

Venice Biennale entitled *Border Device(s) Call*, exhibited at the Institute for Contemporary Art in Berlin, in which he uses video, amongst other media, to depict a route from Berlin to Venice to Jerusalem.[5] My office in Zurich has produced landscape projects in Italy and Switzerland that integrate video not only as a tool of observation but also as a tool of design synthesis.[6] The resulting projects have been used in a variety of important decision-making processes, and it is clear that this new form of vision is beginning to have an impact on the way that we shape the landscape [FIG. 12].

Landscape design teaching at several schools in Europe has integrated video as a tool of observation. Both the University of Hanover in Germany and the ETH in Zurich, Switzerland, have gone so far as to create a specialty in this field, training young generations of designers in this new form of visual thinking. They are exploring how video analysis can also influence design development. In the autumn of 2002, the ETH staged a joint exercise on urban landscape design and video on the Kasern Areal of Zurich, showing the correlative potential of video works in design.[7] The post-graduate program in landscape design at the ETH, inaugurated in 2003, makes it mandatory to correlate the video tool with design. It requires students to think differently and to better incorporate temporal and spatial considerations in their work [FIG. 13].

FIG. 13 Aerial view of Affoltern, Zurich

THE SPACES IN BETWEEN

Our way of seeing the landscape has been considerably altered by the various forms of movement that we presently experience through a site.[8] The moving picture frame, the rolling motion of a car or train, the dashing takeoff of an airplane—all entitle us to question a visual tradition that we have grown to accept, one that has accustomed us to an understanding of landscape through a series of fixed frames and vistas. In light of the discussion on landscape and movement, the French historian Michel Conan recently produced a thought-provoking essay on the premises of the static foundations of landscape scenography.[9] He argues that the art of the picturesque forwarded a static understanding of landscape where movement was absent, or at least not acknowledged as such. The picturesque landscape was experienced rather as a succession of immobile scenes, as in the example of the romantic promenade of Ermenonville designed by the Marquis René de Girardin, which did not incorporate movement as a significant part of its landscape experience. Referring to the French philosopher Henri Bergson, Conan suggests that a voyage through the landscape could only be understood as a succession of immobile scenes lending themselves to memory and aesthetic interpretation. Any movement in between these successive "immobilities" conferred no sentiment of landscape whatsoever. If this particular interpretation of landscape thinking has transcended into our times, as

FIG. 14   Aerial view of Affoltern, Zurich

epitomized by tourism, we can ask ourselves what the black holes in between the scenes really signify, and to what extent they are not in fact part of the overall key to a new way of thinking and looking [FIG. 14].

Why should the black holes, the in-between scenes of landscape beauty, be of such interest to us? Is it not preferable to remain true to polite society and espouse the notions of landscape beauty inherited from our forefathers? The fact is that we travel daily through a multitude of unexplained black holes. They have become the dominant feature of peripheries and urbanized countries, as in many examples of the Swiss *Mittleland*. We need to consider these long non-entities as probably equally significant as the most celebrated vistas of the Alps. These black holes require a long process of aesthetic acceptance. They need more time and memory to decant their specific identity and to operate a veritable change in our appreciation of them. Numerous artists have attempted to integrate such places into their work, and it is rather ironic that these unplanned and nameless landscapes have achieved suddenly such a high level of aesthetic fashionability. In the case of Switzerland, photographic studies on the Zurich suburbs by the Swiss artists Peter Fischli and David Weiss, and landscape images of Affoltern by the Swiss photographer Georg Aerni, are but a few examples of

FIG. 15 Zuriberg Park, Zurich

works that contribute toward the pictorial integration of such nondescript places.[10] The French artist Jean-Marc Bustamante, with his *tableaux* of half-destroyed landscapes in residential areas of Catalunia, further epitomizes the visual acceptance of this *fait accompli*. But this artistic approach implies two major risks: the first is the unabashed aesthetic consecration of the urban production of the last decades that has in fact negated the very idea of spatial composition; the second is the pursuit of static picture framing, which denies the notion of movement and flux inherent to such landscapes. The works of these artists are veritable *tableaux* or *vedutas*, in the strict sense of the word. They describe these very ugly and banal places in their finest intricacies, and tend to make us accept them as such, after the fact. We have reached a point where we can probably learn quite a lot from these new topologies, but we must also question our contemporary vision of landscape in all its picturesque and static might, to reinvent a grammar of visual sensations that enables us to better understand and act preventively [FIG. 15].

Urban landscapes have in great part become *sui generis* environments—that is to say that sites are no longer composed as such, but rather produced and transformed by abstract rules and regulations. These blind "after the fact" environments—call them landscapes if you will—require both discernment and an exquisite intuition to make any kind of sense out of them. The tools used to decipher the production of contemporary cities must engage us on the path of a renewed conquest of urban space and natural structures. Urban landscapes today are generally decomposed and fragmented, and we need to identify the modes of representation that have led to such inadequacies. By acquiring new tools with which to question city landscapes through different conformities, and learning from the so far hidden parts of the urban portrait, it is possible to understand the very limits of our knowledge. Knowing and accepting these limits will undoubtedly foster new forms of empirical investigation, as suggested by Michel Foucault in his text on the limits of representation.[11] This will bring us to the threshold of a vision capable of transcending the present condition, drawing on unforeseen priorities that may enable us finally to think and compose urban landscapes anew.

Notes

1. Stefano Boeri and Giovanni Lavarra, "Mutamenti del territorio," in Alberto Clementi, ed., *Interpretazioni di paesaggio* (Rome: Meltemi editore, 2002), 96–106.
2. The recent suburbanization of French landscapes has led to a variety of site interpretive theories. Among these is Sébastien Marot's latest book on the topic of "suburbanism." Here Marot postulates a complete role reversal between site and program, where site becomes somehow endowed with the capacity to yield a regulatory idea for a project. See Marot, *Suburbanism and the Art of Memory* (London: AA Publications, 2003).
3. Volko Kamensky, *Divina Obsesion*, Germany 1999, 16mm, color, Magnetton, 27:30 min.
4. Brigitte Franzen and Stefanie Krebs, *Mikro-Landschaften, Studien zu einer dynamisierten Kultur der Landschaft* (Hannover, Germany: VW Stiftung, 2003).
5. Stefano Boeri, *Border Device(s) Call*, in the exhibition Territories, Kunst-Werke—Institute for Contemporary Art, Berlin, June 1–August 25, 2003.
6. Christophe Girot and Mark Schwarz, *Feltre, Imagine, Imagini, Imagina* (Zurich: Vues SA, 2001). Christophe Girot and Mark Schwarz, Die Nordküste, Affoltern (Zurich: Vues SA, 2003).
7. The project under the direction of Christophe Girot was led jointly by the ETH Landscape Design Lab under the supervision of Julian Varas, and the Landscape Media Lab under the supervision of Jörg Stollmannand Fred Truniger.
8. See Christophe Girot, "Movism," in *Cadrages 1, Le Regard Actif*, ed. Christophe Girot and Marc Schwarz (Zurich: GTA Carnet Video, Professur für landschaftsarchitektur, NSL, ETH Zürich, 2002), 46–53. The text first appeared in the proceedings of the Herrenhausen Congress of 2001. It was subsequently integrated into the GTA, ETH publication.
9. Michel Conan, "Mouvement et métaphore du temps," in Philippe Pulaouec Gonidec, *Les temps du paysage, Paramètres* (Montréal : Les Presses de l'Université de Montréal, 2003), 23–35.
10. Peter Fischli, and David Weiss, *Siedlungen, Agglomeration* (Zurich: Ed. Patrick Frey, 1993). Georg Aerni, *Studie Öffentliche Raüme Affoltern*, Amt für Stadtebau Zürich, 2003.
11. "Il n'est sans doute pas possible de donner valeur transcendentale aux contenus empiriques ni de les déplacer du côté d'une subjectivité constituante, sans donner lieu, au moins silencieusement, à une anthropologie, c'est à dire à un mode de pensée où les

limites de droit de la connaissance (et par conséquent tout savoir em pirique) sont en même temps les formes concrètes de l'existence, telles qu'elles se donnent précisément dans ce même savoir empirique." Michel Foucault, "Les limites de la représentation," *Les mots et les choses* (Paris : Ed. Gallimard, 1966), 261.

Looking Back at Landscape Urbanism: Speculations on Site

Julia Czerniak

FIG. 1 Mies van der Rohe, Project for Chicago Convention Center, photo collage, 1939

To think about landscape is to think about site. This seemingly transparent proposition is anything but—for the potential of site in landscape design is often overlooked. Most designers quite successfully embrace a site's conventional characteristics, such as its highly valued ecologies, views, and terrain, but only a few creatively address a site's contemporary challenges, such as remediating its brownfields. An even smaller number draw from a site's specific organizational systems, performative agendas, formal languages, material palettes, and signifying content for use when generating landscape design work.

One reason for this oversight is the convention of equating sites with building lots—available parcels bound by legal demarcations driven by property ownership—as opposed to understanding them as large complex landscapes—relational networks of artifacts, and organizations and processes that operate at diverse spatial and temporal scales. Design strategies for a building lot, one scale of site, expand enormously when conceptualized in relation to other, nested scales of reference, like the neighborhood, city, and region of which the site is a part.[1] Conceiving of site in this way suggests that landscape design projects can not only draw from an expanded field of information, they can impact areas larger than their own physical extent (say by cleansing storm water before releasing it into a watershed), making ecological sense.

The architect Carol Burns makes a convincing examination of the status of site in her influential 1991 essay "On Site: Architectural Preoccupations." Burns distinguishes between cleared and constructed sites; thinking about a site as "cleared" equates the ground with a *tabula rasa*, which Burns illustrates by a photo-collage of Mies van der Rohe's project for the Chicago Convention Center of 1939 [FIG. 1].[2] The import and influence of the existing site, in this case the historic fabric of Chicago, is neutralized and then overlaid with the designer's proposition. Extending this example to both past and present landscape work, I would suggest that ordering architectural intentions over the surface of the ground mimics cleared-site thinking by accommodating particularities such as steep slopes and degraded soils rather than generating from more complex conceptions of site.[3] Although nowhere near as radicalized as Mies's *tabula rasa*, many landscape works, as diverse as Raphael's Villa Madama and OMA/Bruce Mau's Tree City, place building and landscape materials *onto* their sites, grafts of a sort that subtly adapt to the nuances of their place [FIG. 2]. These renowned projects nonetheless intentionally overlook the significant impact that site organizations, events, and ecologies can have on design projects. As ironic as it may seem, not all landscape works are site-specific.[4]

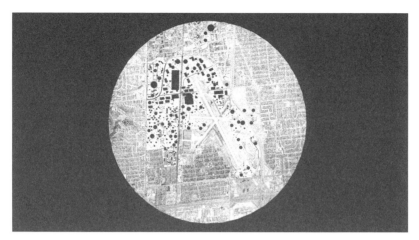

FIG. 2 Bruce Mau, Tree City, 2000; figure ground

In apparent opposition to this approach, Burns suggests, are attitudes and practices which actively "construct" a site, where designers select and represent valued aspects of a place with no pretense of totalization in order to foreground their influence on a project, positioning this information as a critical and creative component of landscape design's advancement. This selection is characteristically biased, as diverse designers privilege at various times geometry over geomorphology, topology over topography, or even conceptual interests over perceptual ones. In this light, seemingly disparate work by Eisenman Architects, known for their brief preoccupation with site, and Hargreaves Associates, whose work on site is ongoing, displays similar sensibilities [FIGS. 3, 4].

THE NOTION OF SITE PROPELLING landscape design work interfaces with the emerging amalgam of practices known as landscape urbanism, a phrase taken here to be the conceptualization of and design and planning for urban landscapes that draw from an understanding of, variously, landscape's disciplinarity (history of ideas), functions (ecologies and economies), formal and spatial attributes (both natural and cultural organizations, systems, and formations), and processes (temporal qualities) impacting many scales of work. Landscape urbanism also suggests a particular culture of and consciousness about the land that refrains from the superficial reference to sustainability, ecology, and the complex processes of our environments in favor of projects that actually engage them. Embedded in landscape urbanism is concern not only with how landscape performs (the agenda of which is most advanced) but how it appears (its latent inescapable counterpart).

This relationship between performative and representational agendas in landscape practice has been a central aspect of several projects of the past two

FIG. 3 Eisenman/Trott Architects,
Wexner Center for the Visual Arts, 1989

FIG. 4 Hargreaves Associates, Byxbee Park, 1991

decades by Hargreaves Associates and Eisenman Architects that both set the groundwork for and are resistant to what I see as the design discipline's current enthusiasm for landscape's performative capacity. The intentions of their examination are three-fold: the first is to observe how site particularities, both physical and discursive, "make their appearance" in design work and the operations used to bring them into being;[5] the second is to speculate on the implications site-generated work poses for landscape and the contemporary city; finally, and most importantly, these projects suggest that the generative capacity of a site—variously construed as a spatial location, a physical and cultural context, and a discursive position which is value-driven—can inform a landscape's representational content all the while addressing its ever-shifting emergent and temporal nature.

In Guadelupe River and Byxbee Parks, projects initiated between 1988 and 1991, Hargreaves Associates approached site as a reserve of processes—from geomorphological forces to landfill engineering practices—that form the surface of the ground. My interest here is to reflect on the specific landforms, such as the braided channels, alluvial fans, and tear-drop shaped mounds, that these preoccupations produce. In the Guadelupe River project, a three-mile linear park and flood control system that passes through downtown San Jose, California, Hargreaves Associates and a team of engineers envisioned the river, a considerable flood threat, as an active part of the city. One aim of the project's program was to make the river visible and legible. Rather than enclose the river in inaccessible concrete culverts, the team controls the water with earth mounds, planted gabions, and undulating concrete stepped terraces that provide for multiple points of access to the flowing water, while designing water features like the Park Avenue Fountain along the park's length that exacerbate water activity. This not only provides wildlife habitat and recreation space, it makes the river landscape—once an urban asset until growth infringed upon its floodplains—seen as a significant component of the city.

FIGS. 5, 6 Braided Channel of the Muddy River, Alaska [LEFT]; Hargreaves Associates, Guadelupe River Park, 1994; landform study model [RIGHT]

More important than simply seeing the river are measures taken that promote an understanding of river landscapes, producing a legibility of its forces, forms, and processes. To facilitate this, Hargreaves Associates used forms produced by the fluvial processes of rivers under specific circumstances, such as tight geometries, weak banks, and high width-to-depth ratios—here, braided channels—as an analog for the landforms of their own park [FIGS. 5–7].[6] The subsequent designed landforms, called "wave-berms," that appear at the downstream end of the river park resemble these formations [FIG. 8]. That this resemblance is carefully constructed through an understanding of how forces produce form (in this case flood flows) eliminates the tendency for the inverse— engineered forms (channels) shaping agencies of change (water). Significant here are the design strategies used to produce the wave-berms.[7] Far from simply scripting a design motif from an image, these forms were first modeled by the team in clay as part of an eighty-foot mock-up of the entire park and then tested by flows of colored water for eddy formation and sand for deposition patterns. The resultant abstracted forms subsequently became the vegetated and stabilized wave-berms in the park that serve to direct both floodwater and, through the circulation network that mimics its geometries, park users.

At Byxbee Park, a thirty-acre park on a capped sanitary landfill in Palo Alto, California—a landform the designers call an "arc-berm"—provides another example of force/form evolution. Added to control the erosion of drainage swales by water runoff in the park, the arc-berm resembles an alluvial fan, a landform feature that takes the shape of a segmented cone and is formed at one end of an erosional-depositional system [FIG. 10].[8] More importantly here is Hargreaves Associates' understanding of the park as the site of sanitary landfill reclamation practices that produced an artificial landform as it accrued household waste. Rising sixty feet out of the site's context of marsh and slough, these

FIGS. 7, 8 Guadelupe River Park: eighty-foot study model (LEFT); view of landforms (RIGHT)

garbage mounds—which form the park's major topography—provide the base for landforms that echo their presence. For example, what the team refers to as the "hillocks"—small tear-drop-shaped mounds clustered on topographic high points—are oriented in the direction of the site's predominant winds. Clearly a human construction on an artificial ground, their form appears to be a reversal of those made by natural aelion processes of wind that tend to narrow on leeward ends, offering a twist on the simple duplication of a natural form [FIGS. 9, 11].[9] The hillocks also intend to resonate with the mounds of discarded shells left by the Ohlone Indians, prior occupants of the region, juxtaposed with the contemporary refuse that they overlay.

In both the Guadalupe River and Byxbee Park projects, Hargreaves Associates' selective attention to park landform, admittedly just small features within large landscapes generated by specific and multiple design motivations, planning strategies, and complex technological and ecological requirements, is what enables a provocative relationship between these landscape's performative and representational concerns. These forms are both instrumental—they guide such things as flood flows, pedestrian movement, and water runoff—and representational, based on an understanding of a site's formative processes, here erosion and deposition in the case of a river, and construction and settlement in the case of a sanitary landfill.[10] The self-conscious abstraction and intensification of site-specific conditions in form reveal their artificiality, and possibly users' perception of their references.[11] Most importantly, these forms participate in larger-scale provisional landscapes that unfold in time and are continually modified by agencies of change. Whereas the wave-berms in Guadelupe River Park are stable, as they have an engineering role to play, flood water will modify the park in ways far greater than the ubiquitous temporal forces that all landscapes are subject to. The mounds and berms in Byxbee Park sit atop an unstable landfill that settles

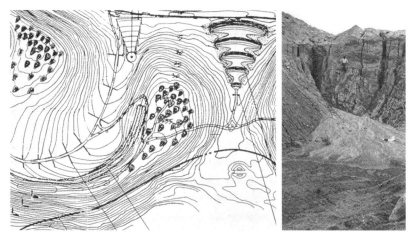

FIGS. 9,10 Byxbee Park; partial plan showing arc-berm and hillocks (LEFT); Alluvial fan (RIGHT)

and shifts as waste decomposes. Figuring the ground in these ways gives parks signifying potential by making local conditions (ecological, geomorphological, social, cultural) legible without limiting preoccupations with processes that can inform readings of the site at a larger scale. This distinction between elements in parks that play representational and/or provisional roles has been provocatively suggested by landscape architect and critic Anita Berrizbeitia. In her discussion of OMA/Bruce Mau's Tree City, the winning competition entry to the Downsview Park, Toronto competition, Berrizbeitia advances ways in which landscape design projects can address environmental and ecological scales while still articulating issues of meaning, artistic expression, and language by their various components being either "open" or "closed" to external perturbations.¹² Using Berrizbeitia's terms, we can think of Hargreaves Associates' specific landforms as closed to the disturbances, such as wind and water, that the rest of the park is open to. Their presence suggests how parks can both accommodate the large-scale concerns of ecological function while holding the potential for meaning.

FIGURING THE GROUND AT GUADELUPE RIVER and Byxbee Parks is based on an understanding of specific processes of their sites. The Rebstockpark Master Plan in Frankfurt—an urban landscape of housing, offices, commercial space, and a large urban park proposed in 1991 by architect Peter Eisenman and landscape architect Laurie Olin—is also generated by an interest in ground, here as a critique of what Eisenman calls the "static urbanism" of figure/ground contextualism.¹³ For both Eisenman/Olin and Hargreaves, *to engage the specifics of site makes the landscape visible and legible.*

With its complex urban and "natural" program, Rebstockpark proposes unconventional relationships between the contemporary city and natural process

FIG. 11 Shrub-coppice dunes

in the late twentieth century. It does so in ways that challenge what landscape architect James Corner suggests are nineteenth-century notions—where nature is seen as separate from the city, is imaged as undulating and pastoral, and acts as a moral antidote to urbanization.[14] Many large urban parks in America—for instance Golden Gate Park in San Francisco, or Central Park in Manhattan—offer examples of this, in short-hand design parlance, "city-versus-nature" condition. With Rebstockpark, the designers purported instead to explore potential relationships between the "city and nature."[15] The project also speculated in important ways on how new parks can build sustainable relationships with their environments while becoming more sociable places, a question still being asked in recent competitions for large urban landscapes.

These promises of the scheme—its alternative figure/ground and city/nature dialogs—are enabled in large part by the conception and use of the site. Evident and inferable information on the building lot such as traces of World War II airfields, swimming pools, lakes, and garden plots, as well as elements of the surrounding context such as athletic fields, tracks, and warehouses, are appropriated and reconfigured as a complex weave of elements that extend into the site's larger context, here the regional greenbelt [FIGS. 12, 13]. Additionally, urban elements of the site's morphology (offices, shops, houses, recreation, and parking) are interspersed with elements drawn from the regional agricultural landscape (orchards, meadows, produce gardens, woodlands, irrigation ditches, hedgerows, and canals), thereby creating an artificial place in the city with characteristics of both. This reconfiguration of site, program, and form is enabled by the structure of a disturbed grid that engages the entire site surface.

Much has been written, by Peter Eisenman and others, on the strategy of folding that forms the fictive structure and promised effects of Rebstockpark.[16]

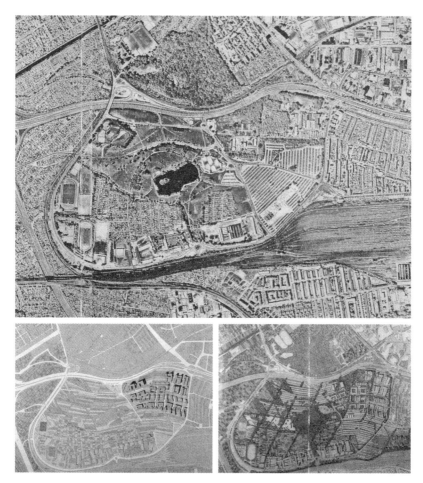

FIGS. 12–14 Eisenman Architects with Hanna/Olin, Rebstockpark, 1991; aerial photo of context (ABOVE);
Rebstockpark: Eisenman Architects' masterplan (LEFT); Hanna/Olin's masterplan (RIGHT)

Little, however, has been written about the development of the landscape. Eisenman refers to the site weave as promoting a "ground surface ... which becomes a topologic event/structure," that inevitably dissolves—yet subsequently reframes—normative relationships of old/new and object/context, as well as figure/ground, supplementing the poverty of choice available in the normative conditions of the latter.[17] Studying the resultant fieldlike continuities between the building and landscape in the representations of this project support these possibilities.

In Laurie Olin's terms, the potential of the project "may afford new and different relationships between people, their daily routines and the environment," a proposition supported by the thoughtful and detailed development of the

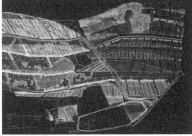

FIGS. 15, 16 Rebstockpark
tree composition for reading folds (ABOVE)
vegetation diagram (LEFT)

landscape plan [FIG. 14].[18] Formally, landscape elements—walks and roads, vegetation, drainage swales, and landform—were used to articulate the folded grid, giving both a new form and image to the park, all the while addressing its social and ecological programs. These programs, developed by Olin, provide respite from increased urbanization (while still providing for large amounts of event parking on site) yet focus on air quality and movement as well as the hydrologic cycle, measures intended to help balance overall regional natural systems of vital importance to the ecology of the city.

To this end, the two principle devices integral to the landscape structure were extensive tree rows and drainage swales. The tree rows were developed as various combinations of canopy, understory, and orchard tree species such as apples, cherries, and peaches [FIGS. 15, 16]. Monoculture plantings evidenced in traditional urban parks—think of Olmsted's promenade of elms in Central Park—are here replaced with rural and agricultural landscape typologies like the farmer's hedgerow. Organized in several orientations and layouts, the trees join patches of fields, shrubs, and grass in an effort to control microclimate. A strong formal element made of the drainage swales and canals form an integrated site network, dramatizing the conservation of rainfall, the cleansing of waste effluents, and the redirecting of water flow back to the earth [FIGS. 17, 18]. This variety of landscape elements and their organization provides moments of interface, or ecotones, where one kind of ecological environment meets another, producing favorable conditions for increased species diversity and wildlife habitat.[19]

One can imagine moving through this landscape where the scheme's unconventional juxtapositions are perceived. The design's provision for park/parking is one such clever moment [FIGS. 19, 20]. For instance, some of the park's circulation routes are aggregate paths under trees rows. These paths are one of a series of strips of meadow, flower field, and stone that simultaneously provide a park

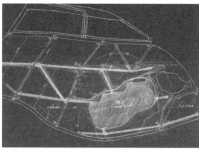

FIGS. 17, 18
Rebstockpark
plan of canal structure (LEFT)
section of canal structure (BELOW)

environment while disguising the infrastructure for large amounts of overflow parking needed on weekends. Another juxtaposition is the park's planting strategies that legibly code public and private space. Areas around the housing units consist of conventional perennial beds and lawns—the latter a much loved and ubiquitous surface composed of grass species, free of weeds and pests, continuously green, and mowed to a low, even height [FIG. 21]. In contrast to this, the park's public open space is developed through an agricultural vocabulary that substitutes meadows and produce gardens for pastoral lawns of parks [FIG. 22]. Maintaining the meadow minimizes those environmentally deteriorating maintenance practices that lawns require, like fertilizing, watering, mowing, and treating for pests. The commercial flowers and vegetables that are part of these fields would require some of these practices. However, they are maintained by the municipality and are intended for productive, not ornamental, uses—in other words, they generate revenue. In these ways, Rebstockpark explores options to imitating nature or recreating the ubiquitous pastoral scene thought by many in the design fields, for quite some time now, too ecologically unsustainable and socially irrelevant.

Certainly Rebstockpark can and has been seen as a project that represents complex processes, driven by a metaphor of nature's forces and cycles. Olin acknowledges that the strategy of folding provides an arbitrary geometric system that is an armature for social, architectural, and poetic development.[20] Although its larger structure is representational, the development of its constituent parts promise nothing less than a landscape that works. Additionally, its experimentation—to embrace, abstract, and use catastrophe theory generatively as an analog of natural process—inevitably reveals Eisenman's and Olin's bias

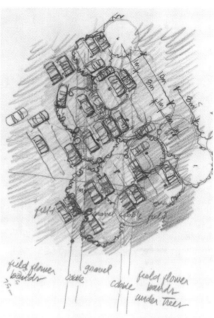

FIGS. 19, 20
Rebstockpark
park/parking plan (LEFT)
material details of parking bands (ABOVE)

FIGS. 21, 22
Rebstockpark
planting detail at housing (LEFT)
detail of site plan showing meadows
and produce plots (BELOW)

for the role accidents, chance, and change play in the formation of alternative urbanisms.[21] Through the weave of urban patterns, site features, and the German countryside, this project yields figure/ground relations of transformed architectural and landscape elements that make a socially and ecologically viable place. Landscape is not simply the background for architecture, it is figured and visible.

IN GUADELUPE RIVER, BYXBEE, AND REBSTOCKPARK, the designers draw from particular aspects of a place for the development of a design project. Hargreaves Associates' Guadelupe River Park already demonstrates its vital role in the social and ecologic communities of San Jose. Conversely, Eisenman's and Olin's Rebstockpark, a competition-winning design developed only through its early stages, remains unrealized. Yet through publication and exhibition, which are no less than additional sites of the project, it continues to inform contemporary architecture, landscape, and urban practice. This distinction is not simply academic, for *to imaginatively construe site is to imagine possibilities for landscape practice.* As suggested, site is at once the specific spatial location for a project, the physical and cultural context it draws from and affects, as well as— in the case of Rebstockpark—a place of discourse and representation which unarguably advances landscape practice.

The projects discussed so far demonstrate how creative thinking about site has affected and generated landscape design. Ultimately, however, the area affecting the design—how the specifics of a site construct the work—is supplanted by the area affected by it—how the work constructs the site.[22] To elaborate on this point through Hargreaves Associates' Plaza Park in San Jose (1989), suggests one final reading of site's potential for landscape urbanism. The 3.5-acre, pill-shaped lot for Plaza Park was the site of an eighteenth-century mission, square, and attendant artesian well that was part of a system of pueblos and missions along the California coast.[23] Although this visible and latent history is important in the design, Hargreaves Associates ignore the conventional limits of property lines and draw additionally from infrastructural connections within the city and the climate and cultural history of the region [FIGS. 23, 24]. The result is an urban landscape that references its extended site in diverse ways. The park's primary circulation echoes that of the former King's Highway, the artery that previously linked the missions. Here, alignments are traced and appear as pathways coded by distinct materials that link analogously significant park program. Additionally, interest in infrastructural connections tie Plaza Park to San Jose's metropolitan plan, designed by Sasaki Associates, where it becomes an integral part of a public framework of arcades, plazas, and courtyards [FIG. 25].[24] Many of the park's elements make reference to specifics of the region: a grid of flowering jacaranda trees displays the landscape's agricultural history of fruit production; a fountain with water cycles alternating from mists to bubblers to jets, set in a gridded glass block, glows at night, simulating the local climate of mist and fog, marking

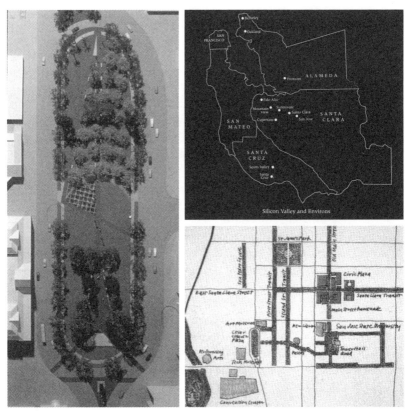

FIGS. 23–25 Hargreaves Associates, Plaza Park, 1989; site plan of lot (LEFT);
Silicon Valley conurbation (RIGHT TOP); Sasaki Associates, San Jose
Metropolitan Plan, 1983; urban linkages (RIGHT BOTTOM)

the location of artesian wells, and referencing through its simulated glow the surrounding high-tech industry, booming at the time of construction.

Positioning work in larger site contexts has been an aspiration in landscape architecture at least since Ian McHarg extolled its ecological virtue in *Design with Nature*. However, the implications for Plaza Park's nested scales of reference— of lot, city, and region—are as much social, political, and economic as they are ecologic, and probably more so. For example, the juxtaposed references of the fountain, a mixed metaphor of water and light, is intended to display the shifting economies of the region, from one based on agriculture and fruit production to a high-tech software industry that has suffered its own setbacks in the last few years. This shift invariably affects the local community, and represents the competing interests of various constituencies and their relationship with the land and the city. During my visit in the summer of 1998, park benches were filled with office workers using laptops, having productive lunches. Alongside them, local families picnicked on the lawn, their children escaping the heat in the fountain. This simple picture of daily life in a socially active and ethnically diverse downtown—a context where successful technology companies were juxtaposed with low-income neighborhoods with gang problems and overcrowded schools—glossed certain tensions. These tensions were exacerbated by a city government who at the time saw no irony in investing billions of dollars in young technology companies while their local United Way branch went broke.[25]

The debate between constituencies and resources evidenced here raises a related point—the promise that multiple scales of reference as a mode of operation holds for the public role of urban landscape in the contemporary city. In her account of the development of site-specific art practices, the art historian Miwon Kwon makes two points relevant to this discussion of landscape's publicness.[26] First, she argues that the distinguishing characteristic of today's site-oriented art is how actuality of location is "subordinate to a discursively determined site that is delineated as a field of knowledge, intellectual exchange or cultural debate."[27] Whereas the area affecting the design of Plaza Park is simultaneously the lot, the city, and the region, the area affected by the project, now built, integrates into the realm of the social, participating in the sites Kwon suggests, here of socio-economic identity and its representation. Promisingly, Kwon's second point is that "the possibilities to conceive site as something more than a place—as a repressed ethnic history, a political cause, a disenfranchised social group—is a crucial conceptual leap in redefining the public role of art and artists."[28] Kwon's point is salient, I would add, to landscape architects as well.

Although the design moves at Plaza Park most certainly represent the constituencies in a cultural debate (the flowering trees, the agricultural industry; the glowing glass, the high-tech industry), it can also be thought to facilitate discourse. Here, unlike nineteenth-century park agendas of social display and reform within the generic pastoral scenes, meaning is regionally located, culturally determined, and produced by the process of use. As such, the project has certain successes as a public park, a landscape type that art critic/activist Lucy Lippard suggests is "probably the most effective public art form there is—the park itself is an ongoing process, the domain where society and nature meet."[29] Landscape's emergent and temporal nature here is not evidenced by the medium itself but by the fluid and shifting occupations that it sponsors, a social fluidity of individual and collective relationships with the land that is too often overlooked in design practice. In this light, Plaza Park may suggest strategies for pursuing public issues in the designed urban landscape.

TO THINK SITE IS TO THINK LANDSCAPE. The projects discussed here creatively construct and construe site, alternatively recuperating or rummaging through the particulars of a place to generate innovative urban landscapes. On one hand, Hargreaves Associates' strategies of site specificity produces work which they describe as having "real meaning for inhabitants."[30] On the other, Eisenman systematically appropriates specifics with the critical motives to displace, dislocate, and subvert objects, places, and scales. Yet whether they engage or oppose determinant site structure, these projects make urbanism specific. They also resonate with the theoretical and practical formulation of landscape urbanism.

To qualify urbanism by landscape is to suggest that landscape's full etymology is engaged. Contemporary practices that favor time over space, performance over appearance, effect over meaning, will nonetheless inevitably confront landscape's representational agenda. In addition to the Germanic variation *landschaft* that signifies a "unit of human occupation" and connotes landscape as a changing system of social and ecological interrelations, its etymological counterpart *landskip* suggests landscape as a picture and a scenic view.[31] To be landscape then, in all its complexity, designers must consider how a landscape looks: its appearance, image and representational concerns. The projects briefly discussed here suggest provocative ways to do so—not as second thoughts or after effects, but as an integral component of landscape's conception and subsequent formation.

Notes

1. Linda Pollak's reading of Henri Lefebvre's provocative diagram of social space (Henri Lefebvre, *The Production of Space* [Oxford: 1991]) suggests a strategy of "nested scales." See Pollak, "Constructed Ground," in this collection.
2. Carol Burns, "On Site: Architectural Preoccupations," in Andrea Kahn, ed., *Drawing Building Text* (New York: Princeton Architectural Press, 1991), 146–67.
3. Useful here are Robert Irwin's working categories for public/site art. Irwin's distinctions between "Site dominant," "Site adjusted," "Site Specific," and "Site conditioned/determined" suggest similar nuances for a site's relationship to the designed landscape. Here, *accommodating* particularities suggests adjustment to the givens of a place. See "Introduction: Change, Inquiry, Qualities, Conditional" in *Being and Circumstance: Notes Toward a Conditional Art*, (San Francisco: The Lapis Press, 1985), 26–27. See also George Hargreaves's discussion of site for the practice of landscape architecture in "Post-Modernism Looks Beyond Itself," in *Landscape Architecture* vol. 73, no. 7 (1983): 60–65.
4. Landscape critic and theorist Elizabeth Meyer has lectured and published widely on the subject of site in landscape architecture and her nuanced thinking has greatly influenced my preoccupations. See her forthcoming book *The Margins of Modernity: Theories and Practices of/in Modern Landscape Architecture* (unpublished manuscript, in progress 2006).
5. For this phrase I thank Mark Linder, who argues that the fundamental theoretical question is how does architecture "make its appearance?" See Linder, *Nothing Less than Literal: Architecture after Minimalism* (Cambridge, Mass.: MIT Press, 2004).
6. For a comprehensive discussion of braided channel formation, see Luna B. Leopold, M. Gordon Wolman, and John P. Miller, "Channel Form and Process," in *Fluvial Processes in Geomorphology* (New York: Dover Publications, 1995), 284–95.
7. The design process for Guadalupe River Park was discussed in a telephone conversation with Hargreaves Associates president Mary Margaret Jones at the American Academy in Rome, July 1998.
8. Michael A. Summerfield, "Fluvial Landforms," in *Global Geomorphology* (Essex: Longman Group Ltd., 1991), 222–24.

9. Ibid., "Aeolian Processes and Landforms," 248–55.

10. For a discussion of the implications of "representation" in Hargreaves Associates' landforms, see Anita Berrizbeitia, "The Amsterdam Bos: The Modern Public Park and the Construction of Collective Experience," in James Corner, ed., *Recovering Landscape: Essays in Contemporary Landscape Architecture* (New York: Princeton Architectural Press, 1999), 187–203.

11. For a discussion the legibility of abstracted landforms in parks, see Hargreaves, "Post-Modernism Looks Beyond Itself," 61.

12. Anita Berrizbeitia, "Scales of Undecidability, in Julia Czerniak, ed., *CASE: Downsview Park Toronto* (Munich: Prestel, Harvard Design School, 2001), 116–125.

13. See Eisenman's discussion of "grounds" in "Folding in time: the singularity of Rebstock." in Greg Lynn, ed., *Folding in Architecture* (London: Academy Editions): 23–26.

14. See James Corner, "Terra Fluxus," in this collection.

15. Laurie Olin, "The Landscape Design of Rebstockpark," September 1992. This essay is published in German in *Frankfurt Rebstock: Folding in Time* (Munich: Prestel, 1992). Translation courtesy of the author.

16. See Peter Eisenman's discussion of the "agency of the fold" and the influence of catastrophe theory on the development of Rebstockpark in "Unfolding Events: Frankfurt Rebstock and the Possibility of a New Urbanism," in John Rachman, ed., *Unfolding Frankfurt* (Berlin: Ernst & Sohn, 1991): 8–17; and Eisenman, "Folding in Time: The Singularity of Rebstock," 23–26.

17. Eisenman, "Unfolding Events," 9.

18. Olin, "The Landscape Design of Rebstockpark," 5.

19. Olin draws from ecological principles to inform the way Rebstockpark works as a system of interrelations. Landscape ecology also serves as an analog or model for many contemporary practices. For example, both landscape architect James Corner and architect Stan Allen cite Richard Forman's principles of landscape ecology (patch, edge and boundary, corridor and connectivity, and mosaic) as useful for the development of urban landscapes. See Olin, "The Landscape Design of Rebstockpark"; and Allen, "Infrastructural Urbanism," *Points + Lines: Diagrams and Projects for the City* (New York: Princeton Architectural Press, 1999).

20. Olin, "The Landscape Design of Rebstockpark."

21. That the project is subsequently read through the discipline of geology and the idea of the picturesque is not surprising. Critic Kurt Forster suggests that Rebstockpark "actualizes the notion of geologic process," due largely, he argues, to Eisenman's operative strategy of "tracings of temporal relationships" in lieu of "static mapping." See Kurt Forster, "Why Are Some Buildings More Interesting Than Others?" *Harvard Design Magazine* no. 7 (Winter/Spring 1999): 26–31. Robert Somol's suggested reading of Rebstockpark through rethinking urbanism from a theory of the "accident" situates it in terms of the picturesque tradition, a landscape reference which foregrounds a project's processes of production over its formal product. See Robert Somol, "Accidents Will Happen," in *Architecture and Urbanism* vol. 252, no. 9 (September 1991): 4–7.

22. In the competition brief written by Andrea Kahn for the 1996 Van Alen Fellowship in Public Architecture, "Public Property: An Ideas Competition for Governors Island," participants were asked to make a distinction between "site" and "building lot" pertinent to the discussion here: "If the building lot is an area of limited physical intervention, the site is an extensive aggregation of interactive scales and programs, where global forces inform local conditions, and metropolitan concerns have regional impact. While all physical design proposals shall be limited to Governors Island (the building lot) it is understood that *the area affected by such proposals (the site)* will not be limited to the island itself"

(emphasis added). See also Kahn's essay "Overlooking: A Look at How we Look at Site...
or Site as 'Discrete Object' of Desire" in Duncan McCorquodale, Katerina Rüedi, and
Sarah Wigglesworth, eds., *Desiring Practices: Architecture, Gender and the Interdisciplinary*
(London: Black Dog Publishing, 1996): 174–85.

23. Reuben Rainey, "'Physicality' and 'Narrative': The Urban Parks of Hargreaves Associates"
    in *Process Architecture 128, Hargreaves: Landscape Works* (Tokyo: 1996): 35.

24. For a detailed description of Sasaki Associates' planning efforts, see Peter Owens, "Silicon
    Valley Solution" in *Landscape Architecture Magazine* 89, no. 6 (June 1999): 52, 54, 56–58.

25. This situation was discussed by Chris Arnold, *Morning Edition*, National Public Radio,
    May 24, 1999.

26. Miwon Kwon, "One Place After Another: Notes on Site Specificity," in *October* 80
    (Spring 1997): 85–110. Kwon's provocative, albeit provisional, paradigms for site-specific
    art practice were very helpful in developing this essay.

27. Ibid., 92.

28. Ibid., 96.

29. Lucy Lippard, "Gardens: Some Metaphors for a Public Art," in *Art in America* 69,
    no. 11 (November 1981): 137, as cited by George Hargreaves in "Post-Modernism
    Looks Beyond Itself."

30. Hargreaves Associates Project Descriptions.

31. The "double identity" of landscapes etymology—a dialectic and dialogic pairing of a
    "view" and a "measured portion of land," of *landskip/landschaft*, picture/process,
    subject/object, and aesthetic/scientific—is discussed in many venues. See Denis Cosgrove,
    "The Idea of Landscape," in *Social Formation and Symbolic Landscape* (New Jersey:
    Barnes & Nobles Books, 1985): 13–38; John Stilgoe, "Landscape," in *Common Landscapes
    of America: 1580 to 1845* (New Haven: Yale University Press, 1982); J. B. Jackson, "The
    Word Itself," in *Discovering the Vernacular Landscape* (New Haven: Yale University Press,
    1984): 1–8; and more recently by James Corner in "Operational Eidetics," in *Harvard
    Design Magazine* (Fall 1998): 22–26.

Constructed Ground: Questions of Scale

Linda Pollak

FIG. 1 Linda Pollak, Sheila Kennedy, and Franco Violich, "Drawing on Site," 1990; aerial view of installation

The discipline of landscape urbanism has emerged primarily from within landscape architecture, widening its focus on processes to include those that are cultural and historical as well as natural and ecological [FIG. 1]. In relation to urban design, which as a discipline has emerged from architecture and planning, part of landscape urbanism's strength lies in this acknowledgment of temporality. It also has the potential to engage architecture in a way that urban design and landscape architecture do not, by challenging architectural conventions of closure and control, which implicitly disavow knowledge of the various incommensurable dimensions of urban reality. In this context, architecture is construed not as an object but as a device that can transform an urban landscape yet at the same time is not in complete control of the relationships between its constitutive elements.

The architectural historian Kenneth Frampton has written that "priority should now be accorded to landscape, rather than freestanding built form" in the making of cities.[1] Yet to build landscape requires the ability to see it, and the inability to do so continues to permeate architectural design culture. This persistent blindness is evident in the still common recourse to the figure/ground plan, which fails to engage the material aspects of a site, representing the ground as a void around buildings. This convention of figure/ground is part of a historically embedded oppositional system of thought—other oppositions include architecture/landscape, object/space, culture/nature, and work/site—which foregrounds and acknowledges the construction of the first paired term while naturalizing the second as unproblematic background. The tendency is to view the second, or what I call *environmental* term, as an abstract container, separate from the objects, events, and relations that occur within it. These second terms often become fused together in some kind of landscape-space-nature-site blur, in contrast to the supposedly clear outlines of architecture.

The objective of what I call *constructed ground* is to engage and focus on these environmental terms in a way that exceeds the oppositional system that continues to contain them. Constructed ground represents a hybrid framework that crosses between architecture, landscape architecture, and urban design, to engage the complexity of contemporary urban landscape. This framework invests in the ground itself as a material for design, using landscape as both a structuring element and a medium for rethinking urban conditions, to produce everyday urban spaces that do not exclude nature. Its goal is to address simultaneously the concerns of architecture, landscape, and city, without having one or more recede in importance, as would happen in a conventional disciplinary framework.[2]

This text will focus primarily on one term, that of space, which exemplifies, in the opposition object/space, architecture's tendency to disacknowledge that which is around it. The French philosopher Henri Lefebvre challenged the unproblematic conception of space in his well-known 1974 book, *The Production of Space*, arguing that such production is concealed by two mutually reinforcing illusions. He defines one illusion as that of transparency—the idea that the world can be seen as it really is. This illusion, which allows the workings of power that produce space to remain invisible, goes "hand in hand with a view of space as innocent."[3] He defines the other as the realistic illusion—the idea that something by seeming natural requires no explanation. This illusion, which is based on the opposition of culture/nature, allows landscape to be used to mask undesirable histories.[4]

The limits imposed by oppositional categories of spatial identity parallel those of subject identity, such as white/black and male/female. If, as geographer Doreen Massey writes, "it is now recognized that people have multiple identities, then the same point can be made in relation to places."[5] While there has been a tendency in contemporary design theory to interpret the mobility of identity in de-territorialized, nomadic terms, I would argue that, while not fixed—that is, permanently determined by one or two preordained traits—identity is indeed grounded, in space, in ways that are geographically and historically specific. To engage this specificity in a design process requires a theory of difference that is performative, an approach based on a conception of the "other" that begins with the premise that identity is relational rather than oppositional. A relational identity is dependent on articulation, in a sociological sense. As the British cultural theorist Stuart Hall has described, articulation is a "form of connection that *can* make a unity of two different elements, under certain conditions."[6] In other words, unity is a possibility rather than an *a priori* assumption. The challenge in design is to develop ways of working that can support and represent a multiplicity of spatial identity, to bring into focus as (constructed) ground that which is usually relegated to background. Such ways of working need to not only recognize the potential of these historically recessive environmental terms in the design of new environments, but also be aware of ways in which their historical marginalization has conditioned the construction of existing environments. The goal, to borrow a statement from the scientist Donna Haraway, is "a knowledge tuned to resonance, not to dichotomy."[7]

Lefebvre's analysis in the *Production of Space* reveals the city in its complexity as what he describes as a "space of differences." This space, far from being a neutral container, is a field in tension which, unlike most representations of urban space, explicitly includes natural processes. He defines social space as the "encounter, assembly, [and] simultaneity... of everything that is produced by nature or by society, either through their cooperation or through their conflicts."[8] This space of differences can be a starting point for constructing ground,

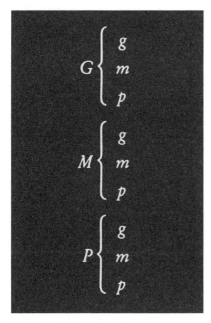

FIG. 2 Henri Lefebvre, diagram of nested scales

understood as a framework for design practice in which the negotiation between the respective scales at which architecture, landscape architecture, and urban design can operate performatively to engage dimensions of difference that characterize the space that is being produced.

The concept of scale as a representation of spatial difference can be used to engage relationships between architecture, landscape, and city across a range of formal, ecological, social and other criteria. These relationships can be apprehended in well-known built projects by Rem Koolhaas/OMA, Andreu Arriola, Catherine Mosbach, Alison and Peter Smithson, and Alvaro Siza; however this discussion of scale may first be introduced in relation to two unbuilt projects from our office, Marpillero Pollak Architects, to outline an approach to design that takes into account the formation of a site by forces acting at multiple scales, often invisible at the physical location of the site itself.

Scale is an issue inherent in all urban landscapes that is barely addressed in design theory or practice. As a conceptual design tool, which can refer to spatial or temporal dimensions of an object or process, it supports a relational approach to built environments—a way of articulating differences that can cross between practices without being subsumed by or allowing any one to dominate. While there is no inherent, assignable scale to architecture, landscape, or city, there is a range of scales associated with each set of practices. Architectural scales traverse a field from the interior to the exterior of a building, from its smallest detail to its overall presence, rarely exceeding the distance from which a project is actually visible. Urban scales extend beyond what is visible from a particular site to scales at which planning has occurred that may have implicated and/or produced that site. Landscape scales also pertain to areas much larger than any specific site, encompassing multiple ecological systems.

At one point in his analysis of space, Lefebvre presents a diagram of nested scales, which he developed through the examination of a Japanese spatial order [FIG. 2].[9] This diagram supports a formulation of the city as a space of differences through two complementary strategies, which together produce dynamic relationships. Its first innovation is to introduce a transitional scale (M), which

Petrosino Park Site
Kenmare Street Cut, 1902
Lafayette Street Cut, 1904

FIGS. 3,4 Marpillero Pollak Architects, Lt. Petrosino Park Design Competition, New York, 1996: diagram of site formation by infrastructural forces [LEFT]; model view [RIGHT]

functions as a mediator between private (P) and global (G). Its second innovation is that each of these scales is integrated within the other two. The diagram provides a basis for a design approach that can support a dynamic and multidimensional differentiation of space. Its overlay of terms recognizes that all scales are internally differentiated, and that while hierarchies of scale exist, they are not fixed or singular.[10] Acknowledging that unity is neither an *a priori* nor a necessarily attainable condition of identity helps to frame it in terms of processes of becoming, with the capacity to include multiple and perhaps contradictory traits.

A site exists at an unlimited number of scales. If a project can be understood to reproduce its site, the potential of a project to operate at different scales relies upon a designer's investment in representing the elements and forces that exist or have existed at those scales, as a precondition for designing ways to foster interdependencies between them. As an architect/landscape designer working in partnership with an architect/urban designer, our practice includes projects for public spaces on disused sites that have been vacant for decades, whose failure can often be traced to the inability of a modernist master-planning framework to recognize the complexity of their position in between multiple scales of use and activity. An approach that engages strategies of scale has the potential to recalibrate such a site in a way that can resonate with its surroundings, to transform a liability in a way that corresponds to a coming together of relational identities.

Tracing the historical processes that produced a site's isolation supported our 1996 proposal for Petrosino Park, a fragment of land in downtown Manhattan [FIGS. 3, 4]. Each side of the site is severed from a different scale fabric, which the park has the potential to reengage on new terms. Historical analysis revealed successive infrastructural interventions, invisible at a local scale, including the construction of the Williamsburg Bridge in 1902, the 4, 5, and 6 subway lines in 1904, and the Holland Tunnel in 1927, respectively isolating the triangle of the site and diminishing its already narrow width, hollowing out the ground beneath it, and increasing traffic congestion alongside it. Understanding how these material processes produced the site supported the conception of four new

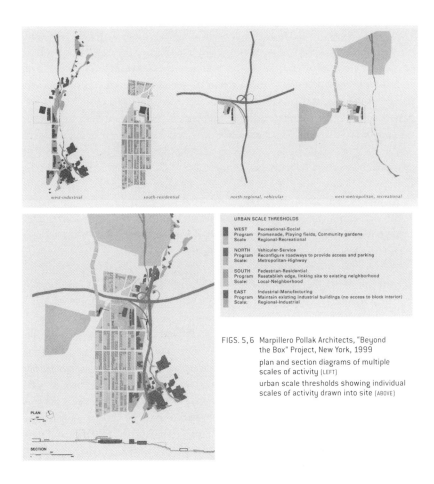

URBAN SCALE THRESHOLDS

WEST — Recreational-Social
Program — Promenade, Playing fields, Community gardens
Scale — Regional-Recreational

NORTH — Vehicular-Service
Program — Reconfigure roadways to provide access and parking
Scale: — Metropolitan-Highway

SOUTH — Pedestrian-Residential
Program — Reestablish edge, linking site to existing neighborhood
Scale: — Local-Neighborhood

EAST — Industrial-Manufacturing
Program — Maintain existing industrial buildings (no access to block interior)
Scale: — Regional-Industrial

FIGS. 5, 6 Marpillero Pollak Architects, "Beyond the Box" Project, New York, 1999

plan and section diagrams of multiple scales of activity [LEFT]

urban scale thresholds showing individual scales of activity drawn into site [ABOVE]

variously scaled thresholds that extend outward from its physical footprint to engage its invisible boundaries. These new thresholds formulate and participate in the park's identity as a "becoming" that occurs through encounters between diverse social groups, economies, ecosystems, and informational webs. The layering of scales embeds a multiplicity of urban and ecological orders, making it difficult for any one group to exclusively appropriate the park.[11]

While the Petrosino Park project addresses only a small fragment of the city, much of landscape urbanism's focus is directed toward large post-industrial sites whose development will have a significant impact on a city's future. Our project for "Beyond the Box," part of a study in 1999 exploring issues of superstore retail development on industrially zoned sites in New York City, addresses the intersection of urban and suburban uses on a derelict two-acre South Bronx superblock [FIGS. 5, 6]. Working with an understanding of the city as a landscape made up of multiple surfaces (rather than its conventional representation as a single surface), the project overlays a range of abstract and material scales onto the site, which has absorbed numerous disjunctures since the construction of the Cross Bronx Expressway in the 1960s. Mapping these disjunctures, in the form of different scales of activity and use that stretch against each other and reverberate on the site, makes it possible to engage their potential in new heterogeneous spaces. These existing scales—to the north, the metropolitan scale of the expressway; to the west, a regional scale of recreation; and to the south, a local, residential/pedestrian fabric—each suggest a kind of access and program. The proposal draws these disparate urban orders into the eviscerated interior of the superblock, intertwining them to situate and scale the foreign entity of the "box," and to produce a variegated set of social and natural spaces, culminating in the topographical device of the Parking Hill, a multilevel infrastructure for cars, people, and landscape. The east side of the site retains the industrial uses that are part of a surviving manufacturing zone.

A built project that accomplishes such an overlay of scales is OMA's Kunsthal in Rotterdam (1992), recalling Rem Koolhaas's formulation of "metropolitanism...a totally fabricated world within which any number of opposing views could co-exist."[12] The simultaneity of scales is present in the Kunsthal's ramp, which shifts identity to become architecture, city, and landscape: at an urban scale, beginning from Westzeedijk Street, it functions as the main entry to the park from the city, the Kunsthal building operating as a portal; by forming a bridge from Westzeedijk Street, elevated on a six-meter-high dike, over the east-west service road, the ramp allows the building to respond three-dimensionally to a regional scale of the Dutch landscape, positioning the visitor to perceive the site's juxtaposition of busy motorway and green idyll [FIGS. 7, 8]. At an architectural scale, the museum appropriates the ramp as it passes through the building by pressing a density of programs against it, including ticket booth, café, gallery, bookstore, and display windows; the ramp also provides the organizing structure of the museum, entering the building and folding over itself repeatedly to become entry, overlook, passageway, room, and roof garden. At a landscape scale, the ramp is one of five similarly scaled movement elements forming a promenade that organizes the experience of the park. Each element controls a field similar in size to the Kunsthal: a bridge crossing a field of flowers, a path through woods and a pond, a hard-surfaced "stage," punctuated with cuts for planting and drainage, and the entry grove with its mirrored wall and ground of white shells.

By participating in multiple scales of its environment, the ramp has the capacity to affect that environment at different levels, through corresponding registers of architecture, landscape, and city. As in Lefebvre's diagram, each scale is nested within the others: the roof garden is a fragment of the park landscape, vertically displaced to become a foreground element within the architecture, yet also the culmination of the architecture; the theater seats are a multicolored garden, in a field that operates at the scale of the park as well as the building [FIGS. 9, 10].

FIGS. 7–10 Office of Metropolitan Architecture, Kunsthal, Rotterdam, 1992: view of ramp, with city beyond [TOP LEFT]; diagrammatic section, showing conception as a continuous circuit initiated by ramp [TOP RIGHT]; sketch of flowers [BOTTOM LEFT]; auditorium with multicolored seats [BOTTOM RIGHT]

A common technique of modernist planning has been to separate functions as a means of resolving conflicts—for instance, suppressing the presence of the car in order to create a pedestrian landscape. This strategy of separation continues to produce sterile environments. Moreover, it cannot support the regeneration of an isolated site, whose derelict condition has been produced, in many cases, by its position between radically different scales. The architect Andreu Arriola layers cars and pedestrians, functions traditionally kept apart, in the multilevel Plaça del Glories Catalanes in Barcelona (1992) to create new spatial configurations [FIG. 11]. The project intertwines local- and metropolitan-scale roadways, a parking structure, a public landscape, and a playground. At a metropolitan scale, it functions as a major interchange, routing cars between principal avenues through its top level. Locally, cars park on the middle and lower levels of the structure, which frames the park at the center, which is entered on foot through large openings in what appears from the outside to be a building, and from the inside a grassy slope. The inscription of vegetation and bodies onto this vehicular infrastructure reappropriates it as everyday urban space at the scale of the neighborhood.

Scale is a key to the development of urban representations that celebrate differences of size rather than suppressing them in an effort to maintain human

FIGS. 11, 12   Andreu Arriola, Plaça del Glories Catalanes, Barcelona, 1992 (TOP)
Catherine Mosbach, Etienne Dolet, outdoor spaces, New York, 1992 (BOTTOM)

FIG. 13 Alison and Peter Smithson, Robin Hood Gardens, the mound, London, 1972

scale, a cultural construction identified exclusively with the measurable and the known. Landscape architect Catherine Mosbach's renovation of outdoor spaces around a ten-story residential tower block on a concrete base brings the issue of being out of scale into design, sometimes even augmenting the distance between scales, engaging the tension between them to produce new interpretations of urban domestic space. Platforms, paths, and benches situate individuals but also stage encounters with scales of building, nature, and city. The wood cladding of these elements evokes intimacy of interior domestic space, effecting a displacement of that space into the urban sphere [FIG. 12]. It also provides a material consistency that allows the project to operate at a much larger scale, as if it was the concrete plinth itself that was clad in its entirety. Mosbach's intervention took on the ambiguity of a place in which architecture, landscape, and city seemed to exist in parallel worlds, recasting these disjunctive realities as a landscape of connections.

Each of the above projects suggests some way in which the scale disparities that are an inevitable part of everyday spaces can contribute to rather than preclude a vital urban realm. A further discussion is that of "bigness," which, in urban and architectural terms, has primarily been framed in terms of monumentality. The concept of the sublime, as it has been associated with landscape, offers an alternative strategy for engaging scalar difference. While American

FIG. 14   Alvaro Siza, Leça Pool, Matushinos, Portugal, 1961

nature and modern landscape have been historically represented in terms of the sublime outside of cities, the strength of these spatial traditions has meant that nature within a situation of perceptible containment (as opposed to, say, the expanse of a large urban park) is often relegated to a background position. Yet sublimity has more to do with the perception of uncontainability than with objectively definable size. It engages the contradiction between the idea of the totality of a thing and the perceived impossibility of understanding the thing in its totality. In other words, as Immanuel Kant has written, the sublime can be found in an object "in so far as its boundlessness is represented in it and yet its totality is also present."[13]

The grass-covered mound at the center of Robin Hood Gardens, the 1970s housing estate designed by the architects Alison and Peter Smithson, represents a condition of boundlessness while still engaging urban boundaries [FIG. 13]. The size of the mound in relation to the two linear buildings that frame it makes it seem to press upward and outward, creating a tension that is both spatial and material. Its virtually uncontainable presence, in combination with its elemental figural quality, shifts the perception of what would usually be a restricted courtyard space to the point of rescaling the repetitive surfaces of the housing blocks themselves.

Alvaro Siza's 1961 Leça de Palmeira Pool complex engages and reproduces multiple scales of architecture, body, city, and landscape, to enable building and

FIG. 15 Adriaan Geuze/West 8, Storm Surge Barrier Landscape, East Scheldt, Netherlands, 1985

beachgoer to inhabit an endless horizon above an uncontrollable sea, without attempting to domesticate the power of these spaces [FIG. 14]. A jetty by the ocean pool meets the breaking waves at high tide to produce a huge spray, re-presenting the open sea's uncontainable processes. The building's striated geological forms operate locally, to intricately traverse its rocky site, but also regionally, at the scale of the coastal landscape, as well as at smaller scales of human action, threading a route through the rocks to reach the sea. The use of concrete as a building material registers the industrial scale of storage tanks visible from the site, rather than ignoring or attempting to screen them out from this set of spaces focused on the enjoyment of nature. It would be easy to ascribe the sublimity of the Leça Pool to its spectacular site, and the architect's activity to one of preservation, if one did not appreciate the difficulties of the location. It is the project that reconstructs a semi-industrial portion of a rocky coast along a busy roadway, by bringing forth and intensifying existing forces and weaving new scales of activity into an existing site.

The project for a storm surge barrier by West 8 represents an uncontainable nature in a different way, by establishing an oscillation between multiple scales of landscape ecology [FIG. 15]. It engages a scale of migration of several species of coastal birds that are not containable within the regional and local landscape for which the barrier is constructed. The infrastructural installation draws the birds onto the barrier island where they arrange themselves by color, corresponding to their species, according to a self-similar attraction, on wide stripes of black mussel shells and white cockle shells. The project sustains a tension between dynamic ethereality and concrete presence; the plateau of colored shells attracts the birds—an uncontainable part of nature—into a field that they inhabit in a way that is unstable even as it reproduces the design.

These strategies each amplify the role of scale to support an inclusive concept of urban landscape that is continually reinvented as it is continually reconstructed. In social terms, this landscape's potential for reinvention means that it is a place that can be appropriated by different constituencies, in such a way as to allow unexpected things to happen. In ecological terms, it offers a means of approaching something too large or complex to be comprehended as a single totality. In either case, it suggests a provisional means of designing the undefinable, through which unanticipated spatial characteristics may emerge from the interplay between elements and through inhabitation.

The instability that characterizes these projects is a positive one that produces and sustains an openness in terms of the meaning or sense of the work. None of these projects blurs the boundary between architecture and landscape. Rather, they inhabit that boundary through their instability, or lack of fixity, constructing as a space by oscillating back and forth across it.

The projects share an emphasis on the ground, in a way that acknowledges its construction, such that it cannot be equated with a fictionally untouched nature. Each project not only amplifies the role of the ground but also multiplies it, to produce or construe it as multiple grounds rather than the single closed surface traditionally associated with "landscape." These grounds, which are variously clad, isolated and warped, inflated, delineated, and made material, perform roles that are simultaneously natural and social, testifying to the possibility of a vital public space, one that does not settle differences but rather allows them to exist.

Notes

1. Kenneth Frampton, "Toward an Urban Landscape," *Columbia Documents* no. 4 (1994): 90.
2. This essay is part of a research on urban outdoor space to develop frameworks that do not rely on polarities such as that of constructed architecture versus natural landscape, and that are not exclusive to any one discipline. This research is supported by grants from the Graham Foundation for Advanced Studies in the Fine Arts and the National Endowment for the Arts.
3. Henri Lefebvre, *The Production of Space*, trans. Donald Nicholson-Smith (Oxford: Blackwell Publishers, 1991): 28.
4. Ibid., 29.
5. Doreen Massey, introduction to *Space, Place, and Gender* (Minneapolis: University of Minnesota Press, 1994), 3.
6. Stuart Hall, "On Postmodernism and Articulation: An Interview with Stuart Hall," *Journal of Communication Inquiry* vol. 10, no. 1 (1986): 91–114.

7. Donna Haraway, *How Like a Leaf* (New York: Routledge, 2000), 71.

8. Lefebvre, *The Production of Space*, 153.

9. Ibid., 155.

10. This recognition precludes the conception of space in the form of a mosaic—a series of different locales each with its own intricacies—a conception that theoretically allows differences to coexist yet fails to represent their interdependence and therefore their potential to act on each other.

11. To understand more about the identity of the thresholds, as well as the design for the park interior, as shown in the model, see Linda Pollak, "City-Architecture-Landscape: Strategies" *Daidalos N° 73: Built Landscapes* (Spring 2000): 48–59.

12. Rem Koolhaas, "Life in the Metropolis or the Culture of Congestion," *Architectural Design* vol. 47, no. 5 (May 1977): 319–25.

13. Immanuel Kant, *Critique of Judgment*, trans. Werner S. Pluhar (Indianapolis: Hackett, 1987), 98.

From Theory to Resistance: Landscape Urbanism in Europe

Kelly Shannon

FIG. 1 Latz and Partners, Piazza Metallica, Duisburg-Nord Park, Germany, 1999; naturalized industrial archaeology

Across the globe, as urbanization continues unabated, territories are often described as seamless artificial landscapes, without physical boundaries.[1] Conceptual boundaries have also been blurred as distinctions between urban and rural, city and countryside, become less relevant to the discussion of the contemporary city. Current discourse on urbanism is awash with "landscape" and its far-reaching conceptual scope—including its capacity to theorize and project urban sites, regional territories, ecosystems, networks, infrastructures, and large organizational fields.[2] The growing range of publications on the subject is evidence of the reemergence of urban landscape into the larger cultural imagination. Although North America lays claim to coining the term and articulating the concept of landscape urbanism, a number of Europeans have recently contributed to this emerging discipline.[3]

The terming of "critical regionalism," as early as 1981 by Alexander Tzonis and Liane Lefaivre, may be viewed as a European preamble to the contemporary interest in landscape urbanism. For them, critical regionalism was a means of criticizing postwar modern architecture and creating a renewed sense of place.[4] Critical regionalism design attributes were derived from regional, circumscribed constraints that produced places and collective representations. Although Tzonis and Lefaivre wrote explicitly of architecture, the environmental determinism accorded to their argument has recently been extended to critical regionalism in the medium of landscape, in an effort to challenge the internationally imposed "generic" models of modernization and urbanization and to resist the homogenizing effects of late capitalism.

The term critical regionalism was popularized by Kenneth Frampton in 1983 through his well-known essay "Towards a Critical Regionalism: Six Points for an Architecture of Resistance."[5] The essay was philosophically based upon Paul Ricoeur's theory that technology was homogenizing the world by facilitating the spread of a single, mediocre culture. Frampton's critical regionalism was an "architecture of resistance," seeking "to mediate the impact of universal civilization" and "to reflect and serve the limited constituencies" in which it was grounded. He alluded to the inherent power of sites and used then recent interventions in the Ticino landscape as an example of a method for constructing meaningful relations with the genius loci:

> The bulldozing of an irregular topography into a flat site is clearly a technocratic gesture which aspires to a condition of absolute placelessness, whereas the terracing of the same site to receive the stepped form of a building is an engagement in the act of "cultivating" the site.[6]

In the 1990s, Frampton went further and concluded that the tools of urbanism alone appear unable to resist the relentless "flattening out" of cultures and places and that perhaps the only remaining plausible instrument is re-engagement with landscape through "megaforms" and "landforms," terms he has used to "stress the generic form-giving potential of such forms and second, in order to emphasize the need for topographic transformation in terms of landscape rather than in terms of self-contained single structures."[7]

In another essay, Frampton explicitly refers to the use of landscape as a vehicle for holding ground for use as reserves of open space and natural resource parks in the midst of what will quickly become low-density urbanized areas. In so doing, he echoes Peter Rowe's formulation of a remedial "middle" landscape, advocating site-specific landscape as an intermediary between built form and the otherwise placeless surfaces of urbanization:

> Two salient factors may be derived from Rowe's thesis: first, that priority should now be accorded to landscape, rather than to freestanding built form, and second, that there is a pressing need to transform certain megalopolitan types such as shopping malls, parking lots and office parks into landscaped built form. . . . The dystopia of the megalopolis is already an irreversible historical fact: it has long since installed a new way of life, not to say a new nature . . . . I would submit that instead we need to conceive of a remedial landscape that is capable of playing a critical and compensatory role in relation to the ongoing, destructive commodification of our man-made world.[8]

The alienation of man from "place" has become a topic widely written about by theorists in the past two decades, and there is no lack of articulate descriptions of the new global landscapes. At the same time, conceptual redefinition and reformulation of the urban—even to the point of dissolving it—have dominated the discourse of the built environment as the imageability, legibility, and particularity of interventions in cities has become less clear. The conventions of urban history, urban planning, and urban design are insufficient to understand and qualitatively intervene in the contemporary condition. Radical rethinking of urbanism's modus operandi is necessary to fundamentally and critically re-engage in the making of cities. The poignant stance of Frampton and his belief in landscape as an operative tool to resist the globalizing and homogenizing tendencies of built environments has provided a platform for the conceptual evolution of landscape urbanism.[9]

THE FRENCH THEORIST OF URBAN LANDSCAPE, Sébastien Marot, has written extensively on the changing role and revival of landscape, posing the formulation landscape sub-urbanism. Marot notes that sub-urbanism is indeed a rich and ancient tradition, replete with its unique morphologies and typologies, and the tools, models, and methods of the suburban tradition are appropriate as springboards for renewing influence on the scenography of public urban spaces.[10]

Marot's lexicographical contribution of "sub-urbanism" to the Grand Larousse of the twenty-first century directly refers to landscape methods and underlines the primacy of sites (as opposed to programs). He uses the words "theoretical hypothesis," "critical," and "genuine laboratories" that place "sub-urbanism experiments and their landscape methods" at the forefront of an alternative to contemporary urbanism:

> Sub-urbanism: n [M. FR. Suburban Italian: suburbia] as opposed to urbanism. 1. Body of experiments and methods of planning and development (landscape, architecture, infrastructure and geotechniques) specifically as these developed in the suburbs and through which the latter have managed to shape their own spaces and physiognomies. 2. Discipline composed of projects first inspired by suburban scenarios and in which the traditional hierarchy imposed by urbanism between program and site (as per the logic of command that prevails in architecture) is reversed, the site becoming the material and the horizon of the project; cf., landscape. 3. Theoretical hypothesis, historiographic and critical, not necessarily exclusive of its obverse that considers development as a movement that goes from the exterior toward the interior, from the outskirts toward the city. By extension: Historiographical approach that considers these suburban experiments and their landscaped methods (especially their gardens) as genuine laboratories of urbanism and land development.[11]

For Marot, European decentralization has led to a proliferation of new public commissions, and regions have begun to view the qualities of their landscape as not only marketable entities but also as reserves of public space. As tourism and recreation rapidly replace agriculture, adaptation to new economies without the complete loss of "identity" demands innovation. In Marot's estimation, contemporary landscape architects—placed at the convergence of agrarian peasantry (low culture) and urban design (high culture) heritages—must take a radically different approach than their predecessors. The specific qualities of sites provide the rationale and raw material for new projects.[12]

Marot identifies four steps in the study and projection of site-based landscapes: anamnesis, or recollection of previous history; preparation for and the staging of new conditions; three-dimensional sequencing; and relational structuring. The first and last stress a possible resistance through landscape. "Anamnesis" views land and public space as an expression of ancient culture, or as a palimpsest that shows all of the unique activities that contributed to the shaping of that particular landscape and no other; sites are inherited and eventual project bequests.

"Relational structuring" refers to the anticipation of future (re)colonized sites. According to Marot, landscapes must be understood as relative spaces.

Landscape strategies have the capacity to challenge the limits of bureaucratic authority while extending the scope of possibilities. Marot writes,

> That landscape as a larger milieu is rarely subject to the control of a single authority means that the forms of relational structuring cannot be so much formal as they are vehicles for negotiation and mediation (among neighboring constituencies, management authorities, etc.).[13]

WHEREAS MAROT HAS ATTEMPTED TO REVIVE landscape through a renewed commitment to public urban spaces, Belgian urban designer and academic Marcel Smets has promoted the landscape tradition as a virtual "savior" to contemporary urban design. Smets has developed a taxonomy of spatial design concepts suggesting how contemporary designers work with the condition of "uncertainty"—interpreted not as a lack of clarity but as indeterminacy regarding future development and the incapacity to shape it is a definitive form. For Smets, the grid (man-made form that provides an underlying structure for development within pre-established regulations), casco (or receptacle, derived from the landscape, reflecting its constitutive form), clearing (landscape as a unifying backdrop assuring freedom of new interventions), and montage (radical superposition of various programmatic and compositional layers) are four design approaches which indirectly reference Frampton's advocacy of new instruments for urbanism.

> [The casco] reflects the constitutive form of the landscape and is based on local geological and hydrological conditions. As such, it can be considered the ideal natural frame that adapts to site conditions. The power of its distinctive pattern allows it to be filled in various ways without losing its fundamental character or identity.[14]

According to Smets, the casco grounds projects in the evident foundations of a physical and geographical logic expressed by the site; it involves the search for a "legitimizing truth in the landscape."[15] Often, minimal interventions seek to render more evident what is already there and incorporates the particular site into its larger setting.

INFRASTRUCTURAL BIAS

Despite such speculations, the landscape urbanism discourse that has developed in Europe has on the whole emerged less as a theory than as a way to innovate at the level of design practice.[16] Landscape is increasingly referenced in regards to infrastructure, ecology, urban de-densification, and sprawl, wherein traditional urban design proves costly, slow, and inflexible. At the same time, a number of landscape urbanism projects have successfully resisted the speculative logics of the private sector and the highly bureaucratic and technically oriented

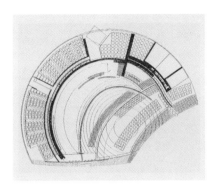

FIG. 2 Joan Roig and Enric Batlle, Nudo-de-la-Trinitat, Catalunia, Spain, 1993; infrastructural landscapes

public sectors. As exurban growth runs wild and post-industrial areas demand clean-up and reprogramming, there is an urge to literally reground the environment with an intelligence of place—interpreted not so much in the conservative sense of Martin Heidegger's and Christian Norberg-Schultz's *genius loci* but more in Elia Zenghelis's contemporary interpretation of uncovering existing logics of reality and finding a site's capacity by distinguishing the junk from the potentials.[17] In a number of recent European projects, landscape urbanism strategies have given voice to the restorative and resistive social and cultural formation of territories—and the evocative power of landscapes. The overlaying of ecological and urban strategies offers a means by which projects create new systems of interconnected networks that complement the existing structures.

The progressive transformation of urban, rural, and peripheral territories into transit areas hosting a modern, amorphous connective web of roads, highways, and railroads has been occurring with relative indifference to geography and the production of qualitative spaces. A notable exception has been France's TGV landscapes and Barcelona's ring roads, both widely published and noted for their integration of state-of-the art civil engineering with urban life. In Barcelona, the city's second beltway, the Ronda de Dalt, was completed for the 1992 Olympics. Following the initiatives of Oriol Bohigas, a team of engineers and architects led by Bernardo de Sola designed a system of collection and distribution among local and regional transport networks that concurrently reconfigured local conditions for new programs and open space by exploiting the section. The highway has literally been embedded in the landscape, with through lanes depressed in a trench. The depression is only covered at strategic urban instances—intersections with the city's major avenues. The covering functions as an extended bridge for local surface traffic and is activated by a recreational facility or public park. Together, landscape and infrastructure frame and create new possible sites for urban activities—both built and unbuilt projects. At one such larger intersection, Enric Batlle and Joan Roig have integrated a transferium, park, and sports facilities [FIG. 2].

ECOLOGICAL BIAS

More and more, the task for European landscape and urban designers is in post-industrial (and post-agricultural) brownfield sites and interstitial terrain vague

FIG. 3 IBA Emscher Park, Northern Ruhr, Germany, 1989–99; ecological stabilization

sites. Germany's 1989–99 International Building Exhibition (IBA)[18] in the Northern Ruhr—once the heartland of Europe's steel and coal industries—confronted regional challenges by simultaneously repairing environmental damage and projecting economic renewal.

Approximately 120 projects were implemented in a program of integrated urban regeneration. The natural landscape was not restored but rather ecologically stabilized, and the region's industrial legacy was recycled, as many of the enormous relics were adapted and reused as centers for cultural activities. Most impressive, however, was the coordinated and regional-scale planning and realization of the project, physically manifested in the Emscher Landscape Park, a green corridor connecting the seventeen cities between Duisburg and Kamen along the ecologically recovered Emscher River and its 350 kilometers of tributaries [FIGS. 3, 4].

The most acclaimed project within the regional strategy is Latz and Partner Architects' Duisburg-Nord Park, a conversion of the Meiderich steel mill and adjacent Thyssen 4/8 mining complex [SEE FIG. 1]. Memory is re-collected in fragments as ruined walls, tracks, underground galleries, and bridges are "naturalized" as industrial archaeology in the 230-hectare park. Demolition materials are recycled as aggregate for new land and concrete structures, while new plants and ecosystems flourish on ash and slag heaps. According to Rossana Vaccarino and Torgen Johnson, Latz's project has become a model for recycling landscapes where "the unseen, the unwanted, the leftover comes back to new life, with the re-engineered sublime qualities of art form."[19]

IBA 2010 will focus on the redevelopment of Saxony-Anhalt, an area in the former German Democratic Republic where agricultural land was dramatically transformed during the twentieth century by large-scale opencast mining for brown coal. Following German reunification, the vast artificial landscapes of gravel and sand mountains, pits, and a regulated river system have been largely abandoned; the mining excavations are turning into interconnected lakes, and

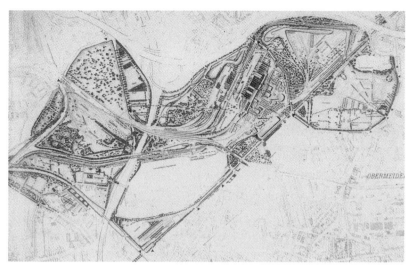

FIG. 4 Latz and Partners, Duisburg-Nord Park; brownfield cleanup and reprogramming

forestry is beginning to cover the man-made topography. British-based Florian Beigel Architects has developed a speculative project for Brikettfabrik Witznitz, Leipzig, which they claim has the potential to become a prototype and a generator for a post-industrial city-landscape within the Halle-Leipzig-Dresden region. Their project provides for initial, interim, and long-term programs for both the former factory buildings and its post-mining landscape. The plateau where the factory buildings are sited has been re-imagined as a series of activity fields, or "carpets," that are able to evolve over time and adapt to the development pressures in the city [FIG. 5].

If no new development is drawn to the city, it will be left with a garden of flowers and ore (derived from the materials found on site). However, these same "carpets" are designed in that they could also become a tapestry of houses, commercial buildings, and reprogrammed industrial buildings [FIG. 6]. The gardens function as an intermediary stage, and their plot sizes correspond to those of eventual building lots. The project is premised upon the uncertainty (as interpreted similarly to Smets' use of the term) of new economic development in the area, while at the same time the post-industrial landscape is renewed and the powerful transformations wrought by mining remain as indelible witnesses to the region's history.

Recovering the landscape though the imposition of a new order of "flexible" organization and reprogramming was a strategy also employed in 1995 by Dominique Perrault to deal with the disappearance of the Unimetal iron and steel plant on the outskirts of Caen, France. The site's 700 hectares along a branch of the River Orle are strategically located for future development of the city,

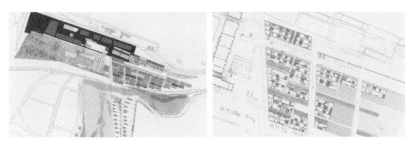

FIGS. 5, 6 Florian Beigel Architects, Brikettfabrik Witznitz, Leipzig, Germany, 1996:
carpets in the landscape [LEFT]; from mines to gardens to buildings [RIGHT]

although no such growth pressures and new programs have yet arisen [FIG. 7].
Perrault therefore developed the site as a "pre-landscape"—a texture that marks
the territory, recovers the river banks and links the city, river, and peripheral
agricultural fields, and establishes an infrastructural backdrop for future developments [FIG. 8].[20] A 100-by-100-meter grid was superimposed on the site, and
the one-hectare fields are alternatively planted with grass and staggered herba-
ceous trees, forming a tapestry that will become urbanized over time [FIG. 9]. The
site's icon, the large refrigeration tower, has been restored along with a select
number of other significant structures, and sits in a 300-by-900-meter void, to
be the central park of future development.

POST-INDUSTRIAL NATURES
Within the more general strategies of recolonizing brownfield sites, a number of
projects have focused on restoring or reintroducing the natural processes and
features of landscapes; the particularities of natural processes within sites are
harnessed in the instigation of interventions. For example, Agence Ter's States
Garden Fair, a conversion of the Osterfeld coal mine and part of Emscher Park,
integrated cultural heritage, ecological recovery, and new development into a
scheme that capitalized on making evident previously unseen natural processes.
A playful staging of the region's underground water sources connects the towns
of Bad-Oeynhausen and Löhne and strengthens the area's spa identity. A hydro-
geological survey outlined fault lines that provide the towns with their sulphur-
and-iron-charged water. The subterranean order was alluded to above ground
as the east-west striations between the towns were marked by "perspiring"
gabions symbolizing the underground crevices through which the water flowed.
The centerpiece of the park is the hollowed-out southern terrain containing an
immense fifteen-meter-deep shaft (three-quarters of which is below ground) that
gushes water from its source at irregular intervals [FIG. 10].

In Zuera, Spain, a project to renew the city's south bank of the River Gallego
was turned into an opportunity to simultaneously solve hydrological and ecological problems as well as expand the public realm and redefine the cultural

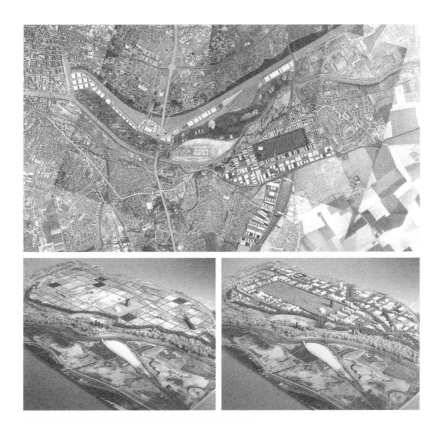

FIGS. 7, 8 Dominique Perrault, Unimetal Park, Caen, France, 1995
superimposed order (TOP)
pre-landscape structure (BOTTOM; LEFT & RIGHT)

FIG. 9
Unimetal Park;
awaiting reclamation

FIG. 10 Agence Ter, Regional Garden Show, Bad Oeynhausen/Löhne, 2000; rhythms of nature

FIG. 11 Inaki Alday, Margarita Jover, and Pilar Sancho, River Gallego, Zuera, Spain, 1999; floodable arena

meaning of the river. Architects Inaki Alday, Margarita Jover Biboum, and Pilar Sancho reconfigured the floodable watercourse of the river by clearly articulating three landscape terraces that are progressively flooded by the natural rhythms of the water regime. The uppermost level, where Zuera's town center is located, is protected by a rubble embankment. The centerpiece of the newly created public promenade is a bullfight arena that is linked to a series of pathways and porous opens areas (capable of absorbing excess water in periods of flooding), remarrying the city with the river [FIG. 11]. The river's island is made accessible via a bridge and functions as an ecological reserve. This low-budget project proves that minimal landscape urbanism interventions can qualitatively impact the public realm and strongly link urban life to yet also protect it from, the cycles of nature [FIG. 12]. Infrastructure demands have been successfully aligned with recreation.

AGRICULTURE AND WEAK URBANIZATION

In addition to the prominent infrastructural and ecological biases in the landscape urbanism discourse, also present are figurative and literal references to agriculture. The countryside is generally shaped neither by aesthetic nor symbolic aims, but instead by pragmatic considerations concerning its productivity. Human capacity to shape the landscape is particularly evident in aerial views of the gigantic patchworks of intensively cultivated land. The clearance of woodland, drainage of marshland and reclamation of wasteland and heath for agriculture originally created the cultivated countryside it represented, in part, the domestication of nature. Clearing, terracing, crop rotation and irrigation were all a part of everyday life for the world's peasantry. However, in quantitative terms of the contemporary world, agricultural land is undergoing a process of devaluation, due to the push for competitive export-oriented farming (exacerbated by increased global competition resulting from the General Agreement on Tariffs and Trade), economies of scale, and agricultural biotechnology, which has the potential to complement and improve the efficiency of traditional selection

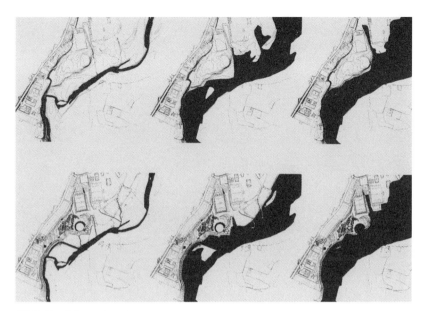

FIG. 12   River Gallego; water regimes

and breeding techniques to enhance productivity. Globally, there has been a massive and silent exodus from farmland as agriculture is further mechanized and societal development is no longer directly tied to productivity of the landscape. As well, the centrifugal growth of cities relentlessly continues to consume once productive territory. Yet agriculture remains predominant not only in trade negotiations but also in spatial terms and cultural identities across the globe. The analogy of agriculture has parallels with landscape urbanism which are interesting at a theoretical level.

Richard Plunz and Inaki Echeverria have written of a "gardener's logic" which builds forward from what exists and deals with the present complexity of cities and territories as entities in constant flux. Large-scale super-impositions, framed by traditional master plans, are relinquished in pursuit of design, policy, and planning, where final forms are open to speculation. The analogies to gardens and agriculture relate to an underlying structure, measure, infrastructure, etc., whose crops are regularly rotated and relate to shifting demands.[21]

Andrea Branzi, the Italian architect and academic who since No-Stop City (1969–72) and the early projects of Archizoom has sought a "permanent avant-garde," refers directly to the contemporary processes of agriculture in his call for "weak urbanization." The process he promotes is of a relational architecture and urbanism which, like agriculture, is able to quickly adjust to changing needs and seasons. In a 2003 lecture at the Berlage Institute in Rotterdam, Branzi elaborated:

FIG. 13   Andrea Branzi, with the Domus Academy, Agronica, Eindhoven,
The Netherlands, 1994; semi-urbanized agricultural park

The industrial agricultural civilization makes a horizontal landscape,
without cathedrals, crossable and reversible: the turn-over of crops man-
ages the agricultural landscape according to a temporary logic, fitting to
the production balance of the earth, to the flow of seasons and of the
market. For all these reasons, contemporary architecture should start to
look at modern agriculture as a reality with which to set new strategic
relations. An architecture that renovates completely its reference patterns,
facing the challenge of a weak and diffused modernity. Setting new relations with a culture that is not constructive in traditional terms, but productive in terms of territorial systems, following bio-compatible logics
and using very advanced support technologies.[22]

Agronica, carried out in 1994 by Branzi through the Domus Academy for Philips
Electronics, experimented with the idea of an architecture based on freely available mobile construction components, laid out in a semi-urbanized agricultural park [FIG. 13]. The Strijp Philips masterplan in Eindhoven, devised five years
later, further developed the ideas of Agronica. The characteristic discontinuous
pattern of the industrial Philips site—to be abandoned and reprogrammed with
sites for new enterprises of the post-industrial economy (the European equivalent to Silicon Valley)—was reenvisioned as an "agricultural park," an experi-
mental territory. Containers for programs were not fixed on the land, but
movable. Their position, number, and contents would shift according to demand
and opportunity. The infrastructure was likewise designed in a manner that
allows for the maximum number of potential spatial configurations, "a sort of
great patchwork quilt of weak and crossed penetrations, laid out on the open
space of the park," Branzi noted, "which constitute a homogenous network of

FIGS. 14–16
François Grether and Michel Desvigne,
confluence of the Saône and Rhône
rivers, Lyon, France, 2001
recoding and relayering (ABOVE)
reclamation by parks (RIGHT)
two-speed landscape (BELOW)

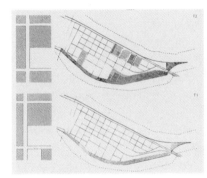
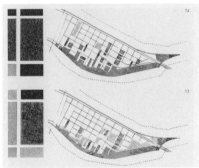

light distribution and make the area totally traversable again."[23] Branzi's "weak urbanization" interprets agriculture as a highly evolved industrial system, capable of adapting to production cycles that change over time and utilize reversible modes of organization.

The agricultural metaphor was also decisive in the "strategy of infiltration" for the Lyon Confluence in France, by the architect/planner François Grether and landscape architect Michel Desvigne. The project for 500 hectares of industrial land under the process of abandonment between the Saône and Rhône rivers is structured by a "dispersed and mobile" system of parks, allowing flexible occupation as parcels become available for new programs [FIG. 14]. During the envisioned thirty-year transformation process, all exterior land will at one time or another be parkland, either provisionally or for the more long term, as described by Desvigne [FIG. 15]:

> We are not envisaging a hypothetical, definitive state but a succession of states that correspond to the different stages of the metamorphosis. Exterior areas will be born, disappear, shift, according to the evolution of the building and the rhythm of the liberation of land, to make up a sort of moving map, like that of crop rotation.[24]

The phasing of the project, as dictated by different industrial parcels made available for new development at dissimilar periods, led to the evolution of a "two-speed landscape" [FIG. 16]. Temporary features instantly enhance the site's public perception—meadows of flowers (as planted at the site's tip), tree nurseries (at the center of the peninsula) and a 2.5-kilometer garden (prefiguring the spinal column of the park system along the Saône) [FIG. 17]. Perennial elements such as lines and clusters of trees, infrastructure and buildings progressively define the projected spatial configuration. Desvigne explains:

> These pieces succeed and displace one another, disappear, compose themselves into a fabric of singular and original forms; as if this landscape was finding its quality in the authenticity and legibility of these construction processes, in the image of an agricultural landscape.[25]

LANDSCAPE COLONIZATION

Resistance to the normative processes of city extension has also been pursued by landscape urbanism strategies. The by-now iconic "Chinese hieroglyph" diagrams of Rem Koolhaas and the Office for Metropolitan Architecture's (OMA) 1987 design entry for the new French town of Melun-Sénart represent a departure of attention given to buildings within the urbanization process [FIG. 18]. The instability of political, cultural, and financial pressures upon the formation of the built environment, according to Koolhaas, is circumvented by a resilient structure of voids:

> At a moment when the complexity of each three-dimensional undertaking is internal, the preservation of the void is comparatively easy. In a deliberate surrender—tactical maneuver to reverse a defensive position—our project proposes to extend this political shift to the domain of urbanism: to take urbanism's position of weakness as its premise.... Instead of a city organized through its built form, Melun-Senart will be formless, defined by this system of emptiness that guarantees beauty, serenity, accessibility, identity regardless—or even in spite of—its future architecture.[26]

FIG. 17 François Grether and Michel Desvigne, Canale de Saône; gardener's logic

The project reverses the formal and structural roles of figure and ground, building and open space. Instead, concentration is directed to the spaces in between—
variously programmed voids are to structure the town. This void framework
resulted from a careful inventory of existing conditions, habitats, historical fragments, existing infrastructure corridors, and new programs [FIG. 19]. The voids
are to be protected from "contamination by the city," while future development
of an archipelago of residue—the leftover, isolated islands—are "surrendered to
chaos."[27] The design offers the future city incredible flexibility, while at the same
time the archipelago model ensures that each island's autonomy ultimately rein-
forces the coherence of the whole.

Architect and urbanist Paola Viganò, who has been working over the past
years in partnership with Bernardo Secchi, has developed a landscape urbanism
strategy for the Salento region in Italy's province of Lecce. The region—1,800
square kilometers, of which 865 are covered with olive trees and vineyards—has
a population of 800,000 and is visited by 2,200,000 tourists annually. In many
aspects it is representative of the città diffusa [FIG. 20], but at the same time it differs in that its modernization has been remote from mainline western development; as a part of Italy's poorer, southern area, the territory of the Salento region
has widely been regarded as marginal. Viganò has designed a series of scenarios
for the region's future development which includes alternative energy and environmental policies, requalification of coastal areas, expanded productive landscapes, increased infrastructure, concentrations of future urbanization, and
collective services [FIG. 21]. At the same time, however, Viganò views this landscape of dispersion as an opportunity for development, and conceives the entirety of the region as one large contemporary park:

> The term "park" as used here in a contemporary sense not only alludes
> to a place of leisure, but is to be understood as a group of environmen-
> tal situations in the broadest sense, whose essential combination will go

towards encouraging the development of some or all the main social activities as affairs…. Contrary to current opinion the porous character of the diffused city presents a great opportunity for paving the way for a correct development of biodiversity and expansion of nature, in order to construct landscape and an environment that will interpret the values of contemporary society.[28]

For Viganò, the larger, existing landscape infrastructures form the basis for later urbanization. This strategy is particularly relevant for contexts in which the productive landscape is extensive and has led to dispersed infrastructure systems—even if they are underdeveloped.

BEYOND RESISTANCE

In North America and Europe, landscape—in both its material and rhetorical senses—has been brought to the fore as a savior of the professions of architecture, urban design, and planning. The theoretical affirmation of landscape as an instrumental tool in urbanism has occupied writers on both sides of the Atlantic. It is only in Europe, however, that the timing of landscape urbanism's discourse has had the fortune to coincide with a fundamental shift in politics—with tangible repercussions for the profession.

Throughout Western Europe, "green" environmental agendas have become mainstream while both popular opinion and political will support a series of robust infrastructural programs and environmental policies.[29] As a result, the once resistive landscape urbanism practices and the projects they produce have recently benefited from investment in public transport systems (particularly the high-speed train networks and highway systems) coupled with a deep commitment to the design and construction of the public realm (evidenced in the proliferation of well-designed open spaces and public amenities) as well as a focus on intelligent stewardship of the natural environment. Many once marginal—even radical—activists, have become "established" players at the highest level of political life.[30]

While the most comprehensive theories of landscape urbanism have been initiated and extrapolated in the context of North America, unless and until there is a significant change in the politics and policy surrounding public work in that context, North American landscape urbanists will no doubt look longingly at the opportunities now available in Western Europe. Landscape urbanism can not only reinvigorate the professions of the built environment with new operative strategies, but, perhaps more importantly, reinstate a critical, resistive capacity of projects in the context of ever-globalizing, homogenizing territories. Frampton's plea for a reengagement with the landscape is an open invitation for investigation into the transformative social and cultural formation of territories and for innovative means to strategically reformulate reality.

FIGS. 18, 19
Rem Koolhaas/Office for Metropolitan
Architecture (OMA), Melun-Sénart, France, 1987
landscape voids (LEFT)
spaces in-between (ABOVE)

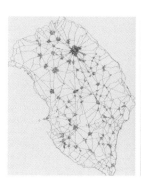

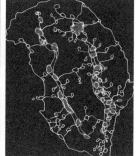

FIGS. 20, 21 Paola Viganò, Salento region, Province of Lecce, Italy:
città diffusa (LEFT); region as park (MIDDLE & RIGHT)

Notes

1. This essay is an edited and reworked portion of the "Landscape Urbanism" chapter of the author's doctorate "Rhetorics & Realities, Addressing Landscape Urbanism, Three Cities in Vietnam," (May 2004, Katholieke Universiteit Leuven, Belgium). The author would like to acknowledge the promoter of the thesis, André Loeckx, whose constructive comments were fundamental to the thesis, and are equally embedded in this essay.

2. A number of recent essays, journals and books could be cited here. Those that have significantly informed the development of this essay include Stan Allen, "Mat-Urbanism: The Thick 2D," in Hashim Sarkis, ed., *CASE: Le Corbusier's Venice Hospital* (Munich: Prestel/Harvard Design School, 2002), 118–26; Henri Bava, "Landscape as a Foundation," *Topos* 40 (2002): 70–77; James Corner, ed., *Recovering Landscape: Essays in Contemporary Landscape Architecture* (New York: Princeton Architectural Press, 1999); Julia Czerniak, ed., *CASE: Downsview Park Toronto* (Munich: Prestel/Harvard Design School: 2001); Mohsen Mostafavi and Ciro Najle, eds., *Landscape Urbanism: A Manual for the Machinic Landscape* (London: AA Publications, 2003); Linda Pollak, "Sublime Matters: Fresh Kills," *Praxis Journal* no. 4 (2002): 40–47; and Charles Waldheim, "Landscape Urbanism: A Genealogy," *Praxis Journal* no. 4 (2002): 10–17.

3. In addition to a growing body of theoretical and built work, landscape urbanism is also becoming a part of educational institutions in Europe. The Architectural Association in London offers a graduate degree in landscape urbanism and the École National Supérieure du Paysage in Versailles and the Institute of Architecture at the University of Geneva have been transformed into laboratories of alternative approaches to landscape and urbanism.

4. Alexander Tzonis and Liane Lefaivre, "The Grid and the Pathway," *Architecture in Greece* 5 (1981).

5. Kenneth Frampton, "Towards a Critical Regionalism: Six Points for an Architecture of Resistance," in Hal Foster, ed., *The Anti-Aesthetic: Essays on Postmodern Culture* (Seattle: Bay Press, 1983), 16–30.

6. Ibid., 26.

7. Kenneth Frampton, "Megaform as Urban Landscape," public lecture at Berlage Institute, Amsterdam, The Netherlands, 1993.

8. Kenneth Frampton, "Toward an Urban Landscape," *Columbia Documents* no. 4 (1994): 83–93. See also Peter Rowe, *Making a Middle Landscape* (Cambridge, Mass.: MIT Press, 1991).

9. Frampton has become a staunch advocate of the landscape urbanism initiative as evidenced in his response to a recent interview, "Nine Questions About the Present and Future of Design," *Harvard Design Magazine* no. 20 (Spring/Summer 2004): 4–52. In response to the question: "What do you consider the strengths and weaknesses of design education? How might it be improved?" Frampton responded "I want to emphasize above all the issue of sustainability and the recently invented synthetic discipline currently subsumed in the Architectural Association School, London, under the title Landscape Urbanism. It seems to me that both of these environmental agendas ought to be strongly emphasized and urban planning faculties in any categorical reformulation of the curricula and methods obtaining in the design studio." He goes on to cite Susannah Hagan, "Five Reasons to Adopt Environmental Design," *Harvard Design Magazine* no. 18 (Spring/Summer 2003): 5–11.

10. Sébastien Marot, *Sub-urbanism and the Art of Memory* (London: AA Publications, 2003).

11. Ibid., 7.

12. See Sébastien Marot, "The Reclaiming of Sites," in Corner, ed., *Recovering Landscape*, 48–49.

13. Ibid., 52.

14. Marcel Smets, "Grid, Casco, Clearing and Montage," in Robert Schafer and Claudia Moll, eds., *About Landscape: Essays on Design, Style, Time and Space* (Munich: Callwey Birkhauser, 2002), 132–33.

15. Ibid., 134.

16. Christopher Hight, "Portraying the Urban Landscape: Landscape in Architecture Criticism and Theory," in Mostafavi and Najle, eds., *Landscape Urbanism*, 9–21.

17. Christian Norberg-Schultz, *Genius Loci: Towards a Phenomenology of Architecture* (New York: Rizzoli International, 1979); Elia Zenghelis, interview by Nicholas Dodd and Nynke Joustra, *Berlage Cahier 2*, (Rotterdam: 010 Publishers, 1993).

18. IBA is the abbreviation for the German term *Internationale Bau-Ausstellung*, or International Building Exhibition. It is not an exhibition in the traditional sense, but IBA exhibits are, or will become, built reality. In 1901, the first German building exhibition took place in Darmstadt followed by a series of well-known building exhibitions including the *Weissenhofsiedlung* in Stuttgart in 1927 and the IBA in West Berlin between 1979 and 1989.

19. Rossana Vaccarino and Torgen Johnson, "Recycling Landscape: Recycling for Change," in *Landscape Architecture: Strategies for the Construction of Landscape* vol. 3, no. 2G (1997): 138.

20. Dominique Perrault, "Park in an Old Siderurgical Plant, Caen (France)," *AV Monographs: Pragmatism and Landscape* no. 91 (2001): 76.

21. Richard Plunz and Inaki Echeverria, "Beyond the Lake: A Gardener's Logic," *Praxis* no. 2, *Mexico City* (2001): 88–91.

22. Andrea Branzi, "Weak and Spread," public lecture at Berlage Institute, Rotterdam, The Netherlands, 2003.

23. Andrea Branzi, "Unpredictable City Planning," *Lotus* 107 (2000): 115.

24. Michel Desvigne, "Infiltration Strategy," *Techniques and Architecture* 456 (2001): 49.

25. Ibid., 53.

26. Rem Koolhaas and Bruce Mau, *S, M, L, XL* (Rotterdam: 010 Publishers, 1995), 974, 981.

27. Ibid., 977.

28. Paola Viganò, *Territories of a New Modernity* (Napoli: Electa Napoli, 2001), 17, 65.

29. Since 1992, "Agenda 21" has been an integral component of the European Commission's environmental policy and is considered fundamental for its "road map to sustainability." "Agenda 21," an 800-page document of the 1992 Rio Declaration, is widely recognized as the "bible of sustainable development."

30. A good example of such a leader is Germany's Joschka Fischer, a radical street-fighting activist of the 1968 protest movement who is one of Germany's most esteemed politicians, as the Green Party leader, former Minister of Environment, and present Foreign Minister.

Landscapes of Infrastructure

Elizabeth Mossop

FIG. 1 Infrastructure as public space as in Spackman and Mossop's Moore Park Bus Interchange, Sydney

The emergence of a discourse based on the relationship between contemporary urbanism and landscape theory and methods signifies an important shift for landscape architecture as a discipline [FIG. 1]. It offers the vehicle by which landscape architecture can reengage with citymaking and take a more significant political role in the debates surrounding urbanization, public policy, development, urban design, and environmental sustainability. The discourse of landscape urbanism establishes the significance of infrastructure and its associated landscape in the development of contemporary urbanism, and in the generation of public space.

Landscape urbanism brings together a number of different landscape-generated ideas in the exploration of contemporary urbanism. Landscape is used as a metaphor for contemporary urban conditions, such as the field scenarios described by James Corner and Stan Allen, the "urbanscape" described by Richard Marshall, or the matrix of landscape described by Rem Koolhaas, all of which refer to an urban type that, unlike the traditional core/periphery model, is not focused on a dense middle but instead is a more fragmented matrix of discontinuous land uses.[1] Landscape is also used to represent and understand the dynamic systems of the city, and is increasingly perceived as the significant medium for citymaking.[2] Strategies have been developed that attempt to make ecological processes operational in design, harnessing natural phenomena such as erosion, succession, or water cycles in the generation of landscapes. Designed landscapes are thus allowed to develop over time as can be seen in recent proposals for Fresh Kills in New York and Downsview Park in Toronto.[3] These proposals and others highlight the way in which the landscape of infrastructure has become the most effective means to explore the relationship between natural processes and the city, which is the integral factor in a truly synthetic landscape urbanism.

As early as the 1880s, Frederick Law Olmsted's proposals for Boston's Emerald Necklace illustrate the intertwining of transport infrastructure, flood and drainage engineering, the creation of scenic landscapes, and urban planning [FIG. 2]. Here the close collaboration between landscape design, urban strategies, and engineering produced a complex project integrating ideas about nature and infrastructure as well as health, recreation, and scenery. The work of Frederick Law Olmsted on major urban projects like Manhattan's Central Park and Brooklyn's Prospect Park, as well as Frederick Law Olmsted, Jr.'s proposals for other major urban park networks, were a significant influence on the urbanism of the time, although their most ambitious urban proposals, such as that for Los Angeles, remain unimplemented.

FIG. 2 Olmsted's design of Boston's Emerald Necklace combined infrastructure, engineering, health, recreation, and scenery.

Walter Burley Griffin's 1911 design for Canberra, national capital of Australia, in which significant features of the natural environment played a key role in locating the city's major axes and key structures, is another example of a strong relationship between city form and the natural landscape structure [FIG. 3]. His designs for residential subdivisions—strongly influenced by Olmsted's work— also illustrate methods for developing urban infrastructure that conserve and enhance the natural landscape, as can be seen at his Castlecrag in Sydney.[4]

In the first half of the twentieth century, ecology and planning were for the first time explicitly linked, in the work Patrick Geddes, in Benton MacKaye's grounding of regional planning in human ecology, in Aldo Leopold's writings on the idea of a land-based ethic, and in Lewis Mumford's description of the city as composed from human processes intricately interwoven with natural processes.[5] This work led to the development of regional environmental planning, and in particular the work of Ian McHarg at the University of Pennsylvania, where he was invited to create a program in landscape architecture and regional planning beginning in 1954. His unique curriculum profoundly influenced the entire discipline of landscape architecture, and has been so thoroughly absorbed into the culture of landscape architecture that it is difficult to properly appreciate its significance at the time. His intellectual leap in comprehensively applying the understanding of ecological processes and natural systems to human settlements and planning was of enormous significance. He was a great communicator and polemical speaker, and his book *Design with Nature* remains one of the most important works shaping our thinking on human settlement.

FIG. 3 Griffin's competition-winning design for Canberra
demonstrates a strong relationship with the landscape.

When professional education in urban design was beginning at Harvard University in the 1960s, Hideo Sasaki, the Chair of the Department of Landscape Architecture, suggested its inclusion within the program. Although this did not transpire, it illustrates the breadth of Sasaki's vision for landscape architects and his assertion of their taking an influential role in shaping the city.[6] This challenge was not effectively taken up, and the discipline has always struggled with its perceived subordinate role to architecture in any discourse on urbanism. Since that time, landscape architects have by and large accepted this, both in practice and within academia, and as a result have increasingly been relegated to a more peripheral or marginal role in debates on urbanization. The mainstream of the profession has been more focused on design at the scale of the individual site, on conservation-based planning, and on visual issues and the amelioration of the impact of development. While there has always been rhetoric calling for a unification of ecology and design, there have been few compelling solutions to urban problems exhibiting this fusion.

There are a number of reasons why this is so. One is that the period spanning from the 1960s through the 1980s saw the transformation of landscape architecture into a full-fledged professional discipline. It has grown in scale and also in scope, and many leading practitioners have been absorbed in the processes of building an academic structure to support the expansion of the discipline and the profession, and in developing organizations and methods for the design and implementation of projects of ever-increasing complexity and scale. Of more significance, however, are two related and powerful paradigms that

FIG. 4 Halprin's Ira Keller Fountain, Portland, Oregon

continue to influence and shape landscape architecture's intellectual trajectory. The first is a worldview that separates the works of humans from the natural world, and the second is the schism within the discipline of landscape architecture, between environment and design.

The perception of the world as "man versus nature," strongly influenced by the ideas of the American transcendentalists, has led to a conceptualization of nature as inherently good and cities and development as inherently bad. These ideas were of profound significance in the nineteenth century, and the designed landscapes that resulted have been most influential on twentieth-century landscape design. This way of thinking also came to the fore after the Second World War in the developing environmental critiques of modernization, for the first time articulated in ecological/scientific terms, most influentially by Rachel Carson in *Silent Spring* and Ian McHarg in *Design with Nature*.

McHarg, in particular, through his teaching and practice in landscape architecture, influenced its intellectual development. His evangelical style reflected a polarized view of the world and of the profession of landscape architecture. He continued to make an absolute distinction between the sustaining, spiritually renewing countryside and the ugly, dirty, brutal industrial city. In *Design with Nature* he describes sprawling suburbs, out of control freeways and traffic, pollution, ugly commercial environments, soulless cities of office towers, and the evils of industrial agriculture. His methods assume an infallibility that produces one objective and replicable answer, and he polarized the profession by insisting that his was the only ethical path for planning and development. But McHarg's methodology fails to account for the significance of design in the planning process, and his scientific rhetoric devalues the expression of art and culture. Much of the work that has followed McHarg in this vein also has a strong tendency to be anti-urban and anti-design. At its crudest, the underlying legacy is the idea that if the process is right, the design solution will also be right. Embodied in this is a fundamental misunderstanding of design, of the relationship between planning and design, and of the complexity of the design process.

FIG. 5 Hargreaves Associates' Northern Water Feature at Olympic Park, Sydney, Australia

In opposition to these views, there has been the ongoing development within the discipline of the art of landscape design. This line of work has continued to be concerned with the creation of spaces for the accommodation of human activity that delight the senses, and has focused on the development and techniques of the creative process, the nature of formal solutions, and the technical and professional issues of implementation, as can be seen in the work of designers such as Lawrence Halprin, Dan Kiley, and more recently Laurie Olin and Peter Walker [FIG. 4]. The impact of postmodernism has forced a greater engagement with social and cultural issues and a reevaluation of the influence of history. It has also been significant in the exploration in the 1980s and 1990s of environmental and land-based art, which has led to an engagement with natural phenomena and processes in design, as can be seen in the work of Hargreaves Associates or Michael Van Valkenburgh Associates [FIG. 5]. Traditionally this more design- and art-focused work has had little overt engagement with the issues of ecological sustainability.

These two schools of thought have tended to separate themselves in terms of scale, with ecological/environmental planning operating at the regional scale and design-focused projects at the scale of individual sites. They tend to be characterized as planning, ecology, sustainability, science, and conservation on one side and art, design, and development on the other. This schism in the discipline, and the territoriality it perpetuates, has led directly to landscape architecture's failure to engage with urbanism and with the bringing together of ecology and design.

There have, however, been some significant attempts to synthesize the ecological systems approach with urbanism. In 1984, two publications developed the discourse relating ecology and the city: Michael Hough's *City Form and Natural Process* and Anne Spirn's *The Granite Garden*. Both attempted the development of theories and methods applying the understanding of ecology and natural processes to a more sophisticated conceptualization of cities and urban processes, and Hough's ongoing work has continued to develop strategies for the application of ecological ideas in urban design.[7] This engagement with the city, although driven by an environmentalist agenda, has forced the development of systems involving both human and natural processes.

BLURRING BOUNDARIES AND HYBRID LANDSCAPES

While it is important to acknowledge the significant intellectual shifts that have informed the development of landscape urbanism, there is much to be gained by building on the strengths of work done by ecological urbanists like Hough and Spirn as well as that of architectural theorists like Kenneth Frampton, Peter Rowe, and Rem Koolhaas. The issue of territoriality is instrumental in our current dilemma of how to deal with contemporary urban development, and disciplinary divisions have only served us ill in coming to terms with the complexity of current patterns of urbanization. One of landscape urbanism's more intriguing aspects is its very crossing of disciplinary boundaries.

The issue of boundaries is also relevant in revisiting the question of the separation of humans from nature and the confusion in discussing the urban landscape often caused by equating "landscape" with nature or naturalness—this in spite of the ongoing and explicit manipulation and construction of the urban landscapes we inhabit. The profession of landscape architecture has been plagued by an unthinking acceptance that nature-landscape is always good and beautiful, which has often replaced a more focused exploration of "solutions" to the design of urban landscapes. Instead we see the ubiquitous creation of mediocre naturalistic pastoral landscapes across every urban or suburban condition. Since the 1980s, however, there has been an investigation of, and focus on, the unnaturalness of the landscape, particularly influenced by the work of designers and commentators from the Netherlands, with its strong tradition of constructed landscapes.[8] In contemporary discussion the difference between natural landscapes and human landscapes is much less clearly defined.

In parallel with this has been the development of the field of urban ecology, the investigation of the characteristics of the plant and animal communities in the urban landscape, subject to natural processes but profoundly shaped by the impact of humans and development. This has led to new design strategies that are based on an acceptance of the disturbed and hybrid nature of these landscapes and the idea that landscape design can be instrumental in working with natural processes to make new hybrid ecological systems. It is clearly not about making approximations of pristine natural environments, but rather making functioning ecologically based systems that deal with human activity and natural processes in the urban environment. Bringing all of the factors together is complex, requiring a synthesis of social, political, and economic factors, as well as issues related to urban wildlife and water management.

In moving these ideas forward to a greater mainstream acceptance, there is a desperate need for successfully functioning prototypes. Architectural critic Bart Lootsma has said, "Designing is not enough: the implementation of schemes and the limitation of undesirable and unsustainable developments are called for."[9] Working against the implementation of projects derived from the ideas of landscape urbanism is that they resist easy communication. The dynamic and systematic quality of projects is much harder to grasp than an individual object or clear formal strategy of more traditional urban landscape designs. One of the characteristics of systems that are trying to work with natural processes is the idea of their development over time, and the formal outcomes of projects that rely on process are difficult to predict, in a way that is often unacceptable to public agencies and other clients.

RECOVERING THE LANDSCAPES OF INFRASTRUCTURE

Explorations in landscape urbanism have focused on infrastructure as the most important generative public landscape. In the course of the twentieth century we have seen the increasing standardization of infrastructural systems as they meet higher standards of technical efficiency. These ubiquitous urban environments have been considered and evaluated solely on technical criteria and somehow exempted from having to function socially, aesthetically, or ecologically. As landscape architect Kathy Poole writes in relation to public infrastructure, "Through roughly 150 years of industrialization we have come to believe that the politics of efficiency are beyond question and that standardization is the ultimate expression of democracy."[10]

Such a reexamination of infrastructural space involves the recognition that all types of space are valuable, not just the privileged spaces of more traditional parks and squares, and they must therefore be inhabitable in a meaningful way. This requires the rethinking of the mono-functional realm of infrastructure and its rescue from the limbo of urban devastation to recognize its role as a part of the formal inhabited city. Designers need to engage with this infrastructural landscape: mundane parking facilities, difficult spaces under elevated roads, complex transit interchanges, and landscapes generated by waste processes. Landscape urbanism also suggests that this happens by an instrumental engagement with ecological processes as well as with the function of infrastructure and the social and cultural needs of the community. This functional engagement with ecological processes is distinct from the representations of natural phenomena and process that have been a significant influence on landscape design in the 1990s. The strategy is an attempt to make the necessities of dealing with human impact a part of the making and generation of urban landscapes.

FIG. 6 At Victoria Park in Sydney, roads and parks form a system of water management.

This relationship between natural systems and the public infrastructure of the city begins to suggest a means of developing urban strategies through the development of networks of landscape infrastructure related to ecological systems. The starting point is that the most permanent and enduring elements of cities are often related to the underlying landscapes—the geology, the topography, the rivers and harbors, and the climate. This does not mean a denial of the realities of globalization or the influence of technology, but recognition of the importance of place and of connection to natural systems.

This suggests there should be a relationship between the underlying structures of topography and hydrology and the major structuring elements of urban form, such as the use of catchments as the basis for physical planning and regulation. There is an obvious synergy between the need to create networks of open space to serve social needs and new approaches to open systems of urban water management.

At the city scale, we see a version of this in historical examples where extreme topographic conditions have controlled the form of development, such as in Rio de Janeiro or Sydney, where very steep topography has prevented development and preserved vegetation in urban areas close to harbors and beaches. In the city of Curritiba, in Brazil, recent planning initiatives undertaken in the 1990s have restructured the city's open-space system to create a network of parks that also regulate floods and collect and treat urban runoff. At the neighborhood and site scales, we are beginning to see the implementation of design strategies that use the matrix of public and circulation space as the drainage and water treatment infrastructure. At Victoria Park in Sydney, the road system has been designed with planted swales that collect and begin the treatment of stormwater, as well as establishing street trees. Water is also collected and held within the neighborhood parks and treated in wetland park areas before being recycled in a series of sculptural water features [FIG. 6]. A similar approach to the integration of public space and water management can be seen in Atelier Dreiseitl's designs for projects at Potsdamer Platz in Berlin, or Scharnhauser Park in Ostinger, Germany.[11]

FIG. 7 Leuven Station in Belgium, design by Smets and Sola-Morales

More traditional networks of open space can also offer the opportunity for the "re-naturalizing" or "day-lighting" of channelized urban streams into functioning hybrid systems. They use the ecological processes of natural streams in making systems that manage flooding, treat stormwater runoff, provide recreation opportunities, and enhance biodiversity. The design by Schaffer Barnsley for the Restoring the Waters project at Clear Paddock Creek in western Sydney is an example of this, as is Hargreaves Associates' Guadalupe River Park in San Jose, California, which created a stylized river channel and recreational landscape in managing urban flooding.[12]

THE LANDSCAPE OF MOVEMENT

One of the biggest challenges is the design of the most mundane landscapes, those dominated by vehicles—carparks, roads, and freeways. The significance of the automobile must be dealt with rather than ignored in a nostalgic yen for a pre-car urbanism or blindly embraced for its romantic associations. It is time to engage with these landscapes that have been so poorly served by design. They have been a kind of shadow city, inhabited only by default. Many solutions to urban conflict between cars, mass transit, and people involve banishing the vehicles to subterranean underworlds, by their nature dark and atmospherically toxic. At the highest densities this separation may be the only solution, and the task is to redefine the nature of these spaces, as can be seen in Marcel Smets and Manuel de Sola-Morales's project for Leuven Station in Belgium [FIG. 7], or in the urban carpark designed by Béal et Blanckaert, in Roubaix Nord, France.[13] In many other instances, however, a reconciliation between the reality of private transport's convenience and the idealized places we want to live in has yet to be tangibly devised.

Road typologies have been distinguished in the past by their relationship to their surroundings. This was determined by their degree of specialization so that the most highly specialized freeways and expressways had almost no relationship to their environment, being corridors for the transit of automobiles only. They were machines for transport, sealed from contamination by their environment, unchanging in section whatever their location, and their form determined solely by the technical requirements of their engineering. Older forms like boulevards and streets permitted different volumes of traffic movement but were also connected into the surrounding fabric and fulfilled a more diverse range of urban functions.

Investigating the design of roads requires understanding their operation at different scales. The plans and longitudinal sections of roads relate to the driver and the experience of movement through their corridors, whereas their cross sections relate the roads to the landscape within which they sit. From within the road we can explore the relationship between the visual and kinesthetic sensations of movement through space provided by the road, and how these can be employed in their design. Instead of only seeing the road from the driver's point of view, designers have recently begun to look at it from the perspective of the landscape through which it passes, responding to it as an element of the urban fabric and an integral part of the city.

Infrastructure increasingly provides the public spaces of our cities, and the infrastructure of movement is an essential presence in the developed world. Whether for cars, bicycles, or people, it is the connection of elements to one another that is the foundation of urban and suburban life. Like other infrastructure, roads are required to perform multiple functions: they must fulfill the requirements of public space and must be connected to other functioning urban systems of public transit, pedestrian movement, water management, economic development, public facilities, and ecological systems. These demands are therefore propelling new design approaches.

Freeways, the most specialized roads, are being designed to perform a more complex range of functions and to be an integrated part of the urban landscapes they traverse. In Melbourne, Denton Corker Marshall's Gateway project heightens the driver's experience of entering the city and also changes the relationship of the freeway to the city, making it a functioning part of the urban fabric. Also in Melbourne, the design of the extension to the Eastern Freeway, by Tract Consultants and Wood Marsh, is designed as part of an integrated strategy for providing open space, the management of urban flooding, and conservation. The design of the roadside landscape also responds to its locality through the use of wall and planting materials. The new design of the Great Western Highway, between Leura and Katoomba in the Blue Mountains west of Sydney, by Spackman and Mossop, responds to the locality by minimizing its impact on the spectacular and rugged terrain through the vertical separation of carriageways, the use of tunnels, and elevated carriageways. It also preserves the historic urban pattern of the relationship between the highway and adjacent towns. The A14 Viaduct in Nanterre in France, designed by Deqc and Cornet, illustrates a more simply architectural solution to diversifying function by adding a Motorway Operations Center to the underside of the elevated viaduct.[14]

The city of Barcelona, in particular, has developed strategies for civilizing urban freeways. A number of projects have been completed implementing strategies dealing with different aspects of the relationships between major arteries and the surrounding city, from the Moll de la Fusta by Manuel de Sola-Morales, completed for the 1990 Olympic redevelopment, to projects such as the Parc Trinitat's attempt to capture the space inside freeway loops for recreational use (Batlle y Roig, 1990–93), or the layered multifunctional strategies developed for the Rambla de la Ronda del Mig by Jordi Heinrich and Olga Tarrasó (1995–2003).

At lower traffic densities, it becomes possible to design roads as spaces to be shared by people and vehicles. In the Netherlands, the design of residential streets as public spaces for play, socializing, and trees, as well as for different kinds of movement, has been a matter of ongoing development in the twentieth century with the realization of many projects, known as *wonerfs*, throughout the country. Across the Atlantic, in Walter Hood's late-1990s design for Poplar Street in Macon, Georgia, public space has been reclaimed from traffic space to create a generous central median or rambla, allowing a range of new uses to enliven the street. The traffic space is unusual in that it is flexible and is explicitly designed to serve the needs of both drivers and pedestrians. To this end the parking areas are designed to operate as shaded spaces opening to the central "yard" areas, places for people to occupy as well as for car storage. These parking areas are designed with the intention of urban amenity and the acknowledgment of their vital role in the urban experience.[15]

Perhaps the most challenging and neglected urban landscape type is the carpark. We are beginning to see many innovative structures for the accommodation of multilevel parking,[16] but for the surface parking ubiquitous in the suburbs, there are only a few projects that suggest non-standard possibilities. Landscape architect Peter Walker has explored the design of roads and parking infrastructure as a seamless extension of the designed landscape. He uses non-standard pavements and architectural planting to create spaces like garden rooms where the needs of people and cars are balanced. At IBM headquarters at Solana, Texas (1984–89), the strong use of architectural planting, skillful planning and use of materials makes the roads and parking areas an integrated and inviting part of the landscape. Parked cars recede under tree canopies, turning circles provide formal building approaches, and the spaces for circulation and car storage become viable public spaces. The Flämingstrasse housing project in Berlin by Büro Keifer also uses non-standard pavement material to change the use and perception of the parking area. Here the surface is strongly patterned to facilitate orderly car parking, as well as encouraging ball games and children's play at other times.[17] A more extensive approach, where the parking area is treated as an orchard or forest planting, is Michel Desvigne and Christine Dalnoky's landscape design for the Thompson factory outside Paris. In this phased design, swales are used to harvest the water needed to establish bands of planting that create an overall impression of a tree-filled space. Over time the bands are replaced with large-canopied trees that dominate the parking.[18]

THESE PROJECTS ILLUSTRATE A POTENTIAL to bridge the divide between ecology and design so persistent since the impact of Ian McHarg's work. We can see designed landscapes where new hybrid systems develop that harness natural processes and strengthen sustainable systems without creating picturesque landscapes. We can also see the possibility of re-examining even the most challenging infrastructural landscapes and a new attitude to infrastructure that goes beyond technical considerations to embrace issues of ecological sustainability, connection to place and context, and cultural relationships.

If we think of landscape as an infrastructure which underlies other urban systems, rather than equating it with nature or ecology we have a much more workable conceptual framework for designing urban systems. This is particularly apt where those systems no longer function in a core/periphery model but as a matrix. This framework of landscape infrastructure should provide the most permanent layer of urban development to preserve the viability of natural systems and regional cultures.

Notes

1. See James Corner's essay, "Terra Fluxus" in this collection; Corner, ed., *Recovering Landscape: Essays in Contemporary Landscape Architecture* (New York: Princeton Architectural Press, 1999); Stan Allen, "Infrastructural Urbanism" and "Field Conditions," *Points and Lines: Diagrams and Projects for the City* (New York: Princeton Architectural Press, 1999); Richard Marshall, "Size Matters," in Rodolphe El-Khoury and Edward Robbins, eds., *Shaping the City: Studies in Urban Design, History and Theory* (London: Routledge, 2003); and Rem Koolhaas, "Urban Operations," *D: Columbia Documents of Architecture and Theory* vol. 3 (1993): 25–57.

2. See Peter G. Rowe, *Making a Middle Landscape* (Cambridge, Mass.: MIT Press, 1991); and Charles Waldheim, "Landscape Urbanism: A Genealogy," *Praxis* no. 4 (2002): 10–17.

3. Competition entries for Downsview Park are described and analyzed in Julia Czerniak, ed., *CASE: Downsview Park Toronto* (Munich: Prestel and Harvard Design School, 2001); and the Fresh Kills competition is available at http://www.nyc.gov/html/dcp/html/fkl/ada/competition/2_3.html.

4. See Peter Harrison, *Walter Burley Griffin, Landscape Architect*, ed. Robert Freestone (Canberra: National Library of Australia, 1995); Richard Clough, "Landscape of Canberra: A Review," *Landscape Australia* 4, no. 3 (1982): 196–201; Malcolm Latham, "The City in the Park," *Landscape Australia* 4, no. 3 (1982): 243–45; and Jeff Turnbull and Peter Y. Navaretti, eds., *The Complete Works and Projects of Walter Burley Griffin and Marion Mahony Griffin* (Melbourne: Melbourne University Press, 1998).

5. See Patrick Geddes, *Cities in Evolution* (London: Williams & Norgate, 1949); Aldo Leopold, *A Sand County Almanac: and Sketches Here and There*, illus. Charles W. Schwartz (New York: Oxford University Press, 1949); Lewis Mumford, *City Development: Studies in Disintegration and Renewal* (New York: Harcourt, Brace

and Company, 1945); and Mumford, "The City, Design for Living," in *Wisdom* 1, no. 11 (Nov. 1956): 14–22.

6. Richard Marshall, speaking at the Symposium "Josep Luis Sert: The Architect of Urban Design," Harvard Design School, Cambridge, Mass., October 25, 2003.

7. Anne Spirn, *The Granite Garden* (New York: Basic Books, 1984); and Michael Hough, *City Form and Natural Process* (London: Routledge, 1984), and *Cities and Natural Process* (New York and London: Routledge, 1995).

8. This idea is discussed in Andreu Arriola, et al., *Modern Park Design: Recent Trends* (Amsterdam: Thoth, 1993), and also by a number of Dutch theorists and practitioners such as Adriaan Geuze of West 8, Hans Ibelings, and Bart Lootsma. See Ibelings, *The Artificial Landscape: Contemporary Architecture, Urbanism, and Landscape Architecture in the Netherlands* (Rotterdam: NAi Publishers, 2000), and Lootsma, *SuperDutch: New Architecture in the Netherlands* (New York: Princeton Architectural Press, 2000).

9. Bart Lootsma, "Biomorphic Intelligence and Landscape Urbanism," *Topos* 39 (Munich, June 2002): 11.

10. Kathy Poole, "Civitas Oecologie: Civic Infrastructure in the Ecological City," in Theresa Genovese, Linda Eastley, and Deanna Snyder, eds., *Harvard Architecture Review* (New York: Princeton Architectural Press, 1998): 131.

11. Victoria Park can been seen at http://www.Hassell.com.au, and the Atelier Dreiseitl projects at http://www.dreiseitl.de, and in Herbert Dreiseitl, Dieter Grau, and Karl H. C Ludwig, *Waterscapes; Planning Building and Designing with Water,* (Berlin: Birkhäuser, 2001).

12. Restoring the Waters is discussed in Landscape Australia, "Australian Institute of Landscape Architects National Awards 1998," *Landscape Australia* 21, no. 1 (1999): supp. folio between 66, 67. Guadalupe River Park is discussed in Jane Gillette, "A River Runs Through It" *Landscape Architecture Magazine* 88, no. 4 (April 1998): 74–81, 92–93, 95–99. See also Julia Czerniak, "Looking Back at Landscape Urbanism: Speculations on Site," in this collection.

13. See Marcel Smets, *Melding Town and Track: The Railway Area Project at Leuven* (Ghent: Ludion Press, 2002); and Francis Rambert, *Architecture on the Move, Cities and Mobility* (Barcelona: Actar, 2003): 133–34.

14. Rambert, *Architecture on the Move,* 57–60.

15. See Raymond W. Gastil and Zoe Ryan, *Open: New Designs for Public Space* (New York: Chronicle Books, 2004).

16. A number of projects for carparks that illustrate innovative approaches were featured in the exhibition *Architecture on the Move, Cities and Mobilities,* and illustrated in the accompanying catalog, Francis Rambert, *Architecture on the Move, Cities and Mobility* (Barcelona: Actar, 2003).

17. Thies Schroder, *Changes in Scenery: Contemporary Landscape Architecture in Europe* (Basel: Birkhauser, 2001).

18. See Michel Desvigne and Christine Dalnoky, *The Return of the Landscape: Desvigne & Dalnoky* (New York: Whitney Library of Design, 1997).

Urban Highways and the Reluctant Public Realm

Jacqueline Tatom

FIG. 1 Aerial view of the boulevard de Sébastopol, between the rue St. Denis and the rue St. Martin. Paris, 1971

The intellectual promise of landscape urbanism to integrate the conceptual fields of landscape architecture, civil engineering, and architecture for the design of the public realm places urban highways squarely within its purview. The realization of limited-access divided highways in the second half of the twentieth century points to many of landscape urbanism's ambitions, notably to strategically engage the urban landscape at a metropolitan scale within the constraints of the prevailing political economy, and to consider environmental and infrastructural systems as primary ordering devices. Highways are public space writ large, in the metropolitan reach of their network as well as their sheer size. They are part structure and part earthwork, occupying a formal position between architecture and landscape. They are conceived as abstract technological artifacts, yet local topographical and hydrological conditions—not to mention local political circumstances—must be accommodated to realize them. As cultural artifacts, finally, they concentrate public resources on a scale that begs a broader definition of the public good that would ensure their diversion for the creation of public space.

The design of urban highways today suggests a transportation "downstairs" of concrete and asphalt, ceded to state agencies and civil engineers, that contrasts markedly with the design of a public space "upstairs" of plazas and streets, the territory of planners and designers. Used by all, the former are nonetheless invisible in public discussions of what makes a "good" city, except in utilitarian terms. While romantic celebration of the rural or wilderness highway prevails in the general public and in the media, urban highways receive harsh treatment. Massive in scale and reductive in scope, they disrupt the physical and social fabric of the neighborhoods they traverse. Their rehabilitation in the eyes of the public and of design professionals, as well as their positioning within the emerging discourse surrounding landscape urbanism, requires that designers and engineers shift the frame of reference for their design from utility to amenity, from infrastructure to urbanism. Building urban highways to provide efficient automobile circulation in cities might then be considered an urbanistic opportunity rather than a planning liability. For this to happen, the design of highways needs to be theorized and situated historically within professional design practice.

A review of canonical urban roadway system designs is the first step in providing the opportunity to reframe familiar narratives. Vehicular circulation in cities has not always received bad press or so little design consideration, nor has it always been considered in purely utilitarian terms. Indeed, the efficient circulation of goods and people as an essential "function" of modern life and modern cities has been a central preoccupation of most theories of urbanism in the last two hundred years. The creation of boulevard systems, parkways, and highways as distinct elements of the urban fabric has been integral to many proposals to make or remake the city in the modern era. Baron Haussman was, in the mid-nineteenth century, the first to formulate a metropolitan-scale response to this function and to recognize the opportunity it provided to "modernize" Paris.[1] The boulevard system was the master element of an urban renovation that included the provision of water, sewers, parks, and housing, as well as cultural and administrative facilities. Frederick Law Olmsted's vision of the Emerald Necklace for Boston and his realization of the Fenway and Jamaicaway offer American counterparts to Haussman's efforts in Paris. For Olmsted, "circulation and respiration" in the nineteenth-century city could be achieved by the realization of parks, parkways, housing, and recreational venues. These were to be realized in conjunction with massive infrastructural works to manage waste and stormwater needs and to control the ecology of natural systems. These projects are remarkable because they suggest a modern urbanism that conceives of efficient circulation not as an independent system within the city but as the defining intervention of an overall project to provide the residential and public spaces necessary for everyday urban life as well as modern sanitation systems.[2]

The advent of the automobile in the early twentieth century spurred many urbanism proposals defined by the requirements of high speed circulation. Le Corbusier's Ville Radieuse and Norman Bel Geddes's Magic Motorways come to mind, as do Frank Lloyd Wright's Broadacre City and Ludwig Hilberseimer's New Regional Pattern.[3] These visions, however, required a *tabula rasa* or green fields for their full expression. In contrast, the limited-access parkway systems developed in the New York City region during this era, including the work of Robert Moses, are remarkable because they are conceived as complements to the existing city. Realizations such as the Henry Hudson Parkway take advantage of an extraordinary site to integrate residential development, recreational facilities, parks, and monuments while accommodating high-speed and local traffic and public transportation.

In the second half of the twentieth century, the potential of roadway design to enhance the continuing urbanization of existing cities is well served by the theoretical work of Christopher Tunnard in his 1963 book *Man-made America: Chaos or Control?*, with its thorough discussion of the technical, visual, and spatial challenges of modern highway design. Lawrence Halprin's *Freeways*, written for the Federal Highway Authority in 1966, remains however the only work to take on the design of highways in cities as a distinct form of urbanism. Halprin diagrams alternative freeway sections for American cities, as well providing a historic overview of roadway precedents. The result is a *de facto* theorization of the formal and functional evolution of urban roads from boulevard to parkway to limited-access parkway to limited-access divided highway. He establishes a historical continuity in the provision of efficient circulation in the modern era while enthusiastically championing the role of these roadways as public spaces in the contemporary city.[4]

Since these two publications, however, the progressive and optimistic inclination of roadway planning has subsided within the engineering and design professions. The sheer magnitude of urban highway construction programs after World War II has shifted the design focus from urbanism to traffic management.[5] In much of North America, Departments of Transportation (DOTs) or their equivalent have established professional hegemony and autonomy, in great part by legislating an independent federal highway trust. Projects are dictated by political and economic ambitions at the state and federal level, and rarely emerge from local planning or citizen demand. The codification of norms of security and efficiency into rigid bureaucratic guidelines has further alienated the civil engineers who design the highways in their interactions with planners, design professionals, and the general public. The functional result today is an uneasy standoff between transportation engineers and designers and planners, and between DOTs and the public, with politicians shifting allegiances according to election timetables. The formal result is an increasingly pervasive yet narrowly defined network of urban highways. They split and marginalize neighborhoods, their physical bulk continues to expand in response to rising automobile use, and they produce an increasingly distressing sensory assault on everyday life.[6]

Critics within the design professions as well as the media have demonized cars and the highways that serve them as the primary culprits in a perceived urban malaise and impending ecological disaster. Anti-sprawl proposals for smart growth, transit-oriented development (TOD), and the design of pedestrian-friendly public spaces have drawn attention away from the design of the highway itself, championing instead the use of traditional urban forms such as street grids and boulevards. Allan Jacobs's documentation, *Great Streets*, fuels the prevailing narrative of lost urbanity that permeates public discourse by proposing these historic urban forms as models to solve contemporary needs for circulation and public space. His more recent *The Boulevard Book* provides nonetheless one of the only comprehensive reviews and documentations of multiway boulevards as alternative roadway systems for contemporary circulation, systematically debunking the arguments of civil engineers and highway designers who reject this form of roadway design.[7] Were it not for its equally nostalgic cast, this book would begin to restore the theoretical continuity in the design of circulation systems that Halprin established when he posited boulevards and parkways not as models to copy but as precursors to the limited-access divided highways of the postwar era. For Halprin, the considered design of these new highways was integral to the creation of a vital and urbane contemporary urbanism, and the precursors provided valuable examples of design innovation.

One recent example of an urban highway, the Barcelona Cinturón, suggests the possibility of picking up the historical narrative where Halprin left off and rediscovering a theoretical continuity in the conception of urban roadways as public space. The Cinturón is a beltway around Cerda's nineteenth-century city that was conceived in the 1980s by the socialist administration that had been elected in the wake of Francisco Franco's death. It was conceived to eliminate the juggernaut of automobile traffic through the central city by diverting circulation from the center. From the outset, the mayoral administration created the powerful Office of Urban Projects (IMPUSA) to carry out the modernization of Barcelona. Politicians, planners, and designers viewed the Cinturón as an opportunity to "complete" the city.[8] It was considered an integral part of a strategic planning initiative that included parks, cultural institutions, and housing, as well as the recreation and sports facilities of the 1992 Olympics. The urbanistic bias of the Cinturón distinguishes it from most highway projects built today, and its design provides insights into how urban highways can enhance the experience of today's cities.

A CRITICAL RECONSIDERATION OF THE PARISIAN boulevards, the Boston parkways, New York's Henry Hudson Parkway, and the Barcelona Cinturón yields a set of possibilities for urban highway design and confirms the theoretical robustness of the topic, exemplifying its relevance for recent discussions of landscape urbanism. While the first two realizations are not highways in the contemporary sense, as they do not have limited access and are only partly divided, they are important to this discussion because they represent early attempts to redirect and concentrate higher-speed traffic in the city on specially designed roadways.

A common characteristic of these four endeavors is that they are inscribed in a complex program of urban renovation. It is formulated within a broad public mandate to redress degraded sanitary conditions and to improve the quality of life for urban dwellers according to modern criteria of efficiency and performance. These realizations are conceived on a metropolitan scale in support of a heterogeneous program of improvements that includes the provision of efficient public and private transportation and the upgrading of essential utilities. It also includes the creation of public spaces for leisure and recreation, the building of cultural facilities, and finally, the upgrading and augmentation of the residential and commercial building stock. While these programmatic elements are common to all comprehensive urban plans, what is exceptional in these instances is that they are addressed under the aegis of a roadway project, and are generally accommodated within the limits of the roadway right of way itself. They constitute, programmatically and morphologically, a complete urbanism that produces new landscapes that are a hybrid of natural and man-made systems. Moreover, this urbanism does not conform to a predetermined formal geometry, despite its realization as a system, but instead emerges from a site-specific diagramming that conforms and deforms according to existing topographical and land-use conditions as well as real property opportunities.

THE BOULEVARDS OF PARIS

In *Les Promenades de Paris* (1867–73), Adolphe Alphand documents his work as designer of the Haussmanian landscape at all scales. In his general plan of the city, he includes the suburban communities outside the Barrières des Fermiers Generaux as well as the Bois de Boulogne and the Bois de Vincennes.[9] Clearly Baron Haussman's vision extended beyond the limits of the mid-nineteenth century city, signaling a new "metropolitan" understanding of urban development. Moreover, Alphand draws the new network of boulevards, parks, places, and monuments as if they were etched into the solid figure of the city, reinforcing the conception of the boulevards as a comprehensive system that is autonomous yet at the same time embedded in the fabric of the city. The new interventions were strategically located to take advantage of existing monuments and amenities, topographical conditions, and real estate opportunities. Haussman also retained customary economic centers such as the neighborhood street markets. The plan reveals a programmatic richness that is enhanced by a careful exploitation of the existing city.

This richness is confirmed in the sectional representations of the proposed boulevards, which include not only the representation of their profile but the landscaping, the street furniture, the building edge, and the utilities below the surface that were built concurrently. The boulevards are conceived three-dimensionally as public places for pedestrian as well as vehicular and utilitarian uses, for leisure as well as for commerce. The apartment buildings that lined the boulevards, and the monuments that crowned them, were also conceived as part of the circulation system. Their architecture is integral to the experience of the system and to its urbanistic "fit" into the fabric of the historic city; they provide a morphological cohesion that allows old and new urbanization as well as old and new social rituals to coexist. The boulevard Sebastopol, for example, cut through historic neighborhoods to link the new Gare de l'Est with the heart of the city while accommodating the new residential apartment blocks of the emerging bourgeoisie and the department stores that served it. The rue St. Denis and the rue St. Martin, however, were preserved intact on either side, and with them the markets, small shops, and dwellings that had lined these streets for centuries [SEE FIG. 1].

The preservation of the continuity of the built fabric and the programmatic heterogeneity of the boulevards make possible a fluid and diverse experience of the city. The *flaneur* strolling about town, the *vendeuse* on her lunch break, and the *bourgoise* about her shopping could move seamlessly between the rituals of the new society and those of traditional custom, from nineteenth-century to

FIG. 2 Imaginary section through the rue
St. Denis, the boulevard de Sébastopol,
and the rue St. Martin

FIG. 3 Park Department City of Boston
Map of Back Bay Fens, Frederic
Law Olmsted, as of 1887

pre-industrial Paris. This is still the case today, as the different morphologies continue to support different uses and rituals. The programmatic breadth of this new
urban form, in plan and section, supports the social breadth of experience [FIG. 2].[10]

BOSTON'S EMERALD NECKLACE

The Emerald Necklace of Frederick Law Olmsted and his partner Charles Eliot
also has utilitarian roots and results from a rich programmatic vision for urban
infrastructure. The Fenway, the first of the "jewels" of the Necklace, was created
to manage the tidal reflux of the Charles River into the Muddy River in Boston's
Back Bay, in order to eliminate the accompanying stormwater and sewer over-
flows. The topographical and hydrological reconfiguration of what had become
a wasted swamp provided the opportunity to create parks and parkways that
served circulation and recreational needs. As in Paris, the spatial cohesiveness of
the system results from a *mise en relation* of diverse urban and natural elements
that is both deliberate and opportunistic. The Necklace's configuration is determined by site conditions—the alignment of the river and whatever land reserves
could be assembled in public hands—rather than by a preconceived rationaliz-
ing geometry, as is generally the case in classical or modernist visions of the city.

In plan view, the Necklace is shown both as an independent realization within the city and as part of a regional system of parks, parkways, and land reser-
vation [FIG. 3]. Like the Parisian boulevards, the system is both local and
metropolitan in its impact, both particular and comprehensive in its scope. The
Fenway and Jamaicaway created a new urban front that increased the value of
real estate along their length and spurred the building of apartment blocks and
cultural institutions, often conforming to the curved alignment of the arbor-
ways. Multiple lanes of circulation that originally separated carriages from horse-
back riders narrow or widen according to available land, shaping the form of the
retention basins within the gardens and parks. The natural landscape varies in
character, from community garden to public garden to recreational and sports
venues. Here too, a sectional representation best captures the multicoordinate
richness of the intervention. Above and below ground, raised or depressed, on

FIG. 4 Ducks along the Fenway, 2004

the surface and to either side, different uses are accommodated within the constructed landscape of the roadway and its edge [FIG. 4].[11]

The result is a work that serves the public good, not only through the provision of needed infrastructure but also through the provision of public place. Commuters or city-dwellers about their business on the parkways, individuals in contemplation on a park bench, or with family or colleagues at a softball game in the parks, or even lost in a crowd on the fairgrounds—all find their space within the right-of-way of the Necklace. While the bucolic nature of Olmsted's aesthetic contrasts with the classical formalism of the boulevards, both realizations are highly constructed urban landscapes in which nature and infrastructure are put to the service of making places for people to be.

NEW YORK'S HENRY HUDSON PARKWAY

In the General Plan of the Park System for New York and its Environs created by the Regional Plan Association in 1938, the Henry Hudson Parkway appears as a small link in a vast network of parkways and parks, boulevards and highways. It is inscribed in a metropolitan conception of the city that melds landscape, infrastructure, and urbanization. As in Paris and Boston, the metropolitan diagram is formalized as a system but remains informal in its expression as a dendridic network resulting from the judicious exploitation of natural features and topographies, as well as opportunistic acquisitions of undeveloped and often marginal land.[12]

The New York parkways marked the evolution in roadway design from multilane, multiuse full-access roadways to limited-access and divided roadways for vehicular traffic only. By the time Robert Moses completed the Henry Hudson Parkway in 1937, most of the parkways had evolved from leisurely driving roads to major commuter routes. However, the multiple agendas of the original Westchester parkways to upgrade transportation, to sanitize creeks and rivers, and to create parks and cultural and recreational amenities while improving residential development, continued to inform the early proposals of Moses's tenure.[13]

The multivalent quality of the metropolitan system is reproduced within the right-of-way of the Henry Hudson Parkway ensemble itself: it incorporates

Olmsted's original Riverside Drive, which creates a residential edge of grand houses and apartment buildings, and the park includes memorials and monuments such as Grant's Tomb and the Cloisters, which rise above the forested slope [FIG. 5]. Moses expanded the park to cover railroad lines converted to commuter traffic and reconfigured the water's edge to include a limited-access divided highway linking Manhattan to the northern suburbs and a public marina. The striking topography facilitated and inspired the rich association of parkways, railroads, recreation areas, cultural institutions, playgrounds, and residences within a section that reached from the bluff to the water's edge. The recreational areas are equally accessible from above and below through a system of trails and overpasses, providing access and views to the mythic Hudson from multiple vantage points.[14]

Driver and pedestrian, commuter and neighborhood resident, all build a cultural identity as city-dwellers through this quotidian intimation of the sublime. The juxtaposition of the experience of tranquility and speed in this landscape

FIG. 6 Promenade along the Henry Hudson Parkway, New York, 1930s

produces a kind of exhilaration for driver and stroller, a contemporary "rush" that is one of the attractions of urban life [FIG. 6]. This experience has been recognized and poeticized in literature and in film, and vulgarized in umpteen car chase scenes. The highway experience is generally presented as having displaced "street" life, but when accommodated within a larger urbanistic agenda, it can be considered an addition to the range of experiences available to city-dwellers.[15]

BARCELONA'S CINTURÓN
The IMPUSA's plan of Barcelona identifies the realization undertaken in the 1980s and 1990s to improve the quality of life in one of Europe's densest cities. Their *Plan d'Urbanismo* complements the strategic economic plan formulated to position the city as a European player with global economic reach. The Cinturón is one element within a comprehensive and metropolitan-scale proposal to improve public and private transportation and to provide greatly needed public amenities. This proposal includes intimate neighborhood parks and plazas, the reconfiguration and redesign of major avenues and larger parks throughout the city, the integration of new subway lines, as well as the beltway. It also includes recreational, residential, cultural, and sports facilities, many built for the 1992 Olympics.[16]

The Cinturón complements both the inner-city network of renovated avenues and the citywide system of parks and plazas. It is located opportunistically to take advantage of marginal sites that remained undeveloped because of difficult topographic conditions along the waterfront and at the base of the

FIG. 7   Aerial view of the Barcelona Cinturón showing depressed roadway, hyper-turning circles, and decked intersections

Tibildado and Montjuic hills. As in Alphand's plan of Paris, park space, circulation, and urban projects are conceived as autonomous systems that are nonetheless physically and culturally integrated to the fabric of the historic city.

As in the earlier projects, the programmatic richness of the metropolitan diagram is reproduced within the right of way of the Cinturón itself. It is in many ways a traditional multiway boulevard that has been folded in on itself. The central four-lane throughway is depressed, while *contre-allées*, or access roads, remain at the surface to distribute entering and exiting vehicles at speeds slow enough to constitute a viable streetfront for the residential and commercial buildings along its length. Leftover land from highway construction was subdivided into parcels for new housing or public facilities, creating a thick urban edge, much like the soldering effect of the Haussmanian apartment buildings. In some locations the access road is cantilevered over the depressed section, further reducing the width and noise and facilitating ventilation. The sectional complexity is compounded by pedestrian bridges treated as promenades, decks treated as plazas or recreational facilities, and signage and lighting designed to accommodate the continuous curve of the roadway. The interchanges are treated as hyper turning circles, creating large enough central spaces to accommodate programs such as intermodal stations, parking, parks, and recreational facilities [FIG. 7].

Careful attention is given to the quality of the materials so that the Cinturón takes on a distinctive formal identity. Palm trees are planted along the depressed median, clearly marking the separation and reducing the glare of oncoming traffic. This accentuates the effect of speed and emphasizes the cinematographic quality of continual highway movement. Only the tops of the palms are visible from the surface roads, adding a humorous touch that signals the presence of the highway below to pedestrians and drivers on the surface. The designers acknowledge that the city can be experienced at multiple speeds: as a driver on business, or a stroller at leisure.

All along the Cinturón, the scaling up and programming of interchanges to include parks and recreation, the selective decking to create plazas and facilities, and the judicious use of grade shifts and separations allow novel adjacencies to

FIG. 8 Aerial view of the Moll de la Fusta

exist between pedestrian and driver, generating for both an experiential identity forged in the comings and goings of everyday life. The Moll de la Fusta, where
the highway aligns with the waterfront, remarkably illustrates the variety of
public places that can be achieved through the articulation of such complex sections [FIGS. 8, 9]. Local circulation, public transportation, pedestrian strolling, and
high-speed traffic are accommodated by the sectional integration of a classic
boulevard, a raised promenade deck above parking, a depressed and partly
decked throughway, and a waterfront esplanade. Here as elsewhere along the
beltway, the driver never loses his sense of place in the city, and remains in touch
with the sky and the seasons as he or she experiences the thrill of speeding
against the backdrop of the city, or the frustration of being blocked in traffic.
The pedestrian slips back and forth across the highway, taking advantage of the
amenities it provides with friends and family, or perhaps alone, strolling across
a bridge and gazing down, slightly mesmerized by the hum of traffic below the
palm trees.[17]

THE DISCUSSION OF THESE FOUR SEMINAL realizations reveals that the
mobilization of public and private resources, political will, bureaucratic structure,

FIG. 9 Night-time view of the Moll de la Fusta, showing sectional relationships of terrace and roadway

and professional vision for modernization, justified variably for "scientific" reasons of sanitation and efficient circulation, or for boosterism in the form of civic identity, can provide the opportunity for a new manifestation of the public realm. In these examples, the introduction of new road morphologies in the historic city constitutes a complete urbanism that allows for the full expression of everyday urban life. Such an urbanism transforms the city in radical ways and provides it with a new formal and experiential identity. However, new forms and new ways of life do not replace so much as supplement existing forms and rituals, augmenting the range of experiences available to the city's inhabitants. The programmatic richness and metropolitan ambition of these realizations insure that the needs that are met and the experiences that are made possible are commensurate with the multiple expressions of individual identity in modern life, in solitude or lost in a crowd. The inclusion of multiple programs within the right of way of the intervention itself through a careful design of the section ensures that the pedestrian and the automobile driver receive equal consideration while maximizing the use of public resources. In addition, it reestablishes a morphological continuity of the urban fabric that rapidly overcomes the social and physical disruptions of the often violent construction effort.

These exceptional realizations were all undertaken in dense, well-established historic cities. They nonetheless remain relevant for the far less dense, more dispersed development of contemporary fringes, or indeed the new twentieth-century American cities in which traditional "urban" rituals are not established. These projects provide a set of assumptions for the realization of a contemporary highway urbanism that would include today's suburban expansion. Such assumptions do not constitute principles or guidelines but rather the foundation for shifting the frame of reference for the design of urban highways, from utility to urbanism, from liability to opportunity.

The discussion of these realizations is a reminder that such an urbanism moves earth on a massive scale. New structures and venues for urban life are achieved through a radical transformation of topography and morphology of large sections of the city. A remarkable bureaucratic and technocratic integration and mobilization of public and private resources is required to sustain this landscape construction, and strong creative personalities battle to maintain the urban integrity of the vision. These personalities establish the theoretical premises of the work but also its operational foundation. It remains to be seen whether these scenarios, as in Paris, Boston, New York, and Barcelona, can be reproduced and whether urban highways of this caliber can be realized without them in the political economy of the United States today. Clearly the theorization of such an intervention and the diffusion of that theory are essential steps in achieving a cultural consensus around this opportunity. The design of urban highways can then truly be conceived as the design of the public realm.

Notes

1. David P. Jordan, *Transforming Paris: The Life and Labors of Baron Haussmann* (New York, The Free Press, 1995).

2. Bruce Kelly, Gail Travis Guillet, et al., *Art of the Olmsted Landscape* (New York: New York City Landmarks Preservation Commission and The Arts Publisher, Inc., 1981); and Albert Fein, ed., *Landscape into Cityscape: Frederick Law Olmsted's Plans for a Greater New York City* (New York: Van Nostrand Reinhold, 1967).

3. See Le Corbusier, *The City of Tomorrow and its Planning* (New York, Dover Publications, 1987); Norman Bel Geddes, *Magic Motorways* (New York, Random House, 1940); Frank Lloyd Wright, *The Living City: When Democracy Builds* (New York: New American Library, 1958); and Ludwig Hilberseimer, *The New City: Principles of Planning* (Chicago: Paul Theobald, 1944).

4. Christopher Tunnard and Boris Pushkarev, *Man-made America: Chaos or Control? An Inquiry into Selected Problems of Design in the Urbanized Landscape* (New Haven and London: Yale University Press, 1963); Lawrence Halprin, *Freeways* (New York: Reinhold Publishing Corporation, 1966); Urban Advisors to the Federal Highway Administration, *The Freeway in the City: Principles of Planning and Design* (Washington, D.C., U.S. Government Printing Office, 1968).

5. This theoretical void has not been compensated by "pop" or postmodern recuperation of the commercial strips in art or architecture, such as Robert Venturi and Denise Scott-Brown's *Learning from Las Vegas* (Cambridge, Mass.: MIT Press, 1977), which addresses a different scale and the more incremental nature of strip development. Recent works of

criticism suggest however a renewal of interest in highways as public space. See Keller Easterling, *Organization Space: Landscapes, Highway and Houses in America* (Cambridge, Mass.: MIT Press, 1999); Peter Rowe, *Making a Middle Landscape* (Cambridge, Mass.: MIT Press, 1990); Jeffrey T. Schnapp, "Three Pieces of Asphalt," *Grey Room* 11 (Spring 2003): 5–21; as well as Clare Lyster, "Landscapes of Exchange" and Pierre Bélanger, "Synthetic Surfaces," both in this collection. Historical accounts of the political and economic issues surrounding the building of the Interstate and Defense Highway system have also been published in the last decade. See Tom Lewis, *Divided Highways: Building the Interstate Highways, Transforming American Life* (New York: Viking Press, 1997).

6. See Lewis, *Divided Highways*; and U.S. Department of Transportation and Federal Highway Administration, *America's Highways 1776–1976: A History of The Federal-Aid Program* (Washington, D.C.: Department of Transportation, 1977).

7. Allan B. Jacobs, *Great Streets* (Cambridge, Mass.: The MIT Press, 1995); Allan B. Jacobs, Elizabeth Macdonald, et al., *The Boulevard Book: History, Evolution, Design of Multiway Boulevards* (Cambridge, Mass.: MIT Press, 2002).

8. Alfons Soldevilla, architect responsible for the signage, pedestrian bridges, and several public space projects along the Cinturón, interview with the author, 30 November 2000.

9. Adolphe Alphand, *Les Promenades de Paris* (Paris: Rothschild, 1867–73; reprinted New York: Princeton Architectural Press, 1984).

10. For further discussion of the Paris boulevards, see Françoise Choay, *The Modern City: Planning in the 19th Century* (New York, George Braziller, 1969); Jean Des Cars, and Pierre Pinon, *Paris-Haussmann: Le Paris d'Haussmann* (Paris, Picard Editeur, 1991); Jean Dethier, and Alain Guiheux, eds., *La ville: Art et architecture en Europe 1870–1993, Ouvrage publié à l'occasion de l'exposition présentée du 10 fevrier au 9 mai 1994 dans la grande galerie du Centre George Pompidou* (Paris: Centre Georges Pompidou, 1994); and Howard Saalman, *Haussmann: Paris Transformed* (New York: Georges Braziller, 1971).

11. For further discussion of the Emerald Necklace, see Walter L. Creese, *The Crowning of the American Landscape: Eight Great Spaces and Their Buildings* (Princeton, N.J.: Princeton University Press, 1985); Kelly, Guillet, et al., *Art of the Olmsted Landscape*; S. B. Sutton, *Civilizing American Cities: A Selection of Frederick Law Olmsted's Writings on City Landscapes* (Cambridge, Mass.: MIT Press, 1971); and Christian Zapatka, *The American Landscape* (New York: Princeton Architectural Press, 1995).

12. The Henry Hudson Parkway Authority, *Opening of the Henry Hudson Parkway* (New York: The Henry Hudson Parkway Authority, 1936); U.S. Department of Transportation and Federal Highway Administration, *America's Highways 1776–1976.*

13. Han Meyer, *City and Port: Urban Planning as a Cultural Venture in London, Barcelona, New York, and Rotterdam, Changing Relations between Public Urban Space and Large-scale Infrastructure* (Utrecht: International Books, 1999); John Nolen, and Henry V. Hubbard, *Parkways and Land Values* (Cambridge, Mass.: Harvard University Press, 1937); Rowe, *Making a Middle Landscape.*

14. Christian Zapatka, "The American Parkways: Origins and Evolution of the Park-road," *Lotus* 56 (1987): 97–128; Zapatka, *The American Landscape.*

15. Jean Baudrillard, *Amériques* (Paris, Editions Grasset et Fasquelle, 1986); Robert Caro, *The Power Broker: Robert Moses and the Fall of New York* (New York: Knopf, 1974); Meyer, *City and Port*; and Zapatka, *The American Landscape.*

16. See Peter Rowe, Henry N. Cobb, et al., *Prince of Wales Prize in Urban Design: The Urban Public Spaces of Barcelona 1981–1987* (Cambridge, Mass.: Harvard University Graduate School of Design, 1991). Mona Serageldin, *Strategic Planning and the Barcelona Example: International Training Program* (Cambridge, Mass.: Harvard University Graduate School of Design, 1995).

17. Guy Henry, Barcelona: *Dix années d'urbanisme, la Renaissance d'une ville.* (Paris: Editions du Moniteur, 1992); Rowe, Cobb, et al., *Prince of Wales Prize in Urban Design; Meyer, City and Port.*

Drosscape

Alan Berger

FIG. 1 California Speedway (former steel mill site), Fontana, California, about 45 miles west of Los Angeles-San Bernadino County

America is deindustrializing. In 2005 more than 600,000 abandoned and contaminated waste sites have been identified within U.S. cities.[1] How did this "waste landscape" come to be? What will we do with it? How will it affect urbanizing areas in the future? Controversial questions like these are difficult to answer, and this subject has produced some of the late-twentieth century's most debated bodies of scholarship.[2] An essay such as this cannot definitively answer these questions. It can and does, however, address the topic of deindustrialization in the context of the relationships between landscape and urbanization. But deindustrialization cannot be discussed in isolation. As America rapidly deindustrializes, it is simultaneously urbanizing faster than at any other time in modern history. What then are the links between urbanization and deindustrialization, and the production of "waste landscapes" in American cities? Most importantly, who is best qualified to deal with the abundance of waste?

Grappling with these questions in the design of the built environment presents a fascinating challenge. Landscape architects in academia give little attention to urbanization, often dwelling instead on the traditional areas of landscape history—site engineering, construction detailing, and project-based design studio education. But beyond and behind these topics is a reality so huge we tend not to see it at all—what I call the *drosscape*, or the inevitable "waste landscapes" within urbanized regions that eternally elude the overly controlled parameters, the scripted programming elements that designers are charged with creating and accommodating in their projects.[3] Adaptively reusing this waste landscape figures to be one of the twenty-first century's great infrastructural design challenges [FIG. 1].[4] This essay chronicles this condition and suggests that those with an understanding of both landscape *and* urbanization will be best positioned to act on these sites in the future.

WASTE LANDSCAPE

The waste landscape emerges out of two primary processes: first, from rapid horizontal urbanization (urban "sprawl"), and second, from the leaving behind of land and detritus after economic and production regimes have ended. From its deindustrializing inner core to its sprawling periphery to the transitional landscapes in between, the city is the manifestation of industrial processes that naturally produce waste. Designers often paint a black-and-white picture of complex industrial processes. A common term, "post-industrial," has been used by landscape architects, architects, and planners to describe everything from

FIG. 2 Downtown Fort Worth, Texas

polluted industrial landscapes to former factory buildings usually found in declining sections of cities. The term itself creates more problems than solutions because it narrowly isolates and objectifies the landscape as the byproduct of very specific processes no longer operating upon a given site (residual pollution aside). This outlook reifies the site as essentially static and defines it in terms of the past rather than as part of ongoing industrial processes that form other parts of the city (such as new manufacturing agglomerations on the periphery). I suggest that it would be strategically helpful for understanding the potential for these sites if designers avoid the term "post-industrial" and its value system when discussing them.

Drosscape is created by the deindustrialization of older city areas (the city core) and the rapid urbanization of newer city areas (the periphery), which are both catalyzed by the drastic decrease in transportation costs (for both goods and people) over the past century.[5] It is an organic phenomenon heedless of the academic and human boundaries that separate environmental from architectural/planning/design issues, urban from suburban issues, and nostalgic definitions of community from actual organizations of people, workplaces, and social structures. I argue that planned and unplanned horizontal conditions around vertical urban centers are intrinsically neither bad nor good, but instead natural results of industrial growth, results that require new conceptualization and

FIG. 3 Housing along south side of Phoenix South Mountain Park, Chandler/Phoenix, Arizona

considered attention, and that these must be in hand before potential solutions to any problem discovered can be effectively addressed or devised [FIGS. 2, 3].

DROSS IS NATURAL

The design world's use of the term "dross" derives from one of the most interesting manifestos written about the urban landscape over the past two decades: "Stim & Dross," a seminal essay by Lars Lerup, Dean of Rice University's School of Architecture.[6] Lerup saw tremendous potential in what most of the design world was ignoring at the time: the "in-between" surfaces left over by the dominant economic forces of urbanization; forces including land investment, development practices, policies and codes, and planning (or the lack thereof). Using Houston, Texas, as his example, Lerup theorized the city's vast stretch of urbanized landscape surface as a "holey plane," the "holes" being currently unused areas:

> This *holey plane* seems more a wilderness than a datum of a man-made city. Dotted by trees and criss-crossed by wo-men/vehicles/roads, it is a surface dominated by a peculiar sense of ongoing struggle: the struggle of economics against nature. Both the trees and machines of this plane emerge as the (trail or) dross of that struggle.[7]

FIG. 4 Plano, Texas

Breaking from pro- and anti-sprawl rhetoric, Lerup momentarily suspended judgment in order to understand the forces creating the horizontal city.

Lerup's "holey plane" is particularly useful for understanding relationships between landscape and urbanization. It reconceptualizes the city as a living, massive, dynamic system, or a huge ecological envelope of systematically productive *and* wasteful landscapes.[8] Films such as *Koyaanisqatsi* and *Baraka* illustrate this by imaging the city and mass-human dwelling and building behavior from aerial overviews and via time-lapse photography to reveal their strikingly organism-like aspects.[9] The city is largely a natural process whose unperceived complexity dwarfs those aspects of it that can be consciously controlled and planned.

The natural process of the city is not unlike that of living organisms, whose hard parts—from the bones and shells of terrestrial vertebrates and marine invertebrates to the iron and other elements and compounds precipitated by cells—originated in the expelling and/or managing of wastes. Calcium, for example, used for that living infrastructure of the human body, the skeleton, is routinely extruded by cells in the marine environment; this striking example is not an analogy, but arguably a homology for how waste becomes incorporated into landscape structure and function. The economies that provide the energy and materials for the growth of cities, such as manufacturing and housing, are less things than processes. And, as is true for organisms, the faster they grow the more (potentially hazardous) waste they produce. This is a natural process that can be ignored, maligned, or embraced, but never stopped. "What is now emerging," writes Nobel Laureate Ilya Prigogine, "is an 'intermediate' description [of reality] that lies somewhere between the two alienating images of a deterministic world and an arbitrary world of pure chance."[10] These words regarding the functioning of complex systems in unpredictable ways apply perfectly to the realm of landscapes in urbanization. Cities are not static objects, but active arenas marked by continuous energy flows and transformations of which landscapes and buildings and other hard parts are not permanent structures but transitional manifestations. Like a biological organism, the urbanized landscape is an open system, whose planned complexity always entails unplanned dross in accord with the dictates of thermodynamics. To expect a city to function without waste (such as in a cradle-to-cradle approach), which represents the *in situ* or exported excess not only of its growth but also of its maintenance, is as naive as expecting an animal to thrive in a sensory deprivation tank. The challenge for designers is thus not to achieve *drossless* urbanization but to integrate inevitable dross into more flexible aesthetic and design strategies.

Contemporary modes of industrial production driven by economical and consumerist influences contribute to urbanization and the formation of waste landscapes—meaning actual *waste* (such as municipal solid waste, sewage, scrap metal, etc.), *wasted* places (such as abandoned and/or contaminated sites), or *wasteful* places (such as oversized parking lots or duplicate big-box retail venues). The phrase "urban sprawl" and the rhetoric of pro- and anti-urban sprawl advocates all but obsolesce under the realization that there is no growth without waste. "Waste landscape" is an indicator of healthy urban growth [FIG. 4].

THE OLD RESPITE IS NEW WASTE

With regards to "waste" it is impossible to isolate recharacterizations of the city from its socioeconomic milieu. Horizontal urbanization is linked to economies and simultaneous modes of industrialization—to what, in 1942, Harvard University economist Joseph Schumpeter characterized as "the process of creative destruction."[11] Schumpeter believed that innovations made by entrepreneurs began with this process, which caused old inventories, technologies, equipment, and even craftsmen's skills to become obsolete. Schumpeter examined how capitalism creates and destroys existing structures of industrialization.[12] Lerup's stim and dross is the physical cognate for creative destruction. Both terms acknowledge the totality of the consumption/waste cycle, and the organic integration of waste into the urban world as the result of socioeconomic processes [FIG. 5].

For much of the late-eighteenth and nineteenth centuries, the American city landscape was designed and built to represent a view opposite to those developed by industrialization, and the professions of landscape architecture and

FIG. 5 Trinity River Corridor, Dallas, Texas. Over $1 billion is invested in the phased redevelopment of this area.

FIG. 6 Fulton/Dekalb County line, Georgia. The "Georgia 400 Corridor" is a commercial corridor mostly composed of non-downtown office space, light industrial businesses, and manufacturing establishments. Downtown Atlanta is in the background.

urban planning were influenced by anti-industrialization offerings. Ebenezer Howard's Garden City, Frank Lloyd Wright's Broadacre City, Le Corbusier's Radiant City, and the City Beautiful movement were all designed under the premise of using landscape as a respite from urban congestion and the pollution created by industrialization. The outcome of these approaches is a net increase in the amount of "waste landscape" in cities. Urban populations continue to decentralize. As a result of fewer constituents, "respite" landscapes in the inner city are now in severe decline and disinvestment. Today the respite landscapes found in older parts of the city, built during periods when the city center was the hub of industry, are in transitional phases of development. Thirty states in 2004 operated with frozen or reduced Parks and Recreation budgets. Currently hundreds of state parks are closed or operate for fewer hours with reduced services, such as maintenance, in order to remain fiscally solvent.[13] In 2003 California's Department of Parks and Recreation, the nation's largest with 274 parks, raised entrance fees to compensate for a $35 million budget cut. Roughly $600 million is still needed for deferred maintenance projects.[14] The U.S. National Park Service also seeks private-sector support for park maintenance in the face of staffing shortages and budget cutbacks of billions of dollars.[15]

CONTAMINATION AND INVESTMENT

Deindustrialization has many meanings, which often refer to topics other than loss of manufacturing jobs. In relation to urbanization, for instance, it reveals how industrial evolution alters the landscape of the city.[16] Its broadest meanings are derived from the history of capitalism and evolving patterns of investment and disinvestment.[17] Manufacturing in America, as in much of the developed world, is decentralized. It takes fewer people located in one central place to make the same or more product than in the past. Fulton County, the central county comprising the city of Atlanta, Georgia, experienced a more than 26 percent decrease in manufacturing establishments from 1977 to 2001, while outlying counties (some seventy miles away from the center of Atlanta) experienced more than 300 percent growth in this sector [FIG. 6].[18] Optimistically, it could be argued that as deindustrialization proliferates, and as industry relocates from central cities to peripheral areas, America's cities will enjoy a net gain in the total landscape (and buildings) available for other uses.[19] Changes in manufacturing and production, new modes of communication, and decreases in transportation costs have resulted in the dispersal and relocation of industrial production to outlying areas, and even to other parts of the world, leaving waste landscape inside the city core while creating it anew on the periphery [FIG. 7].

There are many other types of waste landscapes, such as those associated with former industrial use. Between 1988 and 1995, the federal government closed ninety-seven major military bases around the country. Most had or still have some type of soil, water, or structural contamination that requires remediation.

FIG. 7 Global III Intermodal Terminal, Rochelle, Illinois, about 80 miles west of Chicago

By 1998 the U.S. Department of Defense had completed thirty-five military base property conveyances (transferring of the ownership title); by 1999 twenty-seven of these properties had undergone subsequent development.[20] In Irvine, California, the nation's third largest home builder, Lennar, won an auction to buy the former El Toro Marine Corps Air Station for a record $650 million, from the Department of Defense. Lennar's proposed redevelopment includes plans for 3,400 new homes in the heart of Orange County, the nation's hottest real-estate market [FIG. 8]. El Toro will be the largest of five major former military bases in California being redeveloped by Lennar. The Department of Defense is continuing its evaluation of some 5,700 military installations for decommissioning or closure in the future. In May 2005 a new round of military site closures was released, and it has already been determined that most of these sites contain some form of contamination. They will be transformed through private redevelopment into a variety of new civilian uses, which will take considerable time and investment [FIG. 9].[21]

Since the 1990s, brownfields have received much attention from the federal government. In 2003 more than $73 million in grants were dispersed to thirty-seven states to promote the redevelopment of contaminated landscapes.[22] Most were former urban industrial-production sites. Today developers seek out contaminated sites instead of clean ones: a former director of the National Brownfield

FIG. 8 El Toro Marine Corps Air Station, Irvine, California

Association noted that developers generate a higher rate of return from contaminated properties than from non-contaminated properties.[23] New federal subsidies for brownfield development make this possible. Tax increment financing, for example, allows for the taxes assessed on property value to be used for redevelopment activities such as infrastructure improvements.[24] One recent example is a 138-acre, 12-million-square-foot mixed-use project on the site of a former Atlantic Steel Mill in midtown Atlanta. A developer paid $76 million to purchase the land in 1999. Even with $25 million in clean-up expenses, the total cost of the improved land was $732,000 per acre. A nearby "uncontaminated" site, purchased for the new home of the Atlanta Symphony, cost $22.3 million for 6.36 acres, or about $3.5 million per acre.[25] City leaders in Chicago, which currently has one of the nation's most aggressive brownfield redevelopment programs, agreed to sell a 573-acre former steel mill site along the shores of Lake Michigan to a team of developers for $85 million [FIG. 10].[26] This site had produced steel for warships and skyscrapers for more than a century. It will be transformed into a mixed-use neighborhood for tens of thousands of residents.[27] Home Depot, the chain of home-improvement stores, actively seeks to develop store locations on urban brownfield sites. Their site-development strategy typically includes the excavation and relocation of toxic soil to the parts of the site planned for the store's vast parking lot. The building footprint is then laid down on the area of

FIG. 9 Ammunition bunkers at Ravenna Arsenal, Portage County, between Ravenna and Warren, Ohio. The arsenal produced and stored artillery and mortar shells for World War II and the Korean and Vietnam wars. The site was decommissioned in 1992.

FIG. 10 Former U.S. Steel Plant Superfund Site, South Side Chicago, Illinois

clean soil or on areas where toxins were removed or reduced below legal levels. This practice is obviously quite lucrative, as Home Depot saves large sums of money on the purchase of land.

Contamination and abandonment may also bring favorable ecological surprises. Ecologists often find much more diverse ecological environments in contaminated sites than in the native landscapes that surround them.[28] Because of their contamination, industrial contexts, and secured perimeters, brownfield sites offer a viable platform from which to study urban ecology while performing reclamation techniques. These sites have the potential to accommodate new landscape design practices that concurrently clean up contamination during redevelopment, or more notably where reclamation becomes integral to the final design process and form.[29]

DROSSCAPE DEFINED

Planning and design cannot solve all problems associated with the vast amount of urban waste landscape. However, the alarm is sounded to those who cope with the increased pessimism and cynicism spawned by the inefficacy of the "big four" design disciplines—landscape architecture, urban design, planning, and architecture—in the face of unfettered, market-driven development. The recent emergence of landscape urbanism may be a reaction to the frustration shared by many people in the landscape, planning, and architectural design arenas.[30] The polarizing rhetorical arguments of the pro- and anti-urbanization contingencies, as well as dynamic economic processes, make traditional masterplanning approaches for future cities seem absurd. But advocating a revolutionary form of urban landscape study and practice, such as landscape urbanism, is *not* exclusive of the current mainstream design disciplines. There is no need to develop an entirely new design discipline in order to rethink landscape's relationship to urbanization. Drosscape has the potential to coexist with the big four, by working within their knowledge structure while constructing a radically different agenda. The traditional way to value urban landscapes is through "placemaking" or by using landscape as a placemaking medium (such as for public parks or plazas). This idea is now blurred. The landscape of the contemporary horizontal city is no longer a placemaking or a condensing medium. Instead it is fragmented and chaotically spread, escaping wholeness, objectivity, and public consciousness—*terra incognita*.[31]

This condition begs for landscape architects and other designers of the urban realm to shift a good amount of attention away from small-scale site design in order to consider how we can improve regional landscape deficiencies of the urban realm. This is the potential for landscape urbanism. If this discipline is to be taken seriously, it must craft a specific agenda that both works with the big four and finds new ground to work on—ground that has been overlooked or bypassed by the status quo, such as Drosscape [FIGS. 11, 12].

FIG. 11 Inman Yard, Norfolk Southern Railroad, Atlanta, Georgia

The term *drosscape* implies that dross, or waste, is scaped, or resurfaced/rein-scribed, by new human intentions. Moreover, the ideas of dross and scape have individual attributes. This is where my use of the term dross departs from its Lerupian origin. The suggestive etymology of the word includes shared origins with the words *waste* and *vast,* two terms frequently used to describe the con-temporary nature of horizontal urbanization, as well as connections to the words *vanity, vain, vanish,* and *vacant,* all of which relate to waste through the form of empty gestures [FIG. 13].[32]

DROSSCAPE PROPOSED

Drosscapes are dependent on the production of waste landscapes from other types of development in order to survive. In this rubric one may describe dross-caping as a sort of scavenging of the city surface for interstitial landscape remains. The designer works in a bottom-up manner, conducting fieldwork while collect-ing and interpreting large-scale trends, data, and phenomena in search of waste. Once waste landscapes are identified, the designer proposes a strategy to pro-ductively integrate them [FIG. 14].

As degraded and interstitial entities, drosscapes have few caretakers, guardians, or spokespersons. The importance of a drosscape is only appreciated through a bottom-up advocacy process.[33] The future of any given drosscape or

FIG. 12 Housing in Irvine, California

any entity that is undervalued lies profoundly in the interaction of human agency and emergent novelty derived from explicit transfers and sharing of knowledge, suggesting therefore that design, as a professional and creative endeavor, is recast to resist closure and univalent expertise. The designer, as the strategist conducting this advocacy process, understands the future as being under perpetual construction. Drosscapes require design to be implemented as an activity that is capable of adapting to changing circumstances while at the same time avoiding being too open-ended as to succumb to future schemes that are better organized.[34]

DROSSCAPE REALIZED

Processes of deindustrialization and horizontal urbanization will continue in the foreseeable future to saturate urbanized regions with waste landscape. Subsequent to these processes, designers will need to rethink their roles in creating built environments. Urbanization will no doubt be controlled by a wider array of factors in the future. As deindustrialization illustrates, analyzing cities can no longer be done by one source, nor by one body of knowledge, nor by one bureaucracy. Designers must identify opportunities within the production modes of their time to enable new ways of thinking about the city and its landscape (whatever form it may take). Landscape architects, architects, and urban planners

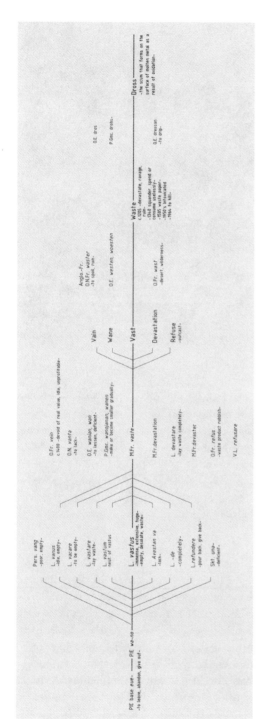

FIG. 13

Etymological Relationships of Vast, Waste, and Dross. The Latin term *vastus* serves as the root for both modern terms: vast and waste. Dross represents that which is left over from a combination of natural and manmade processes. (vast: 1570's, from M.Fr. *vaste*, from L. *vastus* "immense, extensive, huge," also "desolate, unoccupied, empty.")

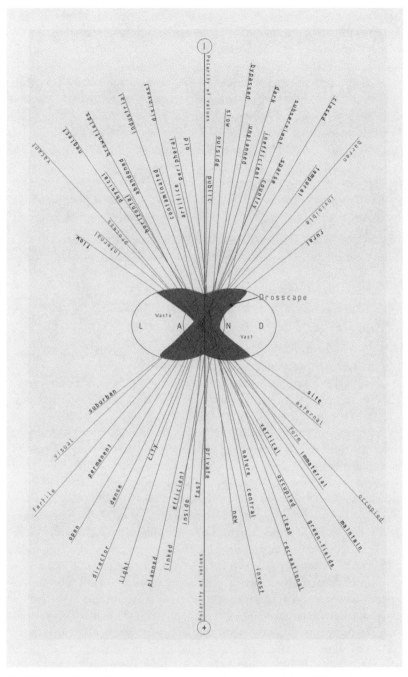

FIG. 14 Drosscape Diagram. Drosscapes emerge out of an amalgamated zone of that which is considered vast (immense, extensive), and that which is waste (squandered, ravaged). Other values stretch the drosscape into an amorphous entity emerging from a wide range of societal values.

often follow too far behind these processes, scavenging commissions from their jetsam as they change course. It is time for designers to find opportunities *within* these processes by advocating more ambitious ways of challenging urbanization, such as landscape urbanism.

As a strategy, drosscape provides an avenue for rethinking the role of the designer in the urban world. Given a constriction of natural and other material resources, politicians and developers alike will shift attention to infill and adaptive reuse development. None of this work will be achieved with a unidisciplinary design approach, nor will the site conditions present univalent environmental solutions. All, however, will be affected by countless unconventional adjacencies and unforeseen complex reclamations.

In his criticism of the scientific world, Bruno Latour states that "soon nothing, absolutely nothing, will be left of [a] top-down model of scientific influence."

> The matter of fact of science becomes matters of concern of politics. As a result, contemporary scientific controversies are emerging in what have been called hybrid forums. We used to have two types of representations and two types of forums: one, science…and another politics…. A simple way to characterize our times is to say that the two meanings of representation have now merged into one, around the key figure of the spokesperson.[35]

Latour's brilliant elucidation leads one out of the lab to discover the city anew. Its composition is part economics, part science, part politics, and part speculation. This new city is reconceptualized from drosscape. As such, it will serve as the stage for the performance of Latour's hybrid forum.

Such ripe conscious design attention mirrors natural environments that are inescapably marked by waste. The continuous material transformation of the environment produces dross, and this waste is most profound in the areas of the highly successful growing organisms and civilizations. Thus dross will always accompany growth, and responsible design protocols will always flag such dross as the expanding margin of the designed environment. The energy that goes into rapid growth, after populations and civilization reach temporary limits, can then be used to refashion and organize the stagnant in-between realm, thus going back like an artist to touch up the rough parts of an otherwise elegant production. Humanity's fantastic growth has inevitably confronted us with commensurate wastelands. Drosscape, the inescapable entropic counterpart to evolution and urbanization, far from marking failure, testifies to previous success and the design challenge for its continuance. Studying how urbanization elegantly co-ops wastes, and reincorporates them in the service of efficiency, aesthetics and functionality, should be at landscape urbanism's center—which is, one need hardly emphasize, increasingly where we find drosscape in the real urban world.

Notes

1. "$76.7 Million in Brownfield Grants Announced," May 10, 2005, and "EPA Announces
$73.1 Million in National Brownfields Grants in 37 States and Seven Tribal Communities,"
June 20, 2003, U.S. EPA Brownfield official web site, http://www.epa.gov/brownfields/
archive/pilot_arch.htm (accessed May 21, 2005); Niall Kirkwood, "Why is There So Little
Residential Redevelopment on Brownfields? Framing Issues for Discussion," paper W01-3,
Joint Center for Housing Studies (Cambridge, Mass.: Harvard University, January 2001), 3–4.

2. Daniel Bell, *The Coming of Post-Industrial Society* (New York: Basic Books, 1999); Barry
Bluestone and Bennett Harrison, *The Deindustrialization of America* (New York: Basic
Books, 1982); Stephen Cohen and John Zysman, *Manufacturing Matters: The Myth of the
Post-Industrial Economy* (New York: Basic Books, 1987); Michael J. Piore and Charles F.
Sabel, *The Second Industrial Divide* (New York: Basic Books, 1984).

3. See Alan Berger, *Drosscape: Wasting Land in Urban America*, (New York: Princeton
Architectural Press, 2006).

4. Further inspiration for this essay came from my students at Harvard Design School, who
over the years have expressed dismay and bewilderment at the lack of critical discourse on
the topic of urbanism and urbanization within the profession of landscape architecture.
Around the world, landscape architecture educational venues lack substantial depth concerning urbanization. As a response to this problem I began offering a course at Harvard
Design School geared toward students in the landscape degree programs, now entitled
"Landscapes of Urbanization," which allows students to study regional and local urban
land issues from a landscape architect's perspective.

5. Edward L. Glaeser and Janet E. Kohlhase, "Cities, Regions and the Decline of Transport
Costs," Harvard Institute of Economic Research, discussion paper 2014, (Cambridge,
Mass.: Harvard University, July 2003), http://post.economics.harvard.edu/hier/
2003papers/2003list.html.

6. Lars Lerup, "Stim & Dross: Rethinking the Metropolis," *Assemblage* 25 (Cambridge, Mass.:
MIT Press, 1995), 83–100.

7. Ibid., 88.

8. Lars Lerup, *After the City* (Cambridge, Mass.: MIT Press, 2000), 59. See also Lerup, "Stim
& Dross," 83–100.

9. *Koyaanisqatsi: Life Out of Balance*, is an independent film by Francis Ford Coppola,
Godfrey Reggio, and The Institute for Regional Education. Created between 1975 and
1982, the film is an apocalyptic vision of the collision of urban life and technology with
the natural environment. *Baraka* (1992) directed by Ron Fricke, uses breathtaking shots
from around the world to show the beauty and destruction of nature and humans.

10. Ilya Prigogine, *The End of Certainty* (New York: The Free Press, 1996), 189.

11. Joseph A. Schumpeter, *Capitalism, Socialism and Democracy*, 3rd ed. (New York: Harper
& Row, 1950), 81–110. See also Sharon Zukin, *Landscapes of Power* (Berkeley: University
of California Press, 1991), 41. Zukin describes Schumpeter's "creative destruction" as a
"liminal" landscape.

12. Schumpeter, *Capitalism, Socialism and Democracy*, 84.

13. Valerie Alvord, "State Parks Squeezed, Shut by Budget Woes," *USA Today*, July 24, 2002;
Kristen Mack, "Police, Fire Departments New Budget's Bid Winners," *Houston Chronicle*,
May 21, 2004; Ralph Ranalli, "Funding Urged to Preserve Ecology," *Boston Globe*, March
31, 2005. Also see "2004 Chicago Park District budget crisis, park advocates requests" at
Chicago's Hyde Park-Kenwood Community Conference Parks Committee (HPKCC) web
site, http://www.hydepark.org/parks/04budcrisisreqs.htm (accessed June 14, 2005); Mike
Tobin and Angela Townsend, "Budget Assumes Flat Economy," in *The Plain Dealer*,

January 28, 2004, http://www.cleveland.com/budgetcrisis/index.ssf?/budgetcrisis/more/1075285840190290.html (accessed June 14, 2005).

14. Ibid. See also Joy Lanzendorfer, "Parks and Wreck," *North Bay Bohemian*, July 3–9, 2003. Project for Public Spaces is an organization that campaigns against landscape budget at http://www.pps.org. A much different picture of open space funding is depicted by The Trust for Public Land. See their LandVote Database at http://www.tpl.org/tier2_kad.cfm? content_item_id=0&folder_id=2607 (accessed June 14, 2005, which reveals that the majority of ballot measures for "conservation" of open space have passed over the last decade.

15. Geoffrey Cantrell, "Critics Fear Park Service Headed Down Wrong Path," *Boston Globe*, March 10, 2005). For national parks, see Stephan Lovgren, "U.S. National Parks Told to Quietly Cut Services," *National Geographic News*, March 19, 2004, http://news.nationalgeographic.com/news/2004/03/0319_040319_parks.html (accessed May 10, 2005).

16. Jefferson Cowie and Jospeh Heathcott, eds. *Beyond the Ruins: The Meanings of Deindustrialization* (Ithaca: Cornell University Press, 2003), 14.

17. Ibid., 15.

18. U.S. Census Bureau State and County Quickfacts, 1998; Georgia Business QuickLinks, http://quickfacts.census.gov/qfd/states/13000lk.html, and Georgia County Business Patterns Economic Profile, 1997, and 2001, http://www.census.gov/epcd/cbp/map/01data/13/999.txt (both accessed July 22, 2004).

19. City of Philadelphia, capital program office, project # 07-01-4371-99, request for proposal for program management services for demolition and encapsulation of vacant and deteriorating buildings, accessed from Philadelphia Neighborhood Transformation Initiative (NTI), http://www.phila.gov/mayor/jfs/mayorsnti/pdfs/NTI_RFP.pdf, March 14, 2001.

20. U.S. Department of Defense official web site, http://www.defenselink.mil/brac (accessed July 14, 2005).

21. Dean E. Murphy, "More Closings Ahead, Old Bases Wait for Hopes to Be Filled," *The New York Times*, May 15, 2005. Sec. 1, p. 1; CNN, "EPA: Closed military bases on list of worst toxic sites," http://www.cnn.com/2005/TECH/science/05/12/base.closings.environm.ap/index.html, May 13, 2005.

22. See note 1"EPA Announces $73.1 Million in National Brownfields Grants in 37 States and Seven Tribal Communities."

23. Leon Hortense, "Squeezing Green Out of Brownfield Development," *National Real Estate Investor* (June 1, 2003).

24. See Brownfields Tax Incentive Fact Sheet, EPA Document Number: EPA 500-F-01-339, http://www.epa.gov/brownfields/bftaxinc.htm.

25. Ibid.

26. Southeast Chicago Development Commission official website, http://www.southeastchicago.org/html/enviro.html (accessed June 18, 2005).

27. Lori Rotenberk, "Chicago Aims to Transform Site of Former Steel Mill," *The Boston Globe*, May 21, 2004.

28. Mike Davis, *Dead Cities*, (New York: The New Press, 2002), 385–86.

29. For a fascinating example see studies for the Berkeley Pit, which is a copper mine in Butte, Montana. Extremophiles have been discovered thriving in the pit's water, which has an extremely acidic pH (around 2.5 to 3.0). Since these organisms persist in such extreme environmental adversity, they are considered by scientists to hold clues for curing our worst diseases and environmental disasters. See United States Environmental Protection Agency, National Risk Management Program, Mine Waste Technology Report on the Berkeley Pit in Butte, Montana. *Activity IV, project 10: pit lake system—Biological Survey of Berkeley Pit Water*, http://www.epa.gov/docs/ORD/NRMRL/std/mtb/annual99g.htm.

30. Graham Shane, "The Emergence of Landscape Urbanism," in this collection.

31. Ann O'M. Bowman, and Michael A. Pagano, *Terra Incognita: Vacant Land and Urban Strategies* (Washington, D.C.: Georgetown University Press, 2004).

32. *The American Heritage Dictionary of the English Language*, Fourth Edition, (New York: Houghton Mifflin Company, 2000).

33. See Jared Diamond, *Collapse*, (New York: Viking Press, 2005), 277–88. Diamond suggests that different societies of the world use a bottom-up approach to deal with environmental problem-solving. His contention is that the most successful bottom-up approaches tend to be in small societies with small amounts of land (such as local neighborhoods) because more people can see the benefit of working together in managing the environment.

34. See James Corner, "Not Unlike Life Itself: Landscape Strategy Now," *Harvard Design Magazine* 21 (Fall 2003/Winter 2004): 32–34. See also Ralph D. Stacy, *Complex Responsive Processes in Organizations* (London: Routledge, 2001).

35. Bruno Latour, "The World Wide Lab," *Wired* vol. 11, no. 6 (June 2003): 147.

Landscapes of Exchange: Re-articulating Site

Clare Lyster

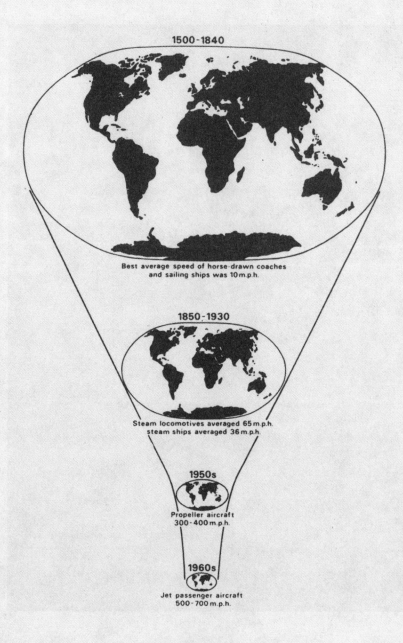

1500-1840

Best average speed of horse-drawn coaches
and sailing ships was 10 m.p.h.

1850-1930

Steam locomotives averaged 65 m.p.h.
steam ships averaged 36 m.p.h.

1950s

Propeller aircraft
300-400 m.p.h.

1960s

Jet passenger aircraft
500-700 m.p.h.

FIG. 1 The shrinking map of the world through innovations in transport

The act of exchange—from ancient trade routes between Asia and Europe to the rapid dissemination of information over the world wide web— has been largely responsible for the articulation of the public realm in the West since antiquity. The optimization of the act of exchange itself has always been directly influenced by the forces that deploy it—horses, railroads, the internet— hence the longstanding relationship between mobility, exchange, and the articulation of territory. This relationship has existed as far back as the Roman Empire. The map of the Roman *viae* serves to remind us of the infrastructural intensity that trade inscribed on its imperial territory, an exchange network that primarily resulted from the power it held over so much continuous land. In the middle ages, the great trade routes combined cartographic knowledge with territorial control (colonization) in the optimization of the act of exchange, marking the origins of organized commercial networks by emphasizing the necessity for both informational expertise and geographic intelligence in the efficient mobilization of trade between previously disparate areas of the world.[1]

In the nineteenth-century city, exchange was further enhanced through the mobilization of labor and technology with the exploitation of railroad transportation, resulting in the explosion of the modern industrial city. Prior to the standardization of the railroads in England and France, production and consumption were still predominantly regional events—goods were produced and exchanged within local geographic areas. The historian Wolfgang Schivelbusch writes, "Only when modern transportation created a definite spatial distance between the place of production and the place of consumption did goods become uprooted commodities."[2] The railroads therefore were responsible for the modern relationship between time, spatial movement, and the value of exchange. In the twentieth century, exchange engineered the erosion of the urban core through zoning ordinances and the removal of manufacturing and production infrastructures to peripheral sites more accessible by car and the expanding interstate highway system.

These exchange networks (Roman, medieval, industrial, and modern) and their corresponding forces of mobilization (power, geographic intelligence, technology, and production) are responsible for the material and operational specificity of territories that have in turn determined the morphology and occupation of our current urban and exurban landscapes. Over the past quarter-century, the process, rate, and basis of exchange has been dramatically altered, causing a corresponding shift in the articulation of territory, or site.

FIG. 2 Diagram mapping the Amazon.com and Federal Express centers involved in the delivery of *Harry Potter and the Order of the Phoenix*, July 2003

JUST IN TIME

At 12:01 am on June 21st, 2003, the largest single-day e-commerce distribution event in history began. It included about 20,000 Federal Express Home Delivery contractors and FedEx Express couriers; 130 scheduled FedEx Express flights; thousands of FedEx Express and Ground delivery vans; specially orchestrated sort operations at FedEx Express and Ground facilities to choreograph the transportation of one product, the third book in the Harry Potter series, *Harry Potter and the Order of the Phoenix*, directly to the homes of Amazon.com customers on the first day the book was available to the public. The logistics were complicated by the fact that the books could be delivered only after offline sales officially began that Saturday at 8:00 am. With a twenty-four-hour operation, FedEx and Amazon capitalized on the 12:01 am deadline, having eight hours of delivery procedure in operation by the time fans began to line up at local bookstores. Leading up to the distribution, FedEx companies transported the orders from five Amazon.com distribution centers located in New Castle, Delaware; Campbellsville and Lexington, Kentucky; Coffeyville, Kansas; and Fernley, Nevada; to FedEx hubs in Newark, Chicago, Indianapolis, Fort Worth, Los Angeles, Oakland, and Anchorage [FIG. 2]; and later onto terminals throughout the country by plane and truck. Extra FedEx Express and Ground personnel conducted specialized sorts of the *Harry Potter* shipments at each hub and automated sort facilities so that they could be transported to local terminals for delivery beginning at 8:00 am.

For 2,000 years, the organization of public space in the city has by and large been predicated on commercial operations, the logistics of production, and trade exchange, which has established an identifiable and corollary typology of public space: the Roman forum, the medieval plaza, and the nineteenth-century street. Even the public park of the early modern city was a commercially resultant typology, albeit a paradoxical one, in so far as it was born out of an attempt to counteract the effects of industrialization on the urban landscape, as well as to further exploit the city's mercantile potential. The public park was as much a consequence of the promotion of commerce as it was the alleviation of it [FIG. 3]. The relationship between these commercial operations (the direct and personal material exchange of goods, money, opinion, or clean air) and their corresponding morphological articulation was one of logistical facility—the optimal containment of the exchange itself, as well as the articulation of the macro-landscape in which the exchange was located. These familiar typologies therefore not only served the function of the commercial event but also visibly, politically, and symbolically organized their host environment: the city. The longevity and fixity of these commercial operations over time and their associated typological identity insured an umbilical relationship between trade, public space, and the hierarchical assembly of the urban landscape. Save the experiment of new forms of urbanism in the 1960s, from an architectural and planning viewpoint, the association between trade and the design of public space in the city centered on the optimal formal and aesthetic consolidation of a single commercial event *at* a singularly specific geographical location, determining the interpretation of public site as a fixed geo-functional artifact.

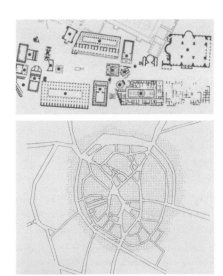

The processes that organize contemporary commercial exchange are not as easily located, interpreted, or contained as their predecessors, and as such the traditional categorization of the "commercial event" as a fixed and reciprocal material

FIG. 3 Diagram of the Roman Forum (TOP); diagram of the medieval town of Lennep, Germany (MIDDLE); photograph of Washington Park, Chicago, Fredrick Law Olmsted, 1890 (BOTTOM)

exchange—that is, the transfer of something in return for something at a specific moment in time at a specific geographic location—is no longer applicable. While the sole criteria of exchange—profit—is still seen as the end product of a commercial transaction, be it virtual or real, the act of exchange or handover and the process by which it occurs is controlled and determined by a series of inseparable determining factors across multiple disciplines, resulting in the multiplication and/or magnification of the scale of the exchange operation. Since the new processes that mobilize and deploy exchange operate through, between, and over multiple sites and disciplines—to the point that urbanism, landscape, infrastructure, economics, and information are now inseparable in terms of their influence on the organization of the public realm—they cannot be solely defined through or against traditional design conventions, resulting in a difficulty, therefore, in synthesizing their operations into a new articulation of public site(s).[3] The plasticity of contemporary ecologies of exchange has resulted in the relationship between public space and commerce progressing from a site/object relationship to a more organizational one that exists "across" or between multiple sites of occupation. It is in acknowledging this shift from "at" (singular) to "across" (plural) site(s), that our uncertainty with the interpretation and territorial articulation of these new processes will be alleviated. It is within this momentary conundrum—architecture's deficiency to decode, interpret, and synthesize the operations of contemporary fluid ecologies of exchange and its subsequent inability to strategize a territorial resolution across site rather than at site—that this essay is located. The scripts documented in this essay attempt to identify these new processes of exchange, to decode the logic behind their operational tactics, and to anticipate a material or performative occupation of the landscape resulting from these operational tactics.[4]

The success of the operational criteria of the aforementioned *Harry Potter* delivery can be empirically determined by the proximity with which each Amazon customer received its pre-ordered copy of the book to the 8:00 am launch time, the "delivery window." Maximum efficiency—instantaneous exchange—would suggest a zero delivery window, or at least one with minimal delay, such that in an ideal world space and time within the commercial landscape are both compressed to and calibrated in nanoseconds. The relationship between FedEx (organizational space) and mobility (delivery time) is exponentially proportional to the performance of the information system that guides the network operation. In fact, an increase in mobility (the output of the space/time relationship) is neither related to the form nor speed of the mobility itself—a FedEx cargo jet plane can only go so fast—but is determined by both the sophistication and synchronization of the controlling information network [SEE FIG. 1]. Maximum efficiency within "just-in-time" protocol is therefore defined not by mobility in the literal sense but by the mobility of information. The resources required for the *Harry Potter* delivery were negligible compared to the pre-delivery choreography, the assembly of data and transport conditions with highly specialized software and a highly complex deployment. The accumulation of deployment procedures creates a highly complex landscape involving the scale and complexity of an intermodal operation. Clearly the public square will not cope. The resources deployed to engage multiple points of exchange at the same time, or within a very short time lag, illustrates that the scale of commercial exchange relative to "place" has been dramatically refigured, a result of how the mobilization of information affects the way in which exchange is deployed across site, rather than the act of the exchange itself—the handover of a children's book.

VIRTUAL MARCH

On Feb. 26th, 2003, the Democratic Senator for California, Dianne Feinstein, deployed six members of staff to deal with 40,000 incoming calls, emails, and

FIG. 4 MoveOn.org, "Win Without War" campaign, 2003

faxes from constituents expressing outrage at the possibility of war in Iraq. In the few days before this, you may have received an email describing the campaign that had more than one million Americans flood the Washington offices of their elected representatives with antiwar messages, electronically timed so as to avoid phone lines jamming. The "Virtual March on Washington" was organized by America's largest antiwar movement, MoveOn.org, a company comprised of four employees operating from a single room on West 57th Street in New York City. MoveOn has over two million participants worldwide and has raised millions of dollars from private and corporate donations. In late 2002 the fringe underground internet organization exploded onto the media with a series of emails urging collective participation in high-profile global peace marches and candlelight vigils. In addition, MoveOn embarked on a series of advertising proposals supporting the UN weapons investigation in Iraq [FIG. 4]. MoveOn's "flash campaigns" were spontaneous initiatives, organized on short notice, comprised of emails with seemingly impossible deadlines for either event organization or contribution assistance—yet MoveOn never once missed an intended publicity target. On March 9th, 2003, the *New York Times Magazine* featured an article by George Packer titled "Smart Mobbing the War," and detailed MoveOn.org as "the fastest-growing protest movement in American history."[5]

The ease with which MoveOn mobilizes spontaneous collective responses to specific political events within a limited time frame enables it to not only "capture the energy of the moment better at the moment"[6] but enables it to maximize its limited resources, financially and logistically, across the largest possible field of play. Remaining flexible across its entire network yet strategically deploying highly specialized exchanges at opportune moments (such as peace marches in Washington, D.C., candlelight vigils, or an airline banner at the 2003 Super Bowl) is its operational strategy. As an economic model, it is superlative in terms of streamline efficiency, perfecting the pursuit of maximum effect with minimal deployment. In this they directly contradict the operational criteria of FedEx, which deploys with minimal impact. MoveOn operates in real time: the space/time interval is compressed almost to the point where it does not exist, as it nimbly adjusts to unanticipated external events without compromising its overall

FIG. 5 X-ray scan of shipping container in transit with illegal immigrants at a border checkpoint

agenda. It is therefore a highly contingent landscape—in fact, the more contingent the circumstances, the more effective its response. That a corporation of two million shareholders can not only capitalize but proliferate under volatility in the marketplace is an interesting phenomenon. It is a reality made possible by information systems and infrastructure that can freely and hospitably navigate multiple transformations. MoveOn's strategy is to have no strategy until a highly specific critical moment occurs and one is created.

HUMAN EXCHANGE

On June 18th, 2000, fifty-seven Chinese immigrants suffocated in a lorry on its way by ferry from Zeebrugge, Holland, to Dover, in the south of England, after it was discovered that a thirty-three-year-old Dutch truck driver, who was since charged with manslaughter and jailed for fourteen years, had deliberately shut off the only air vent to stop noise from filtering out. Most of the victims had paid upward of $20,000 to "snakehead" gangs who netted over $1.2 million from the human cargo. The trucker's cut was $500 for each passenger. Criminal networks in Beijing, in cooperation with snakehead gangs in Budapest together secure false passports with Hungarian entry visas for would be emigrants who are charged $9,000 up front and are put on an Aeroflot plane to Budapest. There, the emigrants rest before boarding a truck that takes them to the Austria–Hungarian border, where they walk across the mountains to a remote location before being ushered into another truck and transported to a port somewhere on the North Sea [FIG. 5]. On arrival in England the emigrant's family in China pays the balance of the money to the local gang, who then distributes a share of the earnings to the entire international criminal network. Unlike other route-based trades, such as drug trafficking, where established hierarchical cartels are run by only a few bosses, the human trafficking networks bracket the different phases of the transit route and subcontract the work out to local companies, much like multinational corporate structures. Both the resilience and at the same time the flexibility of trafficking networks have thus made them virtually undetectable and as a result the world's fastest growing criminal enterprise. The network is therefore both highly specialized and fragmented, a necessity for survival, so as to remain flexible to resist infiltration by police and customs officials.

Human trafficking is an example of a network that is highly resilient, but unlike MoveOn its resilience is not the result of the consolidation of control by a few persons able to mobilize high-performance decision-making in a short period of time, but conversely due to its fragmentation and dispersion of control across a larger field of activity, enabling critical adjustments to be made along the trajectory of the exchange process that ensures the survival of the network in the event that volatile or contingent events such as security checks or border controls threaten the transit route. The non-hierarchical parceling of territorial control makes it nimble and resilient. The materialization of the exchange often mutates depending on the local forces in play at each particular exchange location as it alters in response to outside forces along the way. It accommodates diversion and continuous adjustment not because it is ambiguous and neutral with respect to its environment but because it has many optional sub-organizations or phases within that enable it to be multiresponsive to site. It capitalizes on geography, while MoveOn and Federal Express deny it. Finally, it exemplifies how the accumulation of local exchange has global consequences since subsequent exchanges within the system can only occur depending on the success of the previous exchange, and that micro-events at a detail-scale when multiplied across a larger field of operation have global significance.

FOUR ARTICULATIONS OF NETWORK AND TERRITORY

1. Collisive Sites and Piggyback Programming

Exchange networks that depend on simultaneous large-scale deployment over a wide field of play colonize territory that enables maximum mobilization as well as an amplification of exchange across other networks—i.e., territory that facilitates interactivity or high collision. High-speed infrastructural networks such as distribution hubs, airports, rail yards, highway interchanges, and inter-modal facilities are natural collisive sites. Collisive territories tend not to occur accidentally but instead accumulate upon each other over time and are commonly coincident to preexisting sympathetic conditions such as infrastructure, geographical features, natural resources, and program; that is, they reconfigure and magnetize existing topography rather than develop it from scratch. Exchange is thus multiplied and accumulated across multiple networks that occupy these

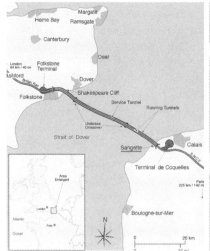

FIG. 6 Map of the English Channel showing the
ports of Sangatte and Folkstone and
the Channel Tunnel route in between

FIG. 7 Photograph of the interior of the retrofitted Red Cross refugee camp at Sangatte

collisive sites, suggesting a larger scale of transfer or inter-exchange at a specific
moment in time. It is in these moments, where excessive accumulation of
exchange already prevails, that design possibilities emerge, staging opportunities for public space and other programmed landscapes that can further occupy
these sites with activities and events other than those that were originally intended. These are parasitical landscapes that both react to and exploit the territorial
accumulation already in place. Occasionally an eccentric, unintended reactionary
landscape emerges.

On September 24th, 1999, the French government, in association with the
Red Cross, opened a settlement camp a half-mile from the seaside town of
Sangatte, near the port town of Calais, on the French side of the channel tunnel,
to cater to immigrants who collected there while they planned their passage to
England either with the help of local smugglers via truck or ferry transport, or
through the tunnel by attempting to jump on the freight trains as they slow
down to enter the tunnel or running through the tunnel's twenty-five-mile
length between trains [FIG. 6]. The camp consists of an old 25,000-square-meter
storage warehouse, retrofitted with prefabricated metal sheds with the addition
of tents in the adjacent ground [FIG. 7]. In total seven hundred beds were provided. A staff of thirty-five manage the camp, which also includes minimal services: a clinic, laundry, showers, and toilets. Two hundred kilometers away in Lille,
2,400 meals a day are prepared and transported to Sangatte, where they are heated up and served. Every afternoon at approximately four o'clock, dozens of camp
residents leave for the coast, in the hope of finding night passage to England.

FIG. 8 Residential and commercial development
at Alliance Land Port, Texas

FIG. 9 Schiphol Airport, Amsterdam

The temporary refugee base in Sangatte exemplifies an unanticipated reactionary landscape, an unintended occupation of territory that emerges as a reaction to a particular collisive context, such that it is not a self-organizing occupation of the landscape but proliferates at the discretion of external forces already in place. In the case of Sangatte, the emergence of the camp is coincident to a series of the following preexisting physical, political, and geographic accumulations: the recent termination of the Euro Tunnel across the English Channel; the fact that the French border police were known not to check foreigners because it was easier to turn a blind eye and aid them to leave French territory than to let them accumulate on French soil; with fierce competition between ports on the North of France, too many checkpoints would slow down both ships and trains out of Calais, thus slowing trade operations; Calais's geographical location, at the narrowest point on the English Channel, logically made it a destination for asylum-seekers hoping to cross to England; and finally, the accumulation of multiple low-cost transport systems (rail, road, and sea) facilitated many route options for the emigrants, such that if one passage route failed then another was quickly opened. No wonder Sangatte became known as the "waiting room for England."

From a planning point of view, the question therefore arises whether there is a way to predict and orchestrate the progressive accumulation of preexisting collisive sites in advance of the emergence of unintended and reactionary occupation, so that the less intentional spatial operations—which are often the most spatially provocative, as illustrated above, can in some way be more appropriately staged. Opportunistic development strategies for the optimization and preparation of preexisting accumulated sites of exchange over time provides a potential opportunity for collaborations within the design, landscape, and economic communities. For example, the exchange protocols out of which Alliance Land Port, a highly collisive site that merges industry, distribution, and transportation systems in Texas, has now spawned housing and commercial initiatives to the point that it is a fully independent urban landscape over and above its initial programming incentive as a distribution hub in the southwest [FIG. 8].[7] Schiphol Airport in Amsterdam exemplifies how increased programming options that accommodate both local inhabitants as well as passengers invigorates the airport not only as a site for global transportation exchange but also for other forms of local commercial and cultural exchange that both relocates as well as reinterprets the occupation of public space [FIG. 9]. Collisive territories of exchange therefore not only erode traditional design approaches with respect to public real estate but have become instrumental in a new articulation of local and national landscapes, bankrupting traditional typological organizations of place and becoming the new magnets of economic, social, and cultural occupation. Silicon Valley in California, Port Elizabeth in New Jersey, the Ranstaad in Holland, The Rhurgebeit in Germany, and the Blue Banana that incorporates land from Liege in Belgium to Milan in the North of Italy, provide additional examples of collisive territories that have begun to cultivate new piggyback territories at the continental and global scale.

2. Surface Accumulation

Exchange-deploying networks expand operation by increasing their own resources to mobilize interchange within or across their trajectories. This does not include a direct expansion of territory or real estate at any one location but the appropriation and organization of themselves across territory, as opposed to previous forms of territorial expansion that were more specifically articulated, such as the addition, infill, or the retrofit of preexisting typologies of space that occurred either by superimposition—the location of the medieval plaza on the site of the Roman forum illustrates how expansion was deployed vertically through layers sequentially supplanted on each other over time—or through addition—the enlargement of an existing superstructure on a specific site. Contemporary exchange networks instead have the tendency to procure a more phased articulation across territory to accommodate the multiple intersections that are now indispensable to their operational success, as much to serve their own internal points of interchange as well as those with, between, and across other points of collision. This new articulation of territory is not formally site-specific but instead encompasses the coordination of material connections via transportation infrastructures and virtual connections through automated transfers and communication systems across larger areas of operation. Thus, the development and striation of territory includes a greater emphasis on performance and organization, such that it has become a valuable *high-performance membrane*—a composite that operates both as information receiver, infrastructure, and superstructure, but at the same time is none of these alone and so falls between traditional typological and morphological perceptions of space. It is a subscape, a territory that structures/serves/hosts multiple possibilities of interchange and occupation across its organization. The significance therefore of

FIG. 10   Woodfield Mall, Schaumburg, Illinois

superstructure (building form), previously the critical (formal and aesthetic) component of public landscape, is eroded, with investment and attention directed
instead to the territory in its midst—not territory as in external environment or
residual space, but territory as a highly charged organizational landscape. High-
performance territory therefore becomes more critical in terms of providing the
necessary logistical functions required to resource the exchange network, while
the traditional superstructural back-up provisions either recede or collapse into
this territory as an embedded logistical layer or dissolve altogether. These organizational territories, which are just as resilient as the exchange ecologies they
attempt to host, therefore have new value, not necessarily in terms of location—
geography or real estate—as was the case in previous typological precedents,
but in their topological resilience to the variables that work across them—infrastructure, information, environmentalism, and so forth. The articulation of site
thus presupposes an organizational rather than aesthetic approach, where design
sensibilities that favor performance and operational efficiency subordinate traditional compositional excellence. Material specificity results from process and
operational flows *across* site rather than formal composition *at* site, redirecting
architectural intervention away from aesthetics and formal indulgence to designs
that merge temporal patterns of connectivity with the logistics of operational

FIGS. 11, 12   FedEx freight-sorting and passenger conveyor systems, Los Angeles (TOP)
Intermodal Freight Facility, Cicero, Chicago (BOTTOM)

tactics that do not suffer the damage resulting from multiple adjustments and fluctuations over time. A territory that hosts a high-tech suburban office park is an accumulated surface type, since parking, lighting, greenery, recreation, and water in the form of reservoirs that collect surface water runoff from the extensive asphalted zones, organize the top layer of the landscape, while sophisticated telecommunication systems embedded within serve an interior landscape that is demarcated primarily with elaborate office furniture systems that interface with the information-embedded exterior landscape via a raised-access floor system, itself an intelligent surface that is just as striated as its exterior counterpart, the only difference being the replacement of rolled sod with commercial grade carpet tiles. Enclosure on this synthetic indo-exo surface accumulation is a mere dumb skin, having minimal impact on the performance of the entire landscape except to serve environmental shelter. Large-scale edge-of-city retail, production plants with mechanized transfers, and handling facilities adjacent to rail and highway infrastructures, also provide examples of accumulated surface space, although with less potential for public appropriation [FIGS. 10–12]. Public space that negotiates complex urban infrastructures such as subterranean parking, with sophisticated lighting and drainage systems and variable soil types embedded within its mass and surface programs above, as in Chicago's Millennium Park or the numerous hybrid connective topographies that bridge residential and commercial districts across Barcelona's ring road, also constitute new urban accumulated surface typologies [FIGS. 13, 14].

FIGS. 13,14 Construction photograph of Millennium Park, Chicago (ABOVE); Bridge over the Barcelona Ring Road, Alfons Soldevilla, architect, 1992 (LEFT)

3. Weak Geography

In more traditional trade routes and organizations, the articulation of the urban landscape was facilitated by capturing the moment at which the point of optimal exchange occurred: the handover. Today the articulation of territory is by way of accommodating the processes of the exchange, or the deployment of the handover. If previously the point of exchange in a commercial operation was considered the optimal expression of that operation, hence its concretization formally and symbolically in the landscape, contemporary ecologies of commercial exchange place minimal emphasis on the handover itself; success instead is determined by the efficiency and optimization of the process of the handover. Adjustments and switches along the exchange route are thus minimized, for they are considered the weak or porous moments in the network. The operational criteria of a sophisticated exchange system is to minimize stoppage and keep the exchange deployment seamless—that is, the most mobilized deployment process should have zero points of adjustment to make along its trajectory, or be so flexible that its fluidity is not compromised by the adjustment. Capturing those moments where the processes that manufacture and deploy the exchange necessitate stoppage, adjustment, or interchange, either across an individual operation or in convergence with another, mark opportunistic moments for design intervention that can yield unique programmatic possibilities. These weak moments in the network's trajectory often have their own real estate and

FIG. 15 Motor Service Plaza on Illinois Tri-state Tollway (Route I-294), Hinsdale, Illinois

FIG. 16 Developer housing adjacent to highway in Hinsdale [TOP]; student housing within highway barrier wall in Utrecht, Holland by Koen van Velsen [BOTTOM]

provide markers that identify the system and can be exploited to present new spatial opportunity, such as programmatic possibilities adjacent to and along transportation infrastructures—a highway rest stop for commuters and commercial truckers on long-haul distribution routes, innovative housing infill on residual verges alongside highway corridors [FIGS. 15, 16]—or the remediation of industrial brownfields for public and commercial development or the reappropriation of landfill sites for recreation. Establishing fertile real estate in the exploitation of weak and underused territory has recently become prevalent in the airline industry that has capitalized on the exploitation of weaker points of exchange as an economic response to the escalating traffic and landing fees at major international hubs. Ryan Air, Europe's most noted low-cost airline, has maximized its profits and destination routes by landing in national cites previously considered of minor consequence such that their route map of Europe constitutes destinations previously ignored or unheard of. Now, rather than entering France through Paris, the gateway is Beauvais, over seventy-five miles away; rather than fly to Venice, one disembarks at the peripheral town of Trevisio; and instead of Stockholm, Goteborg becomes Sweden's low-cost air hub. Peripheral underused geographic areas that may previously have only retained local or national recognition are now global transportation gateways on the international travel loop. The commercial predisposition to ignore and resist the development of poor real estate is now dissolved with the circumstances of a new commercial climate bringing economic and design potential to new zones of influence.

4. Territorial Mergers
All the above examples describe the importance of mergers and collaborations, whether it be an economic merger, as seen between Amazon and Federal Express—a cross-disciplinary merger that included the interplay of technology,

culture, commerce, and distribution—or, and of specific interest, the merger between communication systems and politics and the subsequent simultaneous global articulation of site, as seen in the anti-war protests and candlelight vigils orchestrated by MoveOn.org and their affiliated organizations in many cities throughout the world during the American invasion of Iraq. Such shortlived articulation of territory dependant on the interplay between many different layers of information results in yet another operative articulation of site. Sites of collective exchange where individuals assemble and find self-expression in specific communal practices that represent their individual social, political, and cultural beliefs is greatly facilitated by the increased sophistication of communication technologies that have helped organize a merger between public expression and private purpose into a tribal appropriation of the landscape. Of related interest is the spinoff and reactionary mergers between different exchange systems, for example, the channel tunnel built as a high-speed link for wealthy Europeans that simultaneously became a secret passage for refugees desperate to make it to England, or the practice of responding to instructions via mobile text messaging, known as "flash mobbing," that results in the instantaneous mobilization of a large number of persons to a particular location for a specific event at a particular moment in time, merging the impact of technology and the occupation of public space. Territory is thus organized less compositionally than it is nomadically, whereby temporal adjustments define the nature of the territory rather than specific context.

CONCLUSION

Familiar typologies of space evolve through time. They only arise after the optimization of a certain event and remain in place until such time when new operations take over and cause their reorganization, rendering them obsolete. The complexity of the exchange process and its intense mobilization across site has resulted in an interrogation of what, up until fifteen years ago, we safely constituted as the public realm. As designers, we embrace the opportunities that offer speculation on how these processes continue to challenge our disciplinary conventions and our professional response as we anticipate new possibilities for the urban landscape and a new context through which "public" exists. Landscape urbanism is not merely a discussion on the design of new territorial morphologies that merge infrastructure, commerce, and information systems, but the exploration of their social, political, and cultural impact in a reinterpretation of public space, wherever and whatever that may be.

Notes

1. The geographer and social theorist David Harvey, in his book, *The Condition of Postmodernity* (Cambridge, England: Blackwell Publishers Ltd., 1990), makes reference

to commercial networks of the medieval period in his discussion of the relationship between money, time, and space, and the resulting articulation of power in society. Of particular interest is his reference to two books, David S. Landes, *Revolution in Time: Clocks and the Making of the Modern World* (Cambridge, Mass.: Belknap Press, 1983) and Jacques Le Goff, *Time, Work and Culture in the Middle Ages*, trans. Arthur Goldhammer (Chicago: University of Chicago Press, 1980). Both discuss the relationship between trade and spatial movement in commercial organizations of the medieval period and the subsequent attaching of price to transported goods by merchant traders that served to initiate a quantifiable relationship between time, space, and money. In addition, Le Goff makes further reference to Landes's text to describe the importance of cartographic intelligence and military endeavors in the success of early medieval trade. Good maps, he writes, were paid for in gold, thus expanding the measurable relationship of time and space to include information.

2. Wolfgang Schivelbusch, *The Railway Journey: The Industrialization of Time and Space in the 19th Century* (Berkeley: University of California Press, 1986). Schivellbusch's comments recall Karl Marx, who wrote in *Grundrisse, Foundations of the Critique of Political Economy* (London: Pelican Marx Library, (1857) 1973): "This locational movement—the bringing of the product to the market, which is a necessary condition of its circulation, except when the point of production is the market—could be more precisely regarded as the transformation of the product into a commodity."

3. See Alejandro Zaera Polo's article, "Order Out of Chaos: The Material Organization of Advanced Capitalism," in "The Periphery," ed. J. Woodroffe, D. Papa, and I. MacBurnie, special issue, *Architectural Design*, no. 108 (1994): 25–29, for his discussion on how traditional commercial models of production produced typological urban topographies that were "metric determinations," i.e., fixed and thus measurable spaces, while fluid systems, i.e., those processes that define late-capitalist production since the 1960s, produce another species of space that is not typological but instead involves the reorganization of the urban topography into unarticulated operations and events, which he terms "hybrids"—complex programmatic accumulations linked together.

4. See Keller Easterling, *Organization Space: Landscapes Highways and Houses in America* (Cambridge, Mass.: MIT Press, 1999). In her introduction, Easterling describes a methodology whereby the description of episodic events (often eccentric ones) are exploited to dispel conventional cultural myths through the use of what she terms "spin." The "spin" operates to dispel or explain these myths, yet themselves become scholarly artifacts in the discussion. My own accounts of Federal Express, MoveOn.org, and human trafficking in this essay are influenced by Easterling's method, as they attempt to reveal larger issues attendant to contemporary commercial networks and to make sense of their spatial and material consequences. See Claudia H. Deutsch "Planes, Trucks and 7.5 million Packages: Fed Ex's Big Night," *New York Times*, December 21, 2003; see also "FedEx Ready to Deliver Harry Potter Magic Directly to Thousands of Amazon.com Customers," www.fedex.com/us/mediaupdate1.html?link=4, June 20th 2003. (accessed August 2003).

5. George Packer, "Smart Mobbing the War," *New York Times Magazine*, March 9, 2003. See http://query.nytimes.com/search/restricted/article?res=F20814F734580C7A8CDDAA084 (accessed August 2003).

6. Ibid., 36.

7. On Sangatte and the Channel Tunnel, see Peter Landesman, "The Light at the End of the Chunnel," *New York Times Magazine*, April 14, 2002. See also www.societyguardian.co.uk/asylumseekers/story/0,7991,433654,00.html (accessed April 2001); www.gisti.org/doc/actions/2000/sangatte/synthese.en.html. (accessed April 2001); and www.lineone.net/telegraph/2001/02/20/news/the_38.html (accessed April 2001). Alliance is a land port

strategically located on 8,300 acres of raw land outside Fort Worth, Texas. It was developed by Ross Perot, Jr. as an international transportation development based around the integration of just-in-time (JIT) manufacturing, ground transportation, and global air freight and hosts many of the countries largest corporations, such as JC Penny and Federal Express. Alliance is a highly planned coincidence and now encompasses more than sixty-five square miles of infrastructure and development.

Synthetic Surfaces

Pierre Bélanger

FIG. 1 Foreign Trade Zone No. 49, New Jersey, 2003; orthoimagery detail. Across from left: Newark Liberty International
Airport (EWR) Terminal A, Pier 3; FedEx Cargo Bay; Runway 4L-22R; Runway 4R-22L; The Peripheral Ditch; New
Jersey Turnpike; and Port Newark/Elizabeth Container Terminal New Jersey, USA, 2003

"[T]he emphasis in the future must be, not upon speed and immediate practical conquest, but upon exhaustiveness, inter-relationship and integration. The coordination and adjustment of our technical effort . . . is more important than extravagant advances along special lines, and equally extravagant retardations along others, with a disastrous lack of balance between the various parts."

—Lewis Mumford

Asphalt may be among the most ubiquitous yet invisible materials in the North American landscape [FIG. 1].[1] Its scale and form practically render impossible the conception of it as a single bounded system, yet its function depends precisely upon the singular continuity of a horizontal surface. Highways, terminals, interchanges, offramps, medians, sidewalks, and curbs are such pervasive components of the built environment that they are often overlooked as influential characteristics of contemporary culture in North America.[2] These seemingly disconnected elements form a distinctly engineered operating system that supports a multitude of regional processes and generates a wealth of contemporary programs, many of which lie outside of the conventional axioms of European-influenced theories of urban design and planning. How then do we account for and articulate the logic of urbanism in North America? An examination of the synthetic processes of contemporary urbanization may shed some light on this question and its potentials for contemporary landscape practice.[3]

Recently, the discourse surrounding landscape urbanism has emerged in North America to elaborate upon the role of landscape in many architects' and urbanists' thinking on the contemporary city. Several authors have recently attempted to articulate the logic of North America's spatial structure as a way of understanding contemporary urbanization. Architect and theorist Stan Allen, for example, compares the evolution of the North American urban landscape to "a radical horizontal urbanism . . . developed as a vast, mat-like field, where scattered pockets of density are knit together by high-speed, high-volume roadways."[4] Alex Wall, an architect and urbanist, refers to this transformation as "the extensive reworking of the urban surface as a smooth continuous matrix that effectively binds the increasingly disparate elements of our environment together."[5]

FIG. 2 US Route #1, 1911

At the smaller scale, a growing number of authors are discussing the influence of material technologies on the conditioning of the urban surface, understood as a landscape. Again, Allen is instructive, articulating the role of synthetic surfaces of landscape as to the materiality of urbanism. "[T]he surface in landscape is always distinguished by its material and its performative characteristics," he writes. "Slope, hardness, permeability, depth and soil chemistry are all variables that influence the behavior of surfaces."[6] One of the most underrepresented materials, and one deserving of greater attention, is asphalt, which may be among the most important materials in the history of North American urbanization. Though the history of this material predates Ancient Rome, one example of the topic's more recent cultural relevance can be found in its inclusion in the 2003 Milan Triennale with an exhibition curated by Mirko Zardini titled "Asfalto." With visual acumen, Zardini's installation examined the synthetic attributes of this usually gray surface by uncovering the historical, technical, cultural, and visual layers of the mundane material "commonly considered an undesired yet necessary skin."[7]

The ultimate impact of this material on the built realm would not be fully inscribed across the North American landscape until the advent of the twentieth century. No other material has been found to be so flexible and so adaptable, capable of absorbing so many functions, enabling so many uses, and producing so many effects. This singular material innovation, coupled with the reflexive mechanisms it supports, can be traced back as the source of some of the most generic and ubiquitous aspects of the North American landscape today—those aspects that are gaining increasing attention by the practices articulated through the prism of landscape urbanism.

PRE-CONDITIONS

The history of urbanism in North America starts in the mud.[8] Well before the advent of oil, steam, or coal, or the invention of the airplane, the train, or the automobile, America was characterized more or less by an agonizing unevenness, a topography primarily composed of potholes and ruts that did very little but pose as obstacles to regional mobility and communication [FIG. 2]. Modern industrialization would soon dismantle the resistance sustained for so long by the environmental medium of mud, dust, and darkness. Slowness, the agonizing paradigm of the nineteenth-century landscape, quickly gave way to speed, the essence of modernity.[9] Henry Adams, no less, described this state of arrested development at the end of the nineteenth century:

> America is required to construct, without delay, at least three great roads and canals, each several hundred miles long, across mountain ranges, through a country not yet inhabited, to points where no great markets existed—and this under constant peril of losing her political union, which could not even by such connections be with certainty secure.... Between Boston and New York is a tolerable highway, along which, thrice a week, light stagecoaches carry passengers and the mail, in three days. From New York a stagecoach starts every weekday for Philadelphia, consuming the greater part of two days in the journey, and the road between Paulus Hook, the modern Jersey City, and Hackensack is declared by the newspapers in 1802 to be as bad as any other part of the route between Maine and Georgia.... In the Northern States, four miles an hour is the average speed for any coach between Bangor and Baltimore. Beyond the Potomac the roads become steadily worse, until south of Petersburg even the mails are carried on horseback.[10]

The state of the roads described by Adams was indicative of a state of geographic and civic emergency. A letter from the League of American Wheelman by Isaac B. Potter in 1891 outlines the economic imperative:

> The United States is the only country in the world, assuming to be progressive, that is so poorly provided with highways; that their condition is a source of amazement to the foreigner; showing by a series of pictures of the splendid roads of Germany, France & Italy, and other European countries, and by way of contrast, some typical pictures of the lines of sticky mud, with ruts hub-deep at certain seasons, that go by the name of country roads, in the most populous and prosperous States of the Union.[11]

FROST ACTION

What differentiated the North American situation from the European context most fully was frost. With mild winters, no European surface was ever exposed to permanent cycles of freezing and thawing, which by and large destroyed dirt highways. Water could therefore be used as the primary binding and compaction agent in European road construction. But a more resilient material was required to combat the swampy, muddy surface of the New World, one that would be capable of withstanding deep-freeze cycles of northern temperate climates and was more robust than the inferior European techniques. Charles Goodyear had already developed the perfect paving material as early as 1844—vulcanized rubber, a confection that could be heated without melting or cooled without cracking—but the material would ultimately prove too expensive for the scale and the scope of an intercontinental highway enterprise.[12] Asphalt came to the rescue of an economy that was anxiously awaiting a drier, smoother future. Cultural historian Jeffrey T. Schnapp describes the paradox of asphalt as an urban catalyst in European cities:

> Asphalt erupts on the scene of modernity to redeem the world of industry of the banes of friction and dust. Dust clouds have been around since the beginning of time. But the coaching revolution of the nineteenth century transformed them into signifiers of accelerated movement long before the appearance of the stream or motion lines that would indicate velocity in twentieth century cartooning and graphics. Dust was also what differentiated driver passengers from pedestrians, the enfranchised from the disenfranchised, within the contours of a nation-state now defined as a transportation grid.... Dust was the pollutant of the nineteenth century. Asphalt came to the rescue. It cleaned up speed.[13]

SURFACE ECONOMIES

The prospect of weatherproofing North America's roadways was first conceived the day Edward Joseph De Smedt, a professor from Columbia University, applied for the first time in the world a modern, engineered, graded, maximum-density asphalt pavement. Laid out in 1872 in front of City Hall in Newark, New Jersey, the Belgian chemist irreversibly launched, with the construction of a 1,400-foot segment on William Street, the industry of roadbuilding as we know it today.[14] Joining the ranks of the "grandfathers of roadbuilding" such as the Scottish inventors John Metcalfe, Thomas Telford, and John Loudon McAdam, De Smedt's technique distinguished itself from his predecessors, in that it synthesized a thousand years of material developments into a simple reproducible technique.[15] The surface technique proposed a hot-in-place, semi-liquid asphalt mix application that could be laid down in a series of lifts according to the desired thickness and density. A technique that could only emerge from the geographical circumstance

FIG. 3 Transcontinental Motor convoy, 1919

of the New World—a continent more than a hundred times the size of Scotland—where issues of scale and operational logistics superseded issues of material quality and resource availability. De Smedt's technique also meant that the surface could be engineered according to types of vehicles and volumes of traffic flow for a range of topographical conditions. His 1870 patent describes the mat-like technique with technical precision:

> [T]he surface on which the road or pavement is to be laid is properly graded and I first put a thin layer of hot sand upon it, about half an inch in thickness, and upon this layer of sand I put a layer of hot sand and asphalt, that which was previously mixed, under a comparatively moderate degree of heat, this last layer being about one inch in thickness. Over this layer... I pass a hot roller, and then apply a thin layer of hot sand, half inch thick, and over the latter a layer, an inch thick... which is rolled with a hot roller, as before. This is repeated until the desired thickness for the road or pavement is obtained. By this process or mode of laying, I obtain in the road or pavement the proper proportions of sand and asphalt without any difficulty whatsoever, and insure that the proper thorough incorporation of the sand and asphalt, and sand layers, so that a homogenous mass is obtained throughout.[16]

De Smedt's overlay technique utterly transformed the roadbuilding industry. According to the first complete survey of America's roads, completed in 1904, of the more than two million miles of rural public roads, fewer than 154,000 miles were surfaced, usually with gravel, stones, or crude paving materials. But soon

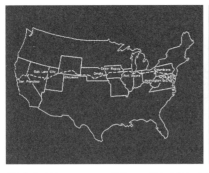

FIG. 4   Pre-highway–era map, 1911 [LEFT]; United States Interstate
& Defense Highway System, 1947 [RIGHT]

after the standardized guidelines of the Federal Road Act of 1916, 4,500 miles of blacktop would soon be laid down. With better tensile strength than concrete and equally good surface traction, asphalt pavement replaced all other forms of road construction. What eventually made it so effective was its regional adaptability. By mid-century, asphalt could be refined from coal or crude oil, blended with virtually any locally available aggregates, from quartzite to granite, to produce a versatile, waterproof, trafficable surface anywhere on the continent.[17]

EXPEDITIONS

In the summer of 1919, a young Lieutenant Colonel named Dwight D. Eisenhower joined a U.S. Army convoy whose objective was to locate and traverse by motorized vehicle a transcontinental route joining the east and west coasts of America. Dubbed the 1919 Transcontinental Convoy, the expedition spanned the continent over sixty-two days. Echoing and outdistancing survey expeditions of Lewis and Clark or King and Hayden, among others, the convoy consisted of thirty-seven officers and 258 enlisted men astride eighty-one motorized vehicles traversing 3,200 miles from Washington, D.C. to San Francisco [FIG. 3].[18] They reached San Francisco via the Lincoln Highway, over a treacherous surface terrain of dirt roads, rutted paths, dark winding trails, and shifting desert sands. Less than ten percent of the country's roads were surfaced with gravel, stone, or some other crude paving materials.[19] The rest was just mud, dust, or sand. Traveling at an average of six miles per hour, Eisenhower witnessed firsthand the frontierlike conditions of the existing roads. "Passing through 350 communities in eleven states," he wrote, "approximately 3,250,000 people witnessed the convoy and its pioneering triumphs. Local publicity exposed the convoy to an additional 33,000,000 people across the country while steadily increasing the number of recruits and good roads partisans" [FIG. 4].[20] The line traced by the transcontinental expedition would later resurface as a preliminary sketch of Eisenhower's greatest and most important achievement.

FIG. 5 Steam-powered roller on asphalt pavement, 1934

AUTOMATION

By the late 1920s, following further developments of De Smedt's technique, the pace was set for the construction of over 4,500 miles of highways [FIG. 5]. As mechanization took command, concrete construction equipment was rapidly adapted to withstand high-temperature liquid emulsions for the purposes of asphalt paving.[21] Everything from dozers, scrapers, graders, millers, screeders, and rollers were enlisted for the cause. Spreading from the roadbuilding industry to manufacturing and housing, no sector of the industry was spared the supremacy of mass-production. *Harper's* magazine reported on the work of Willliam Levitt in the 1920s, a brilliant example of streamline progress, using machinery whenever possible in the name of efficiency:

> Beginning with a trenching machine, through transit-mix trucks to haul concrete, to an automatic trowler that smoothes the foundation-slab, Levitt takes advantage of whatever economies mechanization can give him. The site of the houses becomes one vast assembly line, with trucks dropping off at each house the exact materials needed by the crew then moving up. Some parts—plumbing, staircases, window frames, cabinets—are actually prefabricated in the factory at Roslyn and brought to the house ready to install. The process might be called one of semi-prefabrication [FIG. 6].[22]

Now that mass-production permeated almost every aspect of the construction process, unprecedented levels of cost-efficiency and speed were now in sight.

FIG. 6 The revolutionary tournapull, 1948. The first integral, articulated wheel
tractor scraper earthmover, developed by Robert G. Letourneau

MOBILIZATION

Hot-mix asphalt was now center stage for a theater of explosive invention. Along with the internal combustion engine, other innovations including vulcanized rubber, refined petroleum, the air tube, the pneumatic tire, the ball bearing, cold pressed steel, die-cast metal, hydraulics, and lubricants led to the eventual motorization of almost every component of the North American landscape: horse-drawn carts were being replaced with motor-wagons, coaches with motorized buses, and bicycles with motorized quadricycles. Crossbred with industrial manufacturing techniques, vehicles were almost surpassing the speed of trains, and with this came the demand for a smoother, more extensive, and more connected system of roads and highways. Now that asphalt roads could be streamlined, highway networks had to be planned. Following the Federal Road Aid Act in 1916, State authorities were now empowered to carry out federal highway projects, so roadbuilding companies could now apply De Smedt's technique on a geographic scale.

The early transformation of dirt to asphalt was slow. Foreign conflicts abroad entirely diverted labor, equipment, and materials toward the effort of the two world wars, placing the roadbuilding project on hold. But soon after World War II, New Jersey Governor Alfred E. Driscoll mobilized the necessary means to spearhead the development of modern freeways. Again, speed was of the essence. So, a World War II Brigadier General, William Wesley Wanamaker, was enlisted to expedite the construction of North America's first asphalt superhighway, the New Jersey Turnpike. Like an allied front, Wanamaker divided the massive project into seven separate contracts with, as the caption to a 1949 map of the turnpike declared, a sole purpose and objective: "118 miles safely and comfortably, without a stop!"

That's what this modern "magic carpet" being built by the New Jersey Turnpike Authority will provide vehicle owners when it is completed late in 1951. Long sight distances, wide travel lanes and shoulders, easy curves and no crossroads assure safety and comfort. With fifteen traffic interchanges where vehicles may enter or leave, the turnpike will connect with leading highways to famous seashore resorts east and to other points west. North-south travelers also will be served more quickly and more economically. Savings in travel time on the Turnpike are estimated at as much as 40 percent versus travel on existing highways.[23]

Mobilizing equipment, extracting aggregates, and mixing materials on site precipitated the next pivotal development: the batch plant. Paragon of roadbuilding logistics, the batch plant process effectively reduced transportation costs and fast-tracked construction schedules by centrally locating all necessary equipment required to construct roadway infrastructure.[24] Round-the-clock dredging operations brought in five million cubic meters of silt material from as far as Coney Island to lay the base course for the 324-foot-wide roadbed on high ground. In its path were the Newark Meadows. Turn-of-the-century ideals of land reclamation epitomized the solution to growing urban density, as illustrated in a press release from the Turnpike Authority:

The prejudicial effect of the proximity of these marshlands upon the healthfulness of the cities on their borders and on the salubrity of the adjacent country districts is the strong argument for their drainage and improvement. They are not only insalubrious, but also comparatively non-productive in an agricultural point of view. The possibilities of these meadows when drained and the sanitary advantages of their reclamation, aside from the aesthetic setting, make a strong impression upon all who have seen the rich and beautiful polders of Holland.[25]

Dubbed "Operation Sand," the pairing of modern hopper dredgers and three-hundred-year-old land-reclamation techniques handed down from the Europeans proved useful for one of the final segments of the turnpike. So-called "unproductive" marshlands and surrounding pig farms were irreversibly drained and filled to make way for what are today the New Jersey Turnpike, Newark Liberty International Airport, and Port Newark/Elizabeth [FIG. 7]. Built in a record twenty-three months, the country's worst swampland—ironically called the Garden State—was turned into the world's most modern express highway route. Aimed at passing through the nation's most densely populated state, the new line—more or less a supersized metropolitan bypass—shaved two hours off the trip between New York and Philadelphia. As proclaimed by Governor Driscoll near the turnpike's completion, the economies of time afforded by the synthesis of transportation surfaces seemed irrefutable:

FIG. 7   Tri-level construction on the turnpike: Route 4 Parkway
& Woodbridge Avenue Interchange, 1950

In 1949, we determined to build in New Jersey the finest highway in the
world, linking the interstate crossings of the Hudson River with the interstate crossings of the Delaware River, for the convenience of the citizens
of New Jersey and our sister states. The project is called the New Jersey
Turnpike. Our Turnpike Authority has substantially completed the project with incredible speed... The Turnpike is designed to strengthen the
economy of New Jersey and to promote the general welfare of our country. Its importance to the defense effort is obvious.[26]

Boasting thirteen toll plazas, ten-foot-wide shoulders, and six twelve-foot-wide
lanes, the implementation of the New Jersey Turnpike resulted from the standardization of highway geometries that are found today in the California Highway
Design Manual.[27] Adopted as a roadbuilding bible, the highway design standards
would serve as a model reproduced throughout the United States, Canada,
Mexico, and nearly everywhere else in the paved urban world. By the time the
Turnpike opened, asphalt covered more than 30,000 square kilometers of surface area, one foot deep over two feet of stone and sand. As retired Turnpike
Authority engineer R. Bruce Noel put it, "we probably had the most outstand-
ing pavement. The Turnpike's original pavement... never had to be torn up [or]
replaced. And it will be there forever."[28] The original New Jersey Freeway model,
epitomized by its novel rest stops, toll booths, gas stations, and drive-in movie
theaters, would soon become the basis of a road-based culture that is today, in
one form or another, generic infrastructure.

FIG. 8 State geological survey [LEFT] and turnpike
alignment with ancillary road network [RIGHT]

SYSTEMATIZATION

However modern, the New Jersey Turnpike was less than perfect. An engineering test bed, the Turnpike was marred by corrective S-curves "because of positioning errors resulting from the inattention (of local surveyors) to official
geodetic references."[29] Pulitzer prize-winning science correspondent for *The New
York Times*, John Noble Wilford recounts in his 1981 book *The Mapmakers* that
the official survey markers had been established by Ferdinand R. Hassler—the
Swiss engineer enlisted by Thomas Jefferson to lead the National Geodetic
Survey—some hundred years prior. "The curves were the only way for the turnpike to connect to some of its cloverleaf turnoffs" [FIG. 8].[30]

The 1956 Federal Aid Highway Act emerged as the nation's infrastructural
palliative. Thirty-seven years after his cross-country military expedition, President
Eisenhower laid out a monumental standard—a 43,000-kilometer surface network with a minimum twenty-four-foot width for two lanes in each direction.
Originally charted by Franklin D. Roosevelt in the late 1930s, Eisenhower's inter-
regional highways would follow existing roads wherever possible:

> More than two lanes of traffic would be provided where traffic exceeds
> 2,000 vehicles per day, while access would be limited where entering

vehicles would harm the freedom of movement of the main stream of traffic. Within the large cities, the routes should be depressed or elevated, with the former preferable. Limited-access belt lines were needed for traffic wishing to bypass the city and to link radial expressways directed toward the center of the city. Inner belts surrounding the central business district would link the radial expressways while providing a way around the district for vehicles not destined for it.[31]

Over the course of those intervening thirty-seven years, Eisenhower was absorbed with visions of continental seamlessness. His presidency singularly focused on surveying the surface of the United States to map the highway system and to raise funds to build it. The U.S. Interstate and Defense Highway System was marshaled as a strategic organizational device. Underpinned by military defense objectives, the basis of the superhighway system was intended to connect major cities spread out across the United States and to overcome five major shortcomings of the existing transportation, spelled out by Eisenhower's Vice President, Richard M. Nixon:

> [T]he annual death and injury toll, the waste of billions of dollars in detours and traffic jams, the clogging of the nation's courts with highway-related suits, the inefficiency in the transportation of goods, and the appalling inadequacies to meet the demands of catastrophe or defense, should an atomic war come.[32]

Eisenhower had apparently witnessed first-hand how smooth highway surfaces had been clear advantages to the Germans in World War II. Pre-war German claims that construction of the Autobahn alone would rapidly invigorate their automobile economy and also diminish unemployment were proven much later to be gross overstatements.[33] Eisenhower's 1956 National System of Interstate and Defense Highways is without a doubt the most significant, and perhaps most understated, public works project in the history of America. Master planned as a national imperative conditioned on geographic accessibility, Eisenhower insisted that the system would recast the role of America:

> [T]he amount of concrete poured to form these roadways would build 80 Hoover Dams or six sidewalks to the moon... To build them, bulldozers and shovels would move enough dirt and rock to bury all of Connecticut two feet deep. More than any single action by the government since the end of the war, this one would change the face of America with straight-aways, cloverleaf turns, bridges and elongated parkways. Its impact on the American economy—the jobs it would produce in manufacturing and construction, the rural areas it would open up—was beyond calculation.[34]

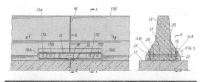

FIG. 9 The New Jersey Turnpike Authority's heavy-vehicle median barrier [TOP]; head-on collision, August 27, 1952 [BOTTOM]

The effect of Eisenhower's diagram was exponential. The construction of the superhighways propelled the United States into five decades of relentless motorization. And with smoothness at a grand scale came speed: in less than fifty years, surface speeds had grown over 1,000%, from six to sixty-five miles per hour. The geotechnical challenge of roadbuilding was now solved, and increasing traffic flows resulted in the foreseeable—governance of speed took the controls. As early as 1954, President Eisenhower described the paradox of speed and mobility during his July 12 Grand Plan speech:

There were 37,500 men, women and children killed in traffic accidents last year, and those injured totaled another 1,300,000. This awful total presents a real crisis to America. As a humane nation, we must end this unnecessary toll. Property losses have reached a staggering total, and insurance costs have become a real burden.... Our first most apparent penalty is an annual death toll comparable to the casualties of a bloody war, beyond calculation in dollar terms. It approaches 40 thousand killed and exceeds one and three-tenths million injured annually.[35]

The first concrete median barrier used in New Jersey was installed in 1955, standing at only eighteen inches tall. An expanded roadside edge, it looked like a low vertical wall with a curb on each side, functioning as a protective divider between opposite traffic flows. From operational observations rather than crash testing, the shape changed and evolved, increasing to twenty-four inches in 1932 and to thirty-two inches in 1959. Going upward from the horizontal, the first two inches from the pavement rose vertically, the next ten inches at a fifty-five-degree angle, and the remainder at an eighty-four-degree angle.[36] With modern slip-forming technologies, the commonly seen shape would be found almost everywhere in North America, now known as the Jersey barrier [FIG. 9].

Jersey barriers prevented collisions, but also prevented crossings. As soon as the u-turn disappeared, the "jughandle" emerged. A spatial invention, this traffic device was conceived to allow unimpeded flow in a practically infinite number of directions by simply raising the surface of a traffic lane over another. This premier engineering strategy at grade separations was adopted wherever two roadways crossed or two transportation modes overlapped. Intended to prevent collisions and fatal accidents at grade, the jughandle evolved into a more

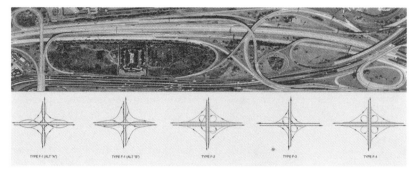

FIG. 10 Typical freeway-to-freeway interchanges (BOTTOM); ensuing highway landscape
of the "mixing bowl" interchange in Newark, New Jersey (TOP)

standard, vertical format of the highway intersection known as the interchange, or the fly-over. Its most classical form, the four-way cloverleaf, allowed for non-stop flow between two high-volume roadways. Unless the interchange was congested, no stopping was required. The first cloverleaf was opened in New Jersey in 1929, on what are now US Interstate 1/9 and NJ State Highway 35. That typology has grown to infamous proportions with junctions on the New Jersey Turnpike such as the Merge, the Tri-Level Interchange, and the Mixing Bowl [FIG. 10].

FOREIGN TRADE ZONES

Urbanism's next obstacle was capacity. By 1995, ninety percent of the system had surpassed its design life. Since the interstate highway system was built to accommodate twenty years of traffic growth for over 100 million people, the capacity of the system was severely overtaxed with a population nearing the 300 million mark in less than fifty years. To address urban congestion, mass transit and aging infrastructure, a series of surface transportation programs were enacted in the late twentieth century, such as the Intermodal Surface Transportation Efficiency Act in 1991 and the Transportation Equity Act for the Twenty-first Century in 1998. By providing federal funds for state and local projects, the acts demonstrated the inextricable bond between transportation and economics to maximize the capacity of existing transportation systems across the continent. The initiatives ranged in scale and in scope: new intermodal travel corridors such as the AirTrain projects established at Newark Liberty International and John F. Kennedy International Airports by the New York/New Jersey Port Authority and new highway trade corridors were being forged with the implementation of the National Corridor Program and the Coordinated Border Infrastructure Program between Mexico, the United States, and Canada by the North American's Superhighway Coalition. Reacting to the growing need for seamless circulation, these intermodal surface programs are synonymous with what Alex Wall refers to as "the reworking of movement corridors as new vessels of collective life."[37]

FIG. 11 Foreign Trade Zone No. 49: Newark Liberty International Airport, the Elizabeth Marine Terminal, and Newark Bay, 2002

The accelerated development of "foreign trade zones" across the United States is a concurrent critical development that took place as a response to the needs for capacity and intermodality. Foreign trade zones are not considered part of the United States' customs territory. Within the zones, companies maintain inventories, factories, or assembling and manufacturing facilities and therefore may defer, reduce, or eliminate import duties. Decentralized and distributed, these zones signal the incubation of a synthetic infrastructure: a polymodal system that fuses truck stops, train stations, harbors, and airport terminals into one undifferentiated land mass of streets, roads, highways, railways, tunnels, shipping lines, and flight paths.

One of the most notable examples is FTZ no.49 in Newark, New Jersey. Located at the convergence of seven major roadways, two of the busiest commercial airports in the world, and the largest seaport in the Western Hemisphere, all linked by the New Jersey Turnpike, FTZ no. 49 stevedores over seven billion dollars of cargo every year and employs 80,000 people, making it the largest and most active zone in the country, with Houston's FTZ no. 84 in close competition. The staging ground for courier companies like Federal Express and UPS, as well as luxury vehicle manufacturers like BMW and Mercedes, the proliferation

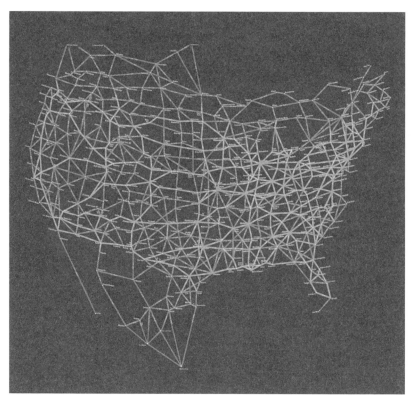

FIG. 12 Terrestrial distances and driving times across Canada, U.S. and Mexico

FIG. 13 Kill van Kull, Newark Bay: Three dimensional sonar image with draped stratigraphy showing depositional zones in the channel bottom. The protruding topography at the base illustrates the bedrock diabase outcroppings that are scheduled for removal by drilling and blasting.

of foreign trade zones is stunning: from 1950 onward the number has increased from 5 to 243 across the United States, handling cargo by air, rail, truck, and sea worth over 225 billion dollars. At almost 10,000 acres in size, the six foreign trade zones in the New Jersey/New York metropolitan region are almost equal the size of Manhattan.[38] Once America's largest suburb, New Jersey has suddenly become its biggest warehouse [FIG. 11].

The multiplying effect of Eisenhower's highway system did not simply end with the proliferation of polymodal transportation. With the advent of the North American Free Trade Agreement in the mid-1980s and the rapid increase in trans-Pacific trade during the 1990s, significant pressure was being placed on the surface capacity of the port facilities of FTZ no.49.[39] Three million tons of cargo were being funneled through the Port of New York and New Jersey each year, heading toward the richest consumer base in the world with a net worth of 80 billion dollars annually. Known as Atlantica, the trade network radiates from New York as far out as Illinois and Ontario, reaching 80 million people lying within a twenty-four-hour truck trip off the mid-Atlantic coast [FIG. 12].

Squeezed in by a major intertidal system, the harbor's precarious situation is nothing new. Since the first recorded landing in New Amsterdam nearly three hundred

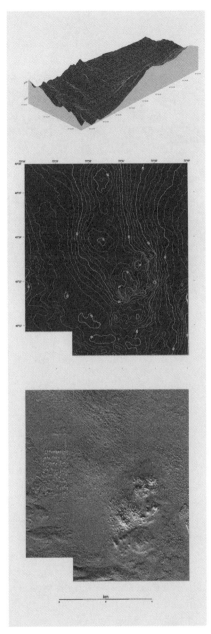

FIG. 14 Mud Dump: The 12-Mile Dumping Ground, now known as the Historic Area Remediation Site (HARS). Shaded relief of seafloor topography, elevational contours, and topographic mesh sampling

FIG. 15 Diversion Strategies. Tipping of a 1962 Redbird rail car to enhance the Shark River Reef, 2003. To date, the New Jersey Artificial Program has made use of 250 rail cars for the creation of fish havens and recreational dive sites [TOP]; Shipping of dredged material from Newark Bay by rail, en route by truck to a pug mill for amendment near the Bark Camp abandoned coal mine in Pennsylvania, 2000 [BOTTOM]

years ago, port facilities have always contended with the pressure from upstream sediment flow that irreversibly fills the harbor's main shipping channels [FIG. 13]. What differentiates the past from the present, however, is the growing size of vessel drafts. At full capacity, Post-Panamax ocean freighters require clear channel depths of at least fifteen meters, nearly double that of the harbor's natural depth. With an annual depositional rate of two million cubic meters of mud and silt filling its harbor, port authorities were now bound by a material conundrum.

To resolve this pressure above and below the surface of the waters, the New York/New Jersey Port Authority embarked on a massive deepening project of its shipping channels for the rapidly growing fleet of Super-Post-Panamax deep-draft ocean freighters that were transforming international maritime trade.[40] Tripling channel depths from six meters to eighteen meant that low water levels posed a unique logistical complexity.[41] Joseph Seebode, environmental engineer and chief of New York/ New Jersey Harbor of the United States Army Corps of Engineers, summarized the paradox in 2001: "Dredging the channels poses an environmental and engineering challenge. There's a lot of blasting, drilling, and dredging to be done, [but] all that material must to be disposed of."[42]

Up until the early 1990s, dredging consisted of little more than digging and dumping. The United States Army Corps of Engineers made use of offshore sites for spoil materials within the vicinity of the Bight of New York for over two hundred years and well into the early '90s. Sites known as the 12 Mile Dumping Ground were used for sewage waste, the Mud Dump for dredge sediment, and the Cellar Dirt Dump for blasted rock from the New York subway system. Those operations came to a grinding halt at the end of the '90s [FIG. 14]. Trig-gered by what is referred to the "Amphipod issue," the 1997 Ocean Dumping Act placed a unilateral ban on the dumping of contaminated sediments in open waters.[43] Diminishing landfill space and skyrocketing landfilling costs on the east coast

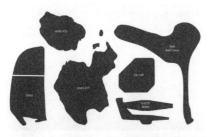

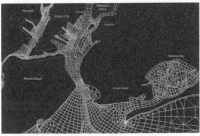

FIGS. 16–18
Placement sites of dredged material (TOP); hydrodynamic mesh model of the dredging contract area in New York Harbor (MIDDLE); Geological Cross-Section of Foreign Trade Zone No. 49. From left: the Garden State Parkway; Interstate Route 78; US Route 22; US Route 1-9; Newark Liberty International Airport; The Peripheral Ditch; New Jersey Turnpike; McLester Street; OENJ Landfill; Jersey Gardens Shopping Centre; Port Elizabeth Marine Terminal; and Newark Bay (BELOW)

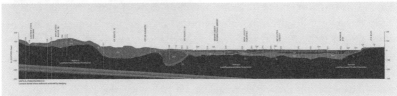

near the turn of this century exhausted all past practices, engendering an important shift in the operational sites and the material flows.

Authorized by the Water Resources Development Act, the Dredged Materials Management Program came to the rescue. Monumental in scale, the program aimed at a "superior industry-standard ocean access to accommodate the demand for international cargo through [the] region."[44] Boiling down to building underwater super highways, the program would effectively result in synthesizing port activities, environmental operations, and urban land uses into one large cohesive landscape operation. Quantitatively, the first phase of the project required the dredging, reprocessing, and distribution of approximately five million cubic meters of mud, silt, and sediment to a multitude of inland sites [FIG. 15].

Diversion strategies soon followed the dredging operations. Coupled with sediment decontamination technologies like soil washing, photo-stabilization, cement binding, and thermal destruction, the economies of scale offered by the program led to the recapitulation of a multitude of infrastructural landscapes with an almost endless array of transformative land uses.[45] Most importantly, the geotechnical characterization of the seven different types of materials determined the logic of their respective post-dredging use within closest possible proximity: red-brown clay toward subaqueous pit encapsulation; silt toward non-aquatic upland sites; and the remaining bedrock (glacial till, serpentinite, diabase, sandstone, and shale) toward artificial reef construction. Once the bane of the highway system, mud was now resurfacing as a rather visible and transformative medium.

SYNTHESIS

Future projections are staggering. Over the next four decades, the United States Army Corps of Engineers will spend over two billion dollars on over two hundred deep-draft seaports to ship and process over two billion annual tons of cargo requiring the relocation of an estimated two billion cubic meters of dredgeate; enough material to entirely bury the states of New Jersey, New York, and Pennsylvania under a one-meter thick layer of mud.[46] The prospects on land are no less dramatic: as of 2006, the United States Federal Highway Administration will have spent over one hundred billion dollars on highway infrastructure and will employ close to twenty-eight million people, keeping three hundred million Americans travelling more than one billion miles every year.

In its century-long search for unimpeded seamlessness, asphalt has become more than a technological panacea. It has effectively become a binding agent whose flexible surface has spawned the growth of what can be called a bionic system—a synthesis of biological, mechanical, and electronic resources—that now spans the entire continent, reaching deep across the sea, the air, and the ground, effectively interlocking global commercial activities, regional transportation infrastructures, regional ecologies, and contemporary land uses [FIGS. 16–18].

Seen from space, the consolidated surface of North America looks less like a landlocked continent and much more like a borderless construction site. Its transportation network resembles a circulation diagram taken from the blueprint of an incomplete factory floor, where the circuitry of highways and shipping channels functions as a load-bearing mechanism and traffic as the surface grease, infinitely optimizing internal urban functions and seeking out new channels of distribution for new inventories of material and access to new sources of energy.[47]

From the sand-pumping and asphalt-paving operations that have led the construction of the transcontinental highway system, to the mud-dredging and materials-management operations of the deepening of New Jersey's seaport in the early twenty-first century, the coupling of transportation networks across North America with the reflexive mechanisms that support them and the topographies they generate, suggest the latent effectiveness of these synthetic surfaces. The contemporary discourse on landscape urbanism suggests that ongoing attention to the seemingly banal surfaces of urban operation is a crucial cultural task.

Notes

Epigraph. Lewis Mumford, *Technics and Civilization* (New York: Harcourt, Brace & Company, 1934), 372.

1. I would like to thank Charles Waldheim for his insightful comments during the production of this essay. For additional background on the topic, see Pierre Bélanger and Dennis Lago, "Highway Surface: A Brief History of the United States Interstate & Defense Highway System" in Francine Houben and Luisa Calabrese, eds., *Mobility: A Room with a View*, (NAI Publishers: Rotterdam, 2003), 397–410.

2. Kevin Lynch strongly advocated for the organizational capacity of circulation systems, and their different constituent parts, throughout his career as author and practitioner. In *Site Planning* (Cambridge, Mass: MIT Press, 1962), Lynch dedicates an entire chapter on systems of movement, establishing "access [as] a prerequisite to the usefulness of any block of space. Without the ability to enter, to leave, and move, within it, to receive and transmit information or goods, space is of no value, however vast or rich in resources. In one sense, a city is a communication net, made up of roads, paths, rails, pipes and wires. This system of flow is intimately related to the pattern of localized activities, or land use. The economic and cultural level of a city is roughly in proportion to the capacity of its circulation system..." (p.118). The recent recapitulation of the discourse on the organizational capacity of circulation systems is owed to two contemporary practitioners: Alex Wall and Keller Easterling. In *Organization Space: Landscapes, Highways and Houses in America* (Cambridge, Mass: MIT Press, 1999), Easterling clearly articulates this latent capacity: "Generic spatial production, for instance, amplifies small adjustments by way of its own banality" (4).

3. Two distinct meanings of the term *synthetic* are employed in this article. In its first and more commonly understood use, synthetic references a state of substitution for a natural occurrence. Underpinning this article, the second meaning is broader in scope since it relates to *synthesis*, the process of the combination and the composition of different elements to form a whole or a complex of parts. The critical meaning of "synthesis" is explored in depth by entomologist Edward O. Wilson in *Consilience: Towards a Unity of Knowledge* (New York: Knopf, 1998) which is based on Julian Huxley's *Evolution: The Modern Synthesis* (London: George Allen & Unwin, 1942). See Massimo Negrotti, *Towards a General Theory of the Artificial* (Exeter: Intellect, 1999) for a comprehensive distinction between the "synthetic" from the "artificial," the "substitute," and the "fake."

4. Stan Allen, "Mat Urbanism: The Thick 2-D," in Hashim Sarkis, ed., *CASE: Le Corbusier's Venice Hospital and the Mat Building Revival* (Munich: Prestel/Harvard Design School, 2001), 118–26.

5. Alex Wall, "Programming the Urban Surface" in James Corner, ed. *Recovering Landscape: Essays in Contemporary Landscape Architecture* (New York: Princeton Architectural Press, 1999), 246.

6. Allen, "Mat Urbanism," 124.

7. See Mirko Zardini ed., Triennale di Milano, *Asfalto: Il Carattere Della Città / Asphalt: The Character of the City* (Milan: Electa Editrice, 2003): jacket note.

8. See Maxwell G. Lay, *Ways of the World: A History of the World's Roads and of the Vehicles that Used Them* (New Brunswick, N.J.: Rutgers University Press, 1992), for an encyclopedic survey on how mud, dust, drainage, erosion, sediment, and transport were central to the transformation of the North American landscape up until the early twentieth century.

9. The impact of speed and accelerated forms of movement on the contemporary landscape has produced two generations of researchers in the latter half of the twentieth century. Philosopher and architect Paul Virilio is one of the most notable proponents. In *Vitesse et*

Politique / Speed & Politics: An Essay on Dromology (Paris: Éditions Galilée, 1977), Virilio is particularly instructive regarding the geopolitical agency of paved surfaces: "Can asphalt be a territory? Is the bourgeois State and its power the street or in the street? Are its potential force and expanse in the places of intense circulation, on the path of rapid transportation?" (4). Dr. Matthew T. Ciolek is another notable practitioner whose research involves the field of "dromography," which involves the synthesis of geography, history, and logistics of trade routes, transportation and communication networks. See Ciolek, "Global Networking: A Timeline," 1999, http://www.ciolek.com/PAPERS/milestones.html.

10. Henry Adams, *History of the United States during the Administrations of Thomas Jefferson and James Madison*, Volume 1 (New York: Charles Scribner's Sons, 1889), 12–13. By 1902, Adams withdrew from politics and converted to the amenities of an eighteen horsepower Mercedes-Benz. He spent more and more time away from Washington; instead, he explored France in his new motor car. Expressed at the end of the eighteenth century, Henry Adams's ideals are a premonition of the future: "My idea of paradise is a perfect automobile going thirty miles an hour on a smooth road to a twelfth-century cathedral."

11. Isaac B. Potter, "The Gospel of the Good Roads: A Letter to the American Farmer from the League of American Wheelman" in *Manufacturer & Builder* 23 (New York: Western and Company, 1891), 1.

12. Charles Goodyear, "Improvement in India-Rubber Fabrics" in *United States Patent No. 3,663* (New York: June 15, 1844): 1–2.

13. Jeffrey T. Schnapp, "Three Pieces of Apshalt," in *Grey Room* 11 (2003): 7.

14. See Edward Joseph De Smedt, "The Origins of American Asphalt Pavements," in *Paving and Municipal Engineering* 5 (December 1879): 251.

15. Of all the historical pavement innovations, the most critical one involved "crowning" the surface of the road whereby creating positive drainage and ensuring dryness. See Irving Brinton Holley, "Blacktop: How Asphalt Paving Came to the Urban United States" in *Technology and Culture* 44 (2003): 703–33. John Loudon McAdam wrote extensively on his findings. An exhaustive description of his work can be found in "Remarks on the Present System of Road-Making" (Bristol: J. M. Gutch, 1816) and "A Practical Essay on the Scientific Repair and Preservation of Public Roads" (London: Board of Agriculture, and internal improvement, 1819). In contrast, Thomas Metcalfe's discoveries resulted from a special advantage that granted him greater freedom to experiment with material coarseness and densities: he was blind.

16. See Edward Joseph De Smedt, "Improvement in Laying Asphalt or Concrete Pavements or Roads," *United States Patent No. 103,581* (New York: May 31, 1870): 1.

17. See Hugh Gillespie, *A Century of Progress: The History of Hot Mix Asphalt* (Lanham, MD: National Asphalt Pavement Association, 1992).

18. Captain William C. Greaney, Expeditionary Adjutant and Statistical Officer of the Transcontinental Convoy, "Principal Facts Concerning the First Transcontinental Army Motor Transport Expedition, Washington to San Francisco, July 7 to September 6, 1919." Dwight D. Eisenhower Archives, Abilene, Kansas; http://www.Eisenhower.archives.gov/dl/1919Convoy/1919documents.html (accessed 26 June 2004).

19. See Joyce N. Ritter, *The History of Highways and Statistics*, U.S. Department of Highway Administration (1994) and United States Bureau of Public Roads, *Highway Statistics: Summary To 1955* (Washington, D.C.: U.S. Government Printing Office, 1957).

20. Dwight D. Eisenhower, *At Ease: Through Darkest America with Truck and Tank* (New York: Doubleday & Company, 1967), 166–67.

21. Although more durable, concrete paving was overcome by the asphalt industry due to its cost effectiveness, homogeneity, and construction speed. The use of concrete made a major comeback with the advent of slipforming technologies in the 1970s.

22. Eric Larrabee, "The Six Thousand Houses That Levitt Built" in *Harper's* 197 (1948): 79–83.

23. Caption (back of map), *1949 New Jersey Turnpike Map*, New Jersey Turnpike Authority, Department of Public Records. New Brunswick, New Jersey.

24. Chief Engineer of the Asphalt Institute, Vaughan Marker, provides an in-depth perspective on the developments of the pavement industry over the past fifty years in Dwight Walker, "A Conversation with Vaughan Marker," *Asphalt Magazine* (Summer 2002): 20–25.

25. DPR, "Operation Sand," *The New Jersey Turnpike Authority—Press Release*, Department of Public Records (Trenton, N.J.: October 12, 1950): 1. For a broader explanation of the 300-year-old unbroken trend of the perception of marshlands as wastelands—a perception that is widely reversed today, see William Cronon, "Modes of Prophecy and Production: Placing Nature in History. *Journal of American History* 76, 1121–31.

26. Paul J. C. Friedlander, "High Road from the Hudson to the Delaware," *The New York Times* (25 November 1951).

27. The geometry of interstate highways is essentially based on a theoretical design speed standard made visible by three main characteristics: flatter horizontal curves, longer vertical curves, and greater sight distances.

28. DPR, "Construction Progress Updates," *The New Jersey Turnpike Authority—Press Release*, Department of Public Records (Trenton, N.J.: November 12, 1956): 1.

29 John Noble Wilford, *The Mapmakers* (New York: Vintage Books, 1981), 356.

30. Ibid. In 1969, a similar circumstance ensued in Pennsylvania, "when the state highway department, used its own reference points on each side of a river, instead of the Geodetic Survey's; construction of a bridge started from each shore, and in midstream the two sections were four metres apart."

31. Dwight D. Eisenhower, "Message to the Congress re Highways", (Abilene, Kansas: Dwight D. Eisenhower National Presidential Library Archives, February 22, 1955), 1. and Joyce N. Ritter, *America's Highways 1776–1976*, (Washington, D.C.: Federal Highway Administration, 1976).

32. Richard M. Nixon, citing Eisenhower, in Dwight D. Eisenhower, "Telegram To Richard Milhous Nixon, 12 July 1954," The Papers of Dwight David Eisenhower, Doc. 976, World Wide Web Facsimile, *The Dwight D. Eisenhower Memorial Commission* (Baltimore, MD: The Johns Hopkins University Press, 1996), http://www.eisenhowermemorial.org/presidential-papers/first-term/documents/976.cfm (accessed July 1, 2004).

33. There are diverging accounts of the geographic and the economic benefits of the German highway system during the middle of the twentieth century. See Eckhard Gruber and Erhard Schütz, *Mythos Reichsautobahn, Bau und Inszenierung der "Straße des Führers 1933–1941* (Berlin: Ch. Links Verlag, 1996) for a compelling interpretation of German military highway infrastructure as tactical propaganda.

34. Dwight D. Eisenhower, *Mandate for Change 1953–1956* (New York: Doubleday, 1963), 548–49.

35. Dwight D. Eisenhower, July 12, 1954, Speech, delivered by Vice President Richard M. Nixon to the Nation's Governors. This speech was given only three months after his famous Domino Theory Speech on April 7, 1954 which discussed the effects of atomic energy research and the arms race. See Richard F. Weingroff, *President Dwight D. Eisenhower and the Federal Role in Highway Safety*, (Washington, D.C.: Federal Highway Administration, 2003).

36. The geometrical objective of the New Jersey profile is to redirect a vehicle upon impact and minimize damage to its wheels and car body. See Charles F. McDevitt, "Basics of Concrete Barriers: Concrete Barriers Appear to be Simple, but in Reality, They are Sophisticated Safety Devices," in *Public Roads Magazine* 5 (March/April 2000). Another innovation in the configuration of the road surface was the "suicide lane." In the 1920s

and '30s, roads were built with three lanes: one lane for each direction and a shared middle lane for passing vehicles in both directions. This presented the very real possibility of head-on collision. The concept behind this lane is similar to the dashed yellow line found on two-lane highways, which permits passing. Suicide lanes were finally phased out by the 1960s, with the roadways being widened to a full four lanes or more.

37. Alex Wall, "Programming the Urban Surface," 246.

38. "Foreign Trade Zone No. 49 Fact Sheet," The Port Authority of New York/New Jersey (2004): 1–2.

39. See Eric Lipton, "New York Port Hums Again With Asian Trade," *The New York Times* (November 22, 2004).

40. The beam length of Post-Panamax and Super-Post-Panamax ships exceeds the maximum allowable width of 32.3 meters of the Panama Canal. These ships navigate the Suez Canal for transoceanic shipping. In the Port of New York and New Jersey, deep-draft ships currently operate at 75% of their capacity due to the shallowness of the waters, resulting in significant losses for both the sea liners and the ports. See Drewry Shipping Consultants, *Post-Panamax Containerships—The Next Generation* (London: Drewry, 2001).

41. See Andrew C. Revkin, "Shallow Waters: A Special Report—Curbs On Silt Disposal Threaten Port Of New York As Ships Grow Larger," *The New York Times* (March 18, 1996): A1.

42. Joseph Seebode, in Gayle Ehrenman, "Digging Deeper in New York," *Mechanical Engineering* (November 2003); http://www.memagazine.org/backissues/nov03/features/deeperny/deeperny.html (accessed 8 November 2004).

43. Amphipods are crustaceans used as bio-indicators for heavy metals in marine environments. See Miller Associates, "Dredging—The Invisible Crisis," *CQD Journal for the Maritime Environment Industry* 1 (January 1996) http://www.cqdjournal.com/html/env__2_1.htm (accessed March 11, 2005)

44. United States Army Corps of Engineers, "Channel & Berth Deepening Fact Sheet," The Port Authority of New York and New Jersey (March 2005): 1.

45. Ibid., and United States Army Corps of Engineers, "Beneficial Uses of Dredged Material," http://www.nan.usace.army.mil/business/prjlinks/dmmp/benefic/habitat.htm (accessed 17 September 2004).

46. Based on facts and figures from the following sources: Committee on Contaminated Marine Sediments, Marine Board, Commission on Engineering and Technical Systems, National Research Council, "Contaminated Sediments In Ports And Waterways—Cleanup Strategies And Technologies" (Washington, D.C.: National Academy Press, 1997): 20; and American Association of Port Authorities and Maritime Administration, "The North American Port Container Traffic—2003 Port Industry Statistics" and "United States Port Development Expenditure Report," (U.S. Department Of Transportation, May 2004).

47. Clare Lyster investigates this process in greater depth in her essay "Landscapes of Exchange," in this collection. In "Programming the Urban Surface" (238), Alex Wall is again instructive: "The importance of mobility and access in the contemporary metropolis brings to infrastructure the character of collective space. Transportation infrastructure is less a self-sufficient service element than an extremely visible and effective instrument in creating new networks and relationships." The project of post-industrial remediation is divided into two main practices. On the one hand, there are practitioners of site-level remediation that rely on measures of inward looking strategies of spatial beautification or surface concealment, employing renderings and property plans aimed solely at visualizing the immediate or short term benefits of design. The other, perhaps more informative practice, lies with regional-scale materials management strategies resulting from logistical, environmental, social and financial complexities. Usually associated with a distribution of sites, in varying sizes and conditions, with a higher magnitude of complexity, these sites often

involve the synthesis of regional transportation infrastructures and ecosystems where strategies must rely on incremental transformation, broader physical impacts and long term effects. See Niall Kirkwood, *Manufactured Sites: Rethinking the Post-Industrial Landscape* (London: Spon Press, 1991). The case of the Dredged Consolidated Materials Management Program at the scale of the mid-Atlantic Region points toward the potential effectiveness of this broader strategy, which simultaneously relies on a more extensive time-scale. Initiated by the U.S. Army Corps of Engineers and the Port of New York and New Jersey as several other environmental agencies with multidisciplinary experts, the overall financial savings balanced by net ecological and social gains, suggests an intelligent strategy for large, complex and open-ended projects. Recently, James Corner has referred to this strategy as "design intelligence" which offers the potential to unlock and seize "opportunism and risk-taking" in contemporary landscape practice. See James Corner, "Not Unlike Life Itself: Landscape Strategy Now" in *Harvard Design Magazine* 21 (Fall/Winter 2004): 32–34, and James Corner, "Terra Fluxus" in this collection.

Public Works Practice

Chris Reed

FIG. 1 Hydrologic Infrastructures, Mt. Tabor Resevoirs, Portland, Oregon, Chris Reed/Stoss Landscape Urbanism

Contemporary landscape practices are witnessing a revival of sorts, a recovery of broader social, cultural, and ecological agendas.[1] No longer a product of pure art history and horticulture, landscape is re-engaging issues of site and ecological succession and is playing a part in the formative roles of projects, rather than simply giving form to already defined projects. Landscape's sheer expanse, especially in terms of the North American continent—whether the vast geological scale of the West or the infrastructural proliferation of landscaped highways and suburban tract developments—is prompting a reconsideration of the role and impact landscape has on the related disciplines of architecture, urban design, and planning. Traces of this evolution can be seen in the regional planning studies of Ian McHarg; the early works of Hargreaves Associates in America and Devisgne and Dalnoky in Europe; work produced during the 1990s at the University of Pennsylvania's Department of Landscape Architecture, led by James Corner and later Anuradha Mathur; innovations in built works of landscape in Europe, first as Barcelona remade itself in preparation for the 1992 Summer Games and later as design practices in the Netherlands flourished in the context of its highly regulated and watery terrains; and projects and written works by the architect Stan Allen in America and generated at the Architectural Association in London, under the leadership of Mohsen Mostafavi.

The strains of this work related to functional and infrastructural agendas are of particular interest, offering departure points for thinking about emerging modes of professional landscape practice or of the discourse of landscape urbanism. In particular, the evolution of public works projects in the United States since their inception in the late nineteenth century offers fuller, more complex, more responsive, and more proactive models for contemporary practice, fully enmeshed in and engaged with contemporary cultural conditions of dispersal, decentralization, deregulation, privatization, mobility, and flexibility.

Public works historians Stanley K. Schultz and Clay McShane offer a useful departure point and baseline overview of public works projects and administration in America: "Twentieth-century economic and political administration emphasized several characteristics, including a centralized permanent bureaucracy staffed by skilled experts, and a commitment to long-range, comprehensive planning."[2] To this we might add that the projects sponsored by such administrations were highly technical, specialized by discipline, economically driven, and discretely bounded. Yet this description is incomplete. In truth, the development of public works projects in the United States during the nineteenth and twentieth centuries was much more diversified and finely grained. Public works evolved from publicly initiated social reforms to multidimensional mega-projects to dispersed, networked initiatives that took on new technical as well as organizational challenges such as research and development, fundraising, and mitigation. Contemporary public works initiatives are caught up in a web of social, logistical, economic, and environmental forces with local and global import.

Landscape practices followed a different trajectory. While initially enmeshed in the social reform movements that spurred on the first sewer and water systems, landscape architects gradually relinquished their social relevance, as scientists and engineers ascended to leadership positions in the agencies formed to implement comprehensive infrastructures. In so doing, newly anointed technocrats assumed an unparalleled social status, one of almost unassailable legitimacy, while landscape architects retreated to the cultural margins. And though public works projects changed radically in terms of management structure, scope, and input, landscape practices eventually congealed into one of two molds: as decorative art, invoked to dress up a site or cover over a problem; or as science-based planning methodology, often co-opted for purely economic development purposes. In other words, landscape succumbed to the conditions outlined above by Schultz and McShane without engaging the economic, political, and logistical forces that radically changed the context for other public and professional practices during the twentieth century.

New conditions necessitate new modes of practice [FIG. 1]. The reformulated context within which public works have evolved is now characterized by dispersal, decentralization, deregulation, privatization, mobility, and flexibility. Project networks are dynamic; infrastructural frameworks are adaptive; management structures are nimble, tactical, and responsive. Expanded and fragmented decision-making processes and entities, competition for resources, multidimensional project typologies (brownfield recovery, for instance), and emerging models of hybrid sponsorship move beyond a capacity for disciplinary distinction and isolation. Dichotomies between top-down and bottom-up planning processes have been obliterated as the roles of infrastructure and ecology have been reconsidered and expanded. These revised conditions invoke a complexly layered landscape urbanist agenda, replete with environmental, urbanistic, social, cultural, ecological, technological, functional, and logistical frameworks and mechanisms. They require a new model for flexible, adaptive, and networked public works practices caught up in the web of sociopolitical, economic, ecological, and global currents in which they operate. To begin, four case studies from the last two centuries trace a trajectory of public works projects and practices from private initiative and corporate sponsorship to complex, multidimensional and multidisciplinary endeavors that spawn new inventions and revolutionize project management structure and practices.

Early public works projects were not centrally organized, top-down initiatives conceived by local and federal governments; rather, they grew as a result of citizen-initiated reform or public pressure exerted upon a central government, or even as private entrepreneurship geared toward the delivery of a new public service. In 1796, the private Aqueduct Corporation, seeing a potentially lucrative enterprise in the making, petitioned the Massachusetts General Court for—and was granted—a charter to supply drinking water to Boston from Jamaica Pond. Three years later, a citizen petition moved the same court to order the city to clean waste from its streets and gutters to prevent disease.[3] Around the same time in New York, doctors, lawyers, businessmen, and other reformers established the Citizens' Association to conduct an investigation into the physical fabric of the city—everything from street pavements and slaughterhouses to brothels and "fever nests" (inner-city areas that, due to their lack of sanitary facilities, were thought to be sources of disease outbreaks)—in order to initiate government-sponsored sanitary improvements.[4] In Philadelphia, political and business leaders, prompted by citizens and private publications, formed a committee that commissioned the country's first municipal Waterworks to prevent epidemics.[5] In Chicago, Daniel Burnham's great plan for remaking the city's physical infrastructure, including its signature boulevards, was commissioned by the Commercial Club, a coalition of business leaders as interested in economic gain from better transportation access as in culturally elevating their emerging city to compete on national and world stages.[6] Shultz and McShane, in characterizing the broad range of citizen- and corporate-driven reform in this era, note that "Sanitarians, landscape architects, and engineers formed a troika that tried to pull citizens and officials alike from the mire of governmental inaction to the higher ground of municipal planning and administration."[7] Social reformers, health workers, business leaders, landscape architects, engineers, and civic groups invented the public works project.

METROPOLITAN DISTRICT COMMISSION

The Metropolitan District Commission (MDC) was formed in 1919, when Boston's Metropolitan Parks Commission, established in 1893 as the first regional parks district in the United States, absorbed the Metropolitan Sewage District, founded four years prior.[8] Multijurisdictional agencies, generally established by legislative charter, were a new, centralized government authority invented to cope with the increasing scope of water, sewage, open space, and transportation systems—usually individually. Yet the MDC's purpose and scope were diverse from the start: open space was initially its first priority, yet the system was sited along the region's water resources—reservoirs used for water supply and rivers used for transportation [FIG. 2]. Designed by landscape architect Charles Eliot,

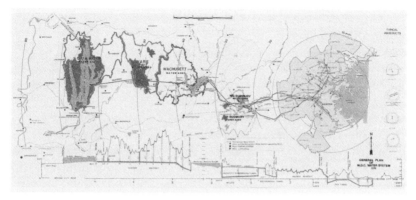

FIG. 2 Metropolitan District Commission, *The Metropolitan Water System*

the open space system was also conceived as a physical framework that would guide public and private development; in this regard, Eliot shared aspirations with his partner Frederick Law Olmsted, who conceived parkways as multilayered, multifunctional landscaped infrastructures and physical urban frameworks, serving transportation, recreation, remedial (with regard to buffering waterways), and urbanistic ends.[9] For much of the twentieth century, the MDC was singularly responsible for a wide variety of services and systems, including the provision of safe drinking water, the treatment of wastewater, the care and upkeep of the region's most critical and comprehensive open-space resources, and the establishment and management of the region's parkways. It has since been dismantled into and absorbed by at least three separate and specialized state agencies.

HOOVER DAM

Projects like the Hoover Dam, at the time the largest construction undertaking in the history of the United States, solidified engineers' prominence in the planning and implementation of public works due to the project's unprecedented scope and technical complexity: in fact, it took a coalition of six construction companies, aptly named Six Companies, to secure the winning bid. Yet the project served other purposes, necessitating other inventions—spinoff initiatives not part of the new dam but required in facilitating its implementation. Astounding engineering feats were achieved, not least of which was the rerouting of the Colorado River through the stone walls of the canyon. New construction techniques emerged, with concrete poured in discrete blocks from an innovative set of transport devices suspended from aerial cables stretched across the canyon [FIG. 3].[10] Impressively, an entire new city—Boulder City—was built in the Nevada desert to house, feed, and educate the five thousand workers and their families required to build the dam.[11] And, though conceived prior to the market crash of 1929, the project became a public employment initiative as thousands of

FIG. 3 Hoover Dam during construction

unemployed workers raced to the desert to fill scarce job openings. In all, the flood control initiative cast in the form of one of the country's largest infrastructural projects served as a catalyst for institutional, technological, and urban advancements—the spawning of "infrastructural ecologies"—and possibly as a model for future government-sponsored work programs.

ARPANET

A radical departure from public works projects directed by a centralized, hierarchical authority, the ARPANET—the predecessor to the current internet—established a new, networked model for project development. In doing so, it manifested a broader series of mid-to-late-twentieth-century trends in global economic and political arenas toward decentralization and privatization. For instance, the developers of the ARPANET took on new roles and were responsible

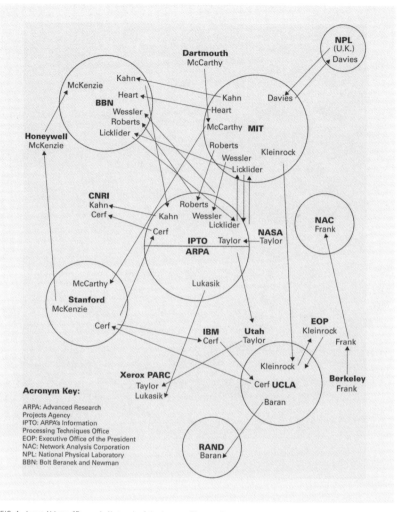

FIG. 4 Janet Abbate, "Dynamic Network of the Arpanet Pioneers"

for project organization and management, research and development, design and engineering, and implementation and maintenance. Project management itself was dispersed and diversified; the ARPANET was created by an evolving coalition of networked entities—some governmental (such as ARPA/ Advanced Research Projects Agency, Information Processing Techniques Office, and National Physical Laboratory), others academic/institutional (such as MIT, UCLA, Stanford, UC Berkeley, and Dartmouth), and still others private/corporate (Bolt Beranek and Newman, Honeywell, and IBM). Hierarchical, single-entity organizations had given way to dispersed matrices of public, private, corporate, institutional, and academic entities; multiple voices, both "official" and traditionally underrepresented, were heard and integrated. Even the individuals at work on the network moved from one organization to another, reflecting in organizational structure and personal mobility the new methodologies and mechanics of project development and information exchange [FIG. 4].

TOGETHER, THESE FOUR INSTANCES OF PUBLIC WORKS initiatives hint at a relatively rapid evolution of project sponsorship, definition, impact, organizational structure, and conception. Yet the work did not evolve in isolation; rather this genealogy of project types and logistics ran parallel with—both influenced by and occasionally impacting on—national and global shifts in domestic market cycles, military-industrial production, worker mobility, the linking of global economies and governments, and trends toward government deregulation and the consequent privatization of public goods and services.

An early characteristic of public works projects, one alluded to in the initial examples, was the rise of the professional engineer in social status and municipal ranks. The unprecedented scale of these projects in the early twentieth century was a factor in this development. Power initiatives such as the Tennessee Valley Authority required new levels of coordination at a scale that stretched across broad regions, or entire states, and between experts in multiple fields— hydrology, dam construction, power generation, and transmission. Barbara Rosencrantz, writing on the water supply situation in Massachusetts, illuminates this national trend:

> Increasingly complex concepts of environmental sanitation... sanctioned the authority of a whole new group of experts to protect the people from the evils accompanying urbanization and industrialization. Meanwhile... [increasing understanding of disease] contributed to shifting responsibility for health from the layman to the trained scientist. As both prevention and cure of disease were removed from the jurisdiction of enlightened common sense, new appeals for sanitary controls were phrased in terms of dependence upon qualified experts—the engineer, the chemist, and the biologist.[12]

The ascendancy of the professional engineer carried with it the pretense of the depoliticization of public works projects, given that issues and decisions were being considered by the most qualified of scientists and engineers and thus were argued to be beyond the realm of politics.[13]

Other factors weighed in. During the 1930s and 1940s, the Works Projects Administration programs and initiatives employed thousands of citizens during a time of economic depression and recovery; the federal government now acted as employer and contractor on its expanding roster of projects and services provided to the public. In fact, 75 percent of all WPA employment between 1935 and 1943 was devoted to the construction of public works projects.[14] Within the context of employment-and economic-driven initiatives, the infrastructure of the United States was radically transformed and expanded. It took only eight years to build:

> 67,000 miles of urban streets; 24,000 miles of new and 7,000 miles of improved sidewalks and paths;...8,000 parks; 3,300 stadiums, grand-stands, and bleachers; 5,600 athletic fields;...500 water treatment plants; 1,800 pumping stations; 19,700 miles of new or repaired water lines; 880,000 consumer water connections; 6,000 new and upgraded water wells; 3,700 storage tanks and reservoirs; 1,500 sewage treatment plants; 200 incinerator plants; 27,000 miles of new and improved storm and sanitary sewers; 639,000 sewage service connections;...350 new and 700 improved landing strips and airports, including 5,925,000 linear feet of runways [and] 1,129,000 linear feet of taxi strips...; a total of 40,000 new and 85,000 improved public buildings...; 572,000 miles of rural roads; 78,000 new and 46,000 improved bridges and viaducts; 1,000 new tun-nels for vehicles, pedestrians, trains, sewers, and cattle; uncounted river control projects, erosion control operations, and mine sealing initia-tives...; forest conservation projects...; 300 new fish hatcheries; and the re-planting of oyster beds with over 8 million bushels of oysters.[15]

Over the course of this tremendous undertaking, the definition of the public works initiative, though still administered by a centralized federal agency, was greatly expanded. As the United States geared up for war at the end of the 1930s and into the 1940s, public works projects assumed a military imperative. A post-World War II government report on the WPA notes that "much of the work done by the Works Projects Administration in peacetime years was later recognized as being of military value to the Nation"—especially projects at air-ports, military establishments, and on roads and highways.[16] By the 1940s, defense and war initiatives were soon given priority in the WPA, and grew to include landing field projects; Reserve Officer Training Corps, National Guard, and naval training facilities; "roads, streets, bridges, and highways forming a part of the national strategic highway network or providing access to military or naval establishments or industrial establishments or industrial plants engaged in war work"; public facilities and utilities and public health projects in areas near defense and war production and activities; radio monitoring stations; and engineering surveys and services.[17] Mid-century and the Cold War witnessed the birth of the Semi-Automated Ground Environment (SAGE) and Atlas missile defense projects, pushing the military-industrial complex forward while simultaneously introducing new, integrated (and eventually non-hierarchical) management structures and research and development initiatives into public works.[18] Importantly, such developments parallel early advances in digital and computing technologies and impact even the way project teams organized themselves within physical settings. Here was a turning point. The scale and complexity of military-related public works initiatives had reached a point where the government could not handle the task itself—and in which its ties to and reliance on the production facilities of private industry was acute and obvious. Systems development was becoming more multidimensional and dispersed.

Simultaneously, mobility of both workers and capital was greatly expanding; structural shifts in the global economy were reflected in national and regional trends away from the old industrial economy toward new, more flexible production arrangements. Broader economic trends in the 1980s and 1990s, perhaps initially spurred on by the energy crisis of the late 1970s, led to decreased investments by governments in infrastructures and public works projects, especially under Reagan and Thatcher. Deregulation of the airlines and energy sectors, and eventually of telecommunications, was one of the factors leading to increased privatization of infrastructural resources and service during this period. Private companies were now racing to compete for access to utilities, phone systems, and communications networks, and were themselves on the forefront of developing emerging technologies.[19]

Decentralization, deregulation, and privatization were factors leading to what Stephen Graham and Simon Marvin define as a "splintering urbanism," characterized by interdependent networked infrastructures, assemblies of "sociotechnical" apparatuses, the physical co-location of unrelated infrastructures (such as optic fiber networks laid along roadways), and the coordination of infrastructural, landscape, and architectural strategies in the emergence of the dispersed, networked city.[20] Sanford Kwinter and Daniela Fabricius have further detailed an expanded view of infrastructure as anything that acts as an "engine of change…, every aspect of the technology of rational administration that routinizes life, action, and property within larger…organizations."[21] Theirs reads like an update to the 1947 WPA report:

> [T]he systematic expression of capital, of deregulated currency, of interest rates, credit instruments, trade treaties, market forces, and the institutions that enforce them;…water, fuel, and electrical reservoirs, routes

and rates of supply;... demographic mutations and migrations, satellite networks and lotteries, logistics and supply coefficients, traffic computers, airports and distribution hubs, cadastral techniques, juridical routines, telephone systems, business district self-regulation mechanisms, evacuation and disaster mobilization protocols, prisons, subways and freeways..., parking garages, gas pipelines and meters, hotels, public toilets, postal and park utilities and management, school systems and ATM machines; celebrity, advertising, and identity engineering; rail nodes and networks, television programming, interstate systems, entry ports and the public goods and agencies associated with them [INS, NSA, IRS, FDA, ATF],... decision engineering pools, wetlands and water basins, civil structure maintenance schedules,... cable delivery systems,... internet scaffolds, handgun regulations,... military deployment procedures.[22]

Beyond mere physical systems and constructions, Kwinter's and Fabricius's view implicates multiple and (surprisingly) diverse administrative entities and agencies; elements of staging and time, via logistics and migrations; economic and political forces; and various decision-making frameworks that allow for the conceptualization and realization of such projects.

These developments can be traced in the birth and evolution of large-scale yet decentralized and increasingly distributed public works initiatives, manifest most profoundly in the example of the ARPANET. According to technology historian Thomas Hughes, such projects required new types of professional managers and management structures, in which

system builders preside[d] over technological projects from concept and preliminary design through research, development, and deployment. In order to preside over projects, system builders needed to cross disciplinary and functional boundaries—for example, to become involved in funding and political stage-setting. Instead of focusing upon individual artifacts, system builders direct their attention to the interfaces, interconnections, among system components.[23]

Public works projects were further catholicized with the broadening of players and issues welcomed to the table. As old urban centers were remade during the 1990s as destinations for entertainment, culture, and recreation, cities began to compete with one another over quality-of-life issues and brand identity. In luring residents, jobs, and tourists, cities remade their physical fabric, restoring old buildings, tearing down highways, building new open space, and resuscitating depleted and polluted natural resources. Environmentalists, social advocates, business leaders, community organizations, and financiers were invited into an ever-increasing fold of citizen and corporate involvement in public works initiatives. "Mitigation projects," often miles away from the main construction site and

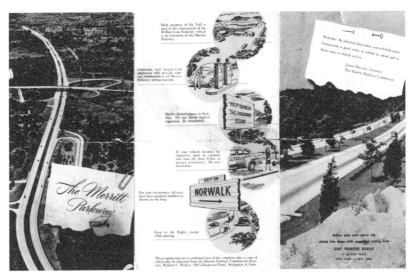

FIG. 5 "The Merritt Parkway: Connecticut's All-Year Gateway to New England."
Connecticut Department of Transportation promotional brochure, 1947

sometimes of tenuous environmental or social relation, were required as part of the project implementation, as an exchange back to landowners, the general public, and the environment for the discomfort of construction and implementation.[24]

Twentieth-century infrastructural and sociopolitical evolutions clearly impacted urbanization, metropolitanization, suburbanization, and the extended urban field. Early-and mid-century highway construction allowed for increased distribution of industrial and residential settlements, spurred on by the return of World War II veterans. Robert Moses's metropolitan New York parkways were early landscaped infrastructures—green highways that responded directly to advancements in automotive technologies and modes of production [FIG. 5]. Levittown and other government-sponsored housing developments were created on cheaper land outside of dense city cores, with each family now able to own a freestanding structure [FIG. 6]. Surrounded by a continuous landscape veneer, these houses and their development structure reflected the landscape ideals of earlier suburban developments, such as Olmsted's plan for Riverside in Chicago and Ebenezer Howard's Garden City, yet were more economically biased and located even further out from the traditional, dense urban core. Frank Lloyd Wright's Broadacre City proposal reveled in the expansive, urban field of green suburban development [FIG. 7]. And more recently, Rem Koolhaas has pointed out that "Atlanta shifted [from center to periphery] so quickly and so completely that the center/edge opposition is no longer the point. There is no center, therefore no periphery. Atlanta is now a centerless city, or a city with a potentially infinite number of centers," rising intermittently from forest expanse.[25]

FIG. 6 Levittown, Pennsylvania, aerial view, ca. 1959

Other fields have witnessed similar developments. Ecological systems are now described by more complex terminologies—matrices, webs, and networks, for instance—and are characterized by adjacencies, overlaps, and juxtapositions.[26] The field itself has experienced a dramatic shift away from an understanding of systems that attempt to achieve a predictable equilibrium condition to systems typically in states of change, adapting to subtle or dramatic changes in inputs, forces, resources, climate, or other variables. Adaptation, appropriation, and flexibility are now the hallmarks of "successful" systems, as it is through their ability to respond to contextual and environmental conditions that they persist.[27]

In seeking to recover the architect's role in "questions of function, implementation, technique, finance, and material practice," Stan Allen offers a constructive model for urbanists and architects operating in the new milieu, one that engages time and process in the "production of directed fields in which program, event and activity can play themselves out." He notes that ecology and engineering are already performance-oriented practices, facilitating "energy inputs

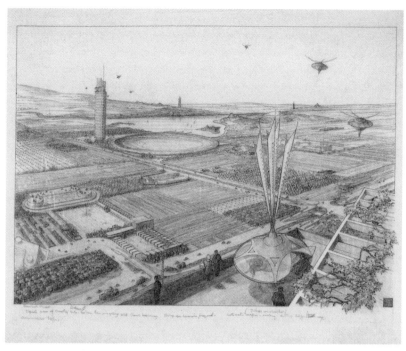

FIG. 7 Frank Lloyd Wright, Broadacre City, 1935

and outputs, the calibration of force and resistance." Allen argues that architecture and urbanism, and by extension landscape, should be "less concerned with what things look like and more concerned with what they do"; he outlines an "infrastructural urbanism" that is strategic, operates at large scales, and is made physical/material when it encounters the local.[28]

DEPARTURE POINTS

Recent and historic advances in public works projects, urbanism, housing, and even ecology point to a new set of professional practices characterized by an emphasis on operational and performance-driven aspects of landscape process and urbanization, and with a focus on logistics and mechanisms. Importantly, though, this interest in the mechanics and mechanisms of project development necessarily extends beyond physical issues to include project conceptualization, funding, implementation, and oversight of maintenance practices. It includes birth processes and the administrative mechanisms of project conception and development, strategies that catalyze growth and succession, and adaptive approaches to long-term implementation and maintenance regimes. Moving forward, at least four trends, as follows.

1. Blurring of Distinctions Between Traditional Fields of Practice

No longer do traditional separations between disciplines hold. The new public works are marked by the integration of functional, social-cultural, ecological, economic, and political agendas. Limited resources demand that interventions satisfy multiple goals, bringing about hybridized solutions, with coordinated urbanistic, infrastructural, ecological, architectural, landscape, economic, artistic, and political agendas. Architecture, landscape architecture, engineering, ecology, art, social programs, environmental remediation, and more are embedded one within the other, resulting in new project typologies irreducible to traditional, singular designations.

2. Appropriation of Infrastructural Strategies and Ecological Tactics for New Civic Programs

While conceived as rational, absolute, and utilitarian, infrastructure has the capacity to be appropriated and transformed toward social, cultural, ecological, and artistic ends. Architectural accretions, layerings of program and use, existing infrastructures made useful—herein lies the basis for a new civic realm, one created by appendage and insertion. Conversely, architecture and landscape can appropriate the utility and serviceability of infrastructure. One could imagine landscape/architectural/urbanistic projects conceived as functional infrastructures, ecological machines that process and perform, public spaces that literally "work." One might also imagine the creation of fertile testing grounds that structure or initiate an unfolding of hydrologic, ecological, social-cultural, and urbanistic processes and adaptations—earthen infrastructures available for appropriation and transformation and whose form is valued for its performative rather than sculptural characteristics.[29]

3. Activation of Multiple, Overlapping Networks and Dynamic Coalitions of Constituencies

Martin Melosi, Stephen Graham, Sanford Kwinter, and others have recognized the decentralized or splintered characteristics of contemporary service provision and decision-making. Local municipalities are coping with limited resources that must fulfill an expanding set of public needs and constituencies; they are also subject to political and administrative changes that often reshuffle economic priorities. Fortunately, funding and organizational resources are not solely available to centralized municipalities; often community groups, arts organizations, research centers, and others have access to as many funding sources, and therefore wield as much power over the definition and playing out of public projects. They also often have political influence. Thus, public works practices must redefine and expand potential constituencies, stakeholders, and clients in the course of a project. Critical is the early establishment of broad networks of potential stakeholders, different coalitions of which can be activated for various stages of project implementation. In such a dynamic matrix of temporary partnerships, strategic coalitions emerge and fade—or at least suspend work—as projects evolve and adapt to local circumstances.

4. Catalytic and Responsive Operations
The key lay in the capacity for installations and operations to catalyze transformations via social, economic, ecological, or hydrologic processes. Understanding that long-term implementation may depend on short-term initiatives to change public perceptions and to generate political will, public works practices set out preliminary smaller-scale events and installations that require few resources. Yet implementation scenarios must also be responsive, such that they accommodate potential changes and diverge from a step-by-step implementation formula. Thus implementation strategies are represented more akin to networks and matrices that allow for both defined and undefined inputs and open-ended futures. Projects with duration of ten or twenty years or more must acknowledge the significant potential impact of changing markets and political agendas, in particular, and any number of forces, in general, that are simply beyond the control of the consultant or clients at the time of project initiation.

LANDSCAPE URBANISM—AS A SET OF IDEAS and frameworks—lays new ground for design and urbanistic practices: performance-based, research-oriented, logistics-focused, networked. Here, the design practitioner is re-cast as urbanistic system-builder, whose interests now encompass the research, framing, design, and implementation of expansive new public works and civic infrastructures.

The four trends outlined above, and the interests and initiatives put forward in this volume, collectively offer a provisional yet optimistic framework for practices in landscape urbanism. These emergent conditions are poised to transform traditional design practices and the roles of those working in the public realm.

Notes

1. This paper evolved from a series of discussions with Charles Waldheim, who was both patient and insightful as I tried to draw coherence from sometimes unrelated strains of thought that have been of interest for a number of years. Waldheim's guidance and friendship, as well as his determination to have me included in this volume of work, are greatly appreciated. Shannon Lee and Chris Muskopf were enormously helpful in assembling and checking sources and images for this article; many thanks to them for their scrupulous work. Finally, I had the opportunity to present portions of early manuscripts at the University of Pennsylvania, at the invitation of James Corner, and at the Harvard Design School, at the invitation of George Hargreaves. Both Corner and Hargreaves were characteristically generous in presenting opportunities to present, develop, and critique my work; I appreciate these specific opportunities, as well as the broader counsel and critical input both have provided for the past decade.

2. Stanley K. Schultz and Clay McShane, "To Engineer the Metropolis: Sewers, Sanitation, and City Planning in Late-Nineteenth-Century America," *Journal of American History*, vol. LXV (September 1978): 390.

3. Fern L. Nesson, *Great Waters: A History of Boston's Water Supply* (Hanover, NH: Brandeis University/University Press of New England, 1983), 2.

4. Eugene P. Moehring, *Public Works and Urban History: Recent Trends and New Directions* (Chicago: Public Works Historical Society, 1982).

5. See Martin Melosi's discussion "Sanitation Practices in Pre-Chadwickian America," in *The Sanitary City* (Baltimore: John Hopkins University Press, 2000), 30–32.

6. Wall Street's economic forecast for the 1893 World's Fair, taken from Mario Manieri-Elia, "Toward an Imperial City: Daniel H. Burnham and the City Beautiful Movement," Giorgio Ciucci et al., eds., *The American City: From the Civil War to the New Deal* (Cambridge, Mass.: The MIT Press, 1983), 15.

7. Schultz, and McShane, "To Engineer the Metropolis," 396.

8. Nesson, *Great Waters*, 36–37. See also *Report of the Board of the Metropolitan Park Commissioners* (Boston: Commonwealth of Massachusetts, January 1893).

9. Schultz and McShane, "To Engineer the Metropolis," 396–97. See also Cynthia Zaitzevsky, *Frederick Law Olmsted and the Boston Park System* (Cambridge, Mass.: Belknap Press, 1982).

10. The skip and cableway system is described by James Tobin in "The Colorado," in *Great Projects: The Epic Story of the Building of America, From the Taming of the Mississippi to the Invention of the Internet* (New York: The Free Press, 2001), 65–66.

11. James Tobin, "Pathways," in *Great Projects*, 226.

12. As quoted by Rosencrantz in Nesson, *Great Waters*, 9.

13. Ibid., 9–10.

14. The Division of Engineering and Construction directed 75 percent or more of the WPA employment until the spring of 1940, according to the United States Federal Works Agency, "Engineering and Construction Projects," *Final Report on the WPA Program*, 1935–43 (Washington, D.C.: US Government Printing Office, 1947), 47.

15. Ibid.

16. United States Federal Works Agency, "War Defense and War Activities" *Final Report on the WPA Program*, 1935–43, 84.

17. Ibid., 84–85.

18. See Thomas P. Hughes's description of systems engineering in *Rescuing Prometheus: Four Monumental Projects that Changed the Modern World* (New York: Vintage Books, 1998), 101.

19. See the discussion on contemporary infrastructure mobilities in the Introduction of Stephen Graham and Simon Marvin, *Splintering Urbanism: Networked Infrastructure, Technological Mobilities, and the Urban Condition* (London: Routledge/Taylor & Francis, 2001), 7–35.

20. Ibid.

21. Sanford Kwinter and Daniela Fabricius, "Urbanism: An Archivist's Art?" in Rem Koolhaas, Stefano Boeri, et al., eds., *Mutations* (Barcelona: Actar, 2001), 495–96.

22. Ibid.

23. Hughes, *Rescuing Prometheus*, 7.

24. Ibid., 221–23.

25. Rem Koolhaas and Bruce Mau, *S, M, L, XL* (New York: Monacelli Press, 1995), 836.

26. Richard T. T. Forman, "Part IV: Mosaics and Flows," *Land Mosaics: The Ecology of Landscapes and Regions* (Cambridge, England: Cambridge University Press, 1995).

27. David Waltner-Toews, James Kay, and Nina-Marie Lister, eds., *The Ecosystem Approach: Complexity, Uncertainty, and Managing for Sustainability* (New York: Columbia University Press, forthcoming). See also Robert E. Cook, "Do Landscapes Learn? Ecology's 'New

Paradigm' & Design in Landscape Architecture," Inaugural Ian L. McHarg Lecture, March 22, 1999.

28. Stan Allen, "Infrastructural Urbanism," *Points + Lines: Diagrams and Projects for the City* (New York: Princeton Architectural Press, 1999), 46–57.

29. Many of these ideas were developed in early form in conversation with Nader Tehrani and Monica Ponce de Leon of Office dA, Boston, Massachusetts.

Pierre Bélanger is Assistant Professor of Landscape Architecture at the University of Toronto.

Alan Berger is Associate Professor of Landscape Architecture at Harvard University and Founding Director of Harvard's Project for Reclamation Excellence.

James Corner is Chair and Professor of Landscape Architecture at the University of Pennsylvania School of Design, and Principal of Field Operations, based in New York City.

Julia Czerniak is Associate Professor of Architecture at Syracuse University and is principal of CLEAR.

Christophe Girot is Principal of Atelier Girot as well as Professor and Director of the Institute of Landscape Architecture at the Swiss Federal Institute of Technology (ETH) Zurich, Switzerland.

Clare Lyster is an architect and Adjunct Associate Professor of Architecture at the University of Illinois at Chicago.

Elizabeth Mossop is Principal of Spackman + Mossop landscape architects and Professor and Director of the School of Landscape Architecture at Louisiana State University.

Linda Pollak is Principal of Marpillero-Pollak Architects in New York and Design Critic in Architecture at Harvard University.

Chris Reed is Principal of Stoss landscape urbanism and Lecturer in Landscape Architecture at the University of Pennsylvania School of Design.

Grahame Shane is Adjunct Professor of Architecture at Columbia University, Visiting Professor at Cooper Union, and Adjunct Professor at City College Graduate Urban Design Program.

Kelly Shannon is Associate Professor at the Department of Architecture, Planning and Urban Design, Katholieke Universiteit Leuven, Belgium.

Jacqueline Tatom is Assistant Professor of Architecture at Washington University in St. Louis.

Charles Waldheim is Associate Dean and Director of the Landscape Architecture Program at the Faculty of Architecture, Landscape, and Design at the University of Toronto.

Richard Weller is Professor and Chair of Landscape Architecture at the University of Western Australia.

Introduction: A Reference Manifesto
FIG. 1: Photo by Andrea Branzi; courtesy Andrea Branzi with the Domus Acadamy.

Terra Fluxus, James Corner
All figures courtesy James Corner/Field Operations.

Landscape as Urbanism, Charles Waldheim
FIGS. 1–3: Courtesy Rem Koolhaas/Office for Metropolitan Architecture (OMA).
FIG. 4: Photo by Luis On; courtesy Joan Roig and Enric Batlle.
FIGS. 5, 6: Photo by Hans Werlemann; courtesy Adriaan Geuze/West 8 Landscape Architects.
FIGS. 7–12: Courtesy Adriaan Geuze/West 8 Landscape Architects.
FIGS. 13, 14: Courtesy James Corner and Stan Allen/Field Operations.
FIGS. 15, 16: Courtesy James Corner/Field Operations.

The Emergence of Landscape Urbanism, Grahame Shane
FIG. 1: Courtesy Cedric Price.

An Art of Instrumentality, Richard Weller
All figures by Richard Weller and Tom Griffiths.

Vision in Motion: Representing Landscape in Time, Christophe Girot
FIGS. 1, 5, 8–12, 15: Photo by Christophe Girot.
FIGS. 2, 4: Photo by Georg Aerni.
FIGS. 3, 13, 14: Video still by Marc Schwarz.
FIG. 6: Photo by Jean Marc Bustamante.
FIG. 7: Courtesy Christophe Girot.

Looking Back at Landscape Urbanism, Julia Czerniak
FIG. 1: Reprinted from Carol Burns, "On Site: Architectural Preoccupations," *Drawing Building Text*, ed Andrea Kahn (New York: Princeton Architectural Press, 1991) 152.
FIG. 2: Courtesy Bruce Mau Design.
FIGS. 3, 14: Courtesy Eisenman Architects.
FIGS. 4, 6–9, 23: Courtesy Hargreaves Associates.
FIG. 5: Reprinted from Luna B. Leopold, M. Gordon Wolman, John P. Miller, *Fluvial Processes in Geomorphology* (New York: Dover Publications, 1995), 285.
FIG. 10: Reprinted from Andrzej Rachocki, *Alluvial Fans* (New York, John Wiley & Sons, 1981), 26.
FIG. 11: Reprinted from Michael A Summerfield, "Fluvial Landforms," *Global Geomorphology* (Essex: Longman Group, 1991), 255.
FIGS. 12, 13, 15–22: Courtesy Olin Partnership.
FIG. 24: Reprinted from AnnaLee Saxenian, *Regional Advantage: Culture and Competition in Silicon Valley and Route 128* (Cambridge, Mass.: Harvard University Press, 1994).
FIG. 25: Reprinted from Peter Owens, "Silicon Valley Solution," *Landscape Architecture Magazine* (June 1999).

Constructed Ground: Questions of Scale, Linda Pollak
FIG. 1: Courtesy Linda Pollak, Sheila Kennedy, and Franco Violich.
FIG. 2: Reprinted from Henri Lefebvre, *The Production of Space*, trans. Donald Nicholson-Smith (Oxford: Blackwell Publishers, 1991).

FIGS. 3–6: Courtesy Marpillero Pollak Architects.
FIGS. 7–10: Courtesy Rem Koolhaas/Office for Metropolitan Architecture (OMA).
FIG. 11: Courtesy Andreu Arriola.
FIG. 12: Courtesy Catherine Mosbach and Etienne Dolet.
FIG. 13: Courtesy Alison and Peter Smithson.
FIG. 14: Courtesy Alvaro Siza.
FIG. 15: Courtesy Adriaan Geuze/West 8 Landscape Architects.

Place as Resistance: Landscape Urbanism in Europe, Kelly Shannon
FIGS. 1, 3, 4: Courtesy Latz and Partners.
FIG. 2: Courtesy Joan Roig and Enric Batlle.
FIGS. 5, 6: Courtesy Florian Beigel Architects.
FIGS. 7–9: Courtesy Dominique Perrault.
FIG. 10: Courtesy Agence Ter.
FIGS. 11, 12: Courtesy Inaki Alday, Margarita Jover, and Pilar Sancho.
FIG. 13: Courtesy Andrea Branzi with the Domus Academy.
FIGS. 14–17: Courtesy François Grether and Michel Desvigne.
FIGS. 18, 19: Courtesy Rem Koolhaas/Office for Metropolitan Architecture (OMA).
FIGS. 20, 21: Courtesy Paola Viganò.

Landscapes of Infrastructure, Elizabeth Mossop
FIG. 1: Photo by Spackman and Mossop.
FIGS. 2–4, 6, 7: Photos by Elizabeth Mossop.
FIG. 5: Photo by Glen Allen/Hargreaves Associates.

Urban Highways and the Reluctant Public Realm, Jacqueline Tatom
FIG. 1: Photo by Michel Brigaud/Sodel; courtesy La Documentation Francaise/ Interphotothèque.
FIG. 2: Montage by Jacqueline Tatom and Julie Villa, 2004.
FIG. 3: Courtesy of the National Park Service, Frederick law Olmsted National History Site.
FIG. 4: Photo by Jacqueline Tatom.
FIG. 5: Photo by William Fried; courtesy New York City Parks Photo Archive.
FIG. 6: Courtesy New York City Parks Photo Archive.
FIG. 7: Courtesy IMPUSA.
FIGS. 8, 9, Courtesy Manuel de Sola Morales.

Drosscape, Alan Berger
All images by Alan Berger.

Landscapes of Exchange, Clare Lyster
FIG. 1: Reprinted from David Harvey, *The Condition of Postmodernity* (Cambridge: Blackwell, 1990).
FIG. 2: Diagram by Clare Lyster. Book cover reprinted from J. K. Rowling, *Harry Potter and the Order of the Phoenix* (New York: Scholastic, 2003).
FIG. 3 (TOP): Reprinted from John W. Stamper, *The Architecture of Roman Temples: The Republic to the Middle Empire* (Cambridge: Cambridge University Press, 2005).
FIG. 3 (MIDDLE): Reprinted from Spiro Kostoff, *A History of Architecture: Settings and Rituals* (New York: Oxford University Press, 1985).

FIG. 3 (BOTTOM): 13 Reprinted from Julia Sniderman Bachrach, *The City in a Garden: A Photographic History of Chicago's Parks* (Washington, D.C.: Center for American Places, 2001).

FIG. 4: Courtesy http://www.moveon.org (accessed August 2003).

FIG. 5: Courtesy the *New York Times*.

FIG. 6: Courtesy http://www.googlemaps.com (accessed March 2004).

FIG. 7: Reprinted from Peter Landesman, "The Light at the End of the Chunnel," *New York Times Magazine*, April 14th, 2002. Courtesy of the *New York Times*.

FIG. 8: Courtesy http://www.alliancelandport.com (accessed August 2003).

FIG. 9: Reprinted from Maarten Kloos and Brigitte de Maar, *Schiphol Architecture: Innovative Airport Design* (Amsterdam: ARCAM, 1996).

FIG. 10: Reprinted from Elmer Johnson, *Chicago Metropolis 2020* (Chicago: The University of Chicago Press, 2001).

FIG. 11 (TOP LEFT): Reprinted from Bruce Mau and the Institute without Boundaries, *Massive Change* (London: Phaidon, 2003); (TOP RIGHT) reprinted from Martha Rosler, *In the Place of the Public: Observations of a Frequent Flyer* (Munich: Hatje Cantz, 1999).

FIG. 12: Courtesy Illinois Department of Natural Resources, http://www.catsiatf.com/linkfiles/gall/pictures/cicero.htm and http://maps.google.com (accessed March 2004).

FIG. 14: Courtesy Alfons Soldevilla.

FIGS. 15, 16 (TOP): Photos by Clare Lyster.

FIG. 16 (BOTTOM): Reprinted from *Abitare* 417, "Olanda" (May 2002).

Synthetic Surfaces, Pierre Bélanger

FIGS. 1, 10 (TOP), 11: Courtesy of The United States Geological Survey.

FIG. 2: Courtesy of the Iowa Department of Transportation and the Farwell T. Brown Photographic Archive (Ames Public Library), Ames, Iowa.

FIG. 3: Courtesy of Kenneth C. Downing Photo Collection, The Smithsonian Institute, Washington, D.C.

FIG. 4 (LEFT): Courtesy of The Dwight D. Eisenhower Library, Abilene, Kansas; (RIGHT) Courtesy of U.S. Department of Transportation, Federal Highway Administration, Washington, D.C.

FIG. 5: Courtesy of the Washington State Department of Transportation.

FIG. 6: © 2003 The State Museum of Pennsylvania; courtesy of the Nassau County Museum, Roslyn Harbor, New York.

FIG. 7: Courtesy of the New Jersey Turnpike Authority.

FIGS. 8, 17, 18: © 1996–2005, New Jersey Department of Environmental Protection, Geographic Information System, Trenton, New Jersey.

FIG. 9 (BOTTOM): Reprinted from Hancock County Journal & Carthage Republican; scanned by Marcia Farina; (TOP) courtesy of the United States Patent and Trademark Office, Washington, D.C.

FIG. 10 (BOTTOM): Courtesy of the California Department of Transportation, Division of Geometric Design, Sacramento, California.

FIG. 12: © 2005, MapQuest.com, Inc.

FIG. 13: © 2005, Earthworks LLC and Theoretical & Applied Geology.

FIG. 14: Courtesy of the Woods Hole Field Center, USGS Coastal and Marine Program, Woods Hole, Massachusetts.

FIG. 15 (TOP): Photo by Captain Steve Nagiewicz; courtesy of NJScuba.com; (BOTTOM) courtesy New York/New Jersey Clean Ocean and Shore Trust.

FIG. 16: Source: United States Army Corps of Engineers & The Port Authority of New York and New Jersey.

Public Works Practice, Chris Reed

FIG. 1: Courtesy Chris Reed/Stoss landscape urbanism.

FIG. 2: Reprinted from Metropolitan District Commission, *The Metropolitan Water System* (Boston: Metropolitan District Commission, 1976).

FIG. 3: Courtesy the United States Department of the Interior, Bureau of Reclamation, Washington, D.C.

FIG. 4: Courtesy Janet Abbate, redrawn with permission of the author from a version published in Thomas P Hughes, Rescuing Prometheus: Four Monumental Projects that Changed the Modern World (New York: Vintage Books, 1998).

FIG. 5: Courtesy Library of Congress, Prints and Photographs Division, Historic American Engineering Record, CONN, 1-GREWI, 2-82, Washington, D.C.

FIG. 6: Photo by Ed Latchman, ca 1959; negative #306-PS-59-13580, National Archives and Records Administration, College Park, Maryland.

FIG. 7: Courtesy of The Frank Lloyd Wright Foundation, Taliesin West, Scottsdale, Arizona.